The Verbum Book of PostScript Illustration

MW00721347

BOB BAILLARGEON VE3MPG
179 MCGILLIVRAY ST
OTTAWA ONT
K1S 1K7

The Verbum Book of PostScript Illustration

Michael Gosney ▌ Linnea Dayton ▌ Janet Ashford

Produced by The Gosney Company, Inc. and Verbum Magazine

670 Seventh Avenue, Second Floor
San Diego, CA 92101
(619) 233-9977

Book and cover design: John Odam
Cover illustration: Jill Malena
Production Manager: Martha Siebert
Production Assistant: Doug Moore
Administrative Manager: Jeanne Lear
Technical Graphics Consultant: Jack Davis
Proofreading, research: Audrey Nimura, Valerie Bayla

Published by M&T Books
A Division of M&T Publishing, Inc.
501 Galveston Drive
Redwood City, CA 94063

ISBN 1-55851-089-3

Printed in the United States of America
First Edition published 1990

Library of Congress Catologing-in-Publication Data
Gosney, Michael
    The Verbum book of PostScript Illustration/Michael Gosney, Linnea Dayton, Janet Ashford
    p. cm.
    ISBN 1-55851-089-3: $29.95
    1. PostScript (Computer program language)
    I. Dayton, Linnea, 1944– . II. Ashford, Janet. III. Verbum (San Diego, Calif.)
    IV. Title.
    QA76.73.P67G57 1990
    005.26'2- -dc20   90-33612
                                                       CIP

© 1990 by Michael Gosney and M&T Books

All rights reserved. No part of this book may be reproduced or transmitted in any form or by any means, electronic or mechanical, including photocopying, recording, or by any information storage and retrieval system, without prior written permission from the Publisher. Contact the Publisher for information on foreign rights.

Notice of Liability: The information in this book is distributed on an "As Is" basis, without warranty. Neither the author(s) nor M&T Publishing, Inc. shall have any liability to customer or any other person or entity with respect to any liability, loss or damage caused or alleged to be caused directly or indirectly by the programs contained herein. This includes, but is not limited to, interruption of service, loss of data, loss of business or anticipatory profits, or consequential damages from the use of the programs.

All brand names, trademarks and registered trademarks are the property of their respective holders. Copyrights on individual artworks reproduced in this book are retained by the originators of the artworks.

Contents

Welcome to the *The Verbum Book of PostScript Illustration*. This book, like the others in the *Verbum Electronic Art and Design Series,* is an instructional graphic design book rather than a technical computer book. We've found that whether in the Mac or MS-DOS environment, the PostScript illustration programs have many of the same capabilities and routines. The book is designed to make it easier for you to be creative with these new electronic illustration tools.

The first two chapters of the book provide an overview of PostScript illustration and some of the outstanding products available for doing it. In the following chapters, you can look over the shoulder of talented designers and illustrators as they demonstrate the electronic art-making process. Each chapter introduces an artist and a project case study, starting with an overview of the project and then re-creating the technical steps taken to complete it. A narrative in the artist's own voice lets you in on the creative thought processes involved in designing and carrying out the project, and the carefully captioned illustrations tell the story along with the text. In general, simpler projects can be found toward the beginning of the book, and more complex ones toward the back. At the end of each chapter is a "Portfolio" of other PostScript illustrations by the artist, with brief descriptions of interesting techniques used to create them.

Throughout the project chapters are sidebars and tips. Sidebars, some written by the featured artists, are explorations, technical or historical sidetrips related to the chapter's project. ▮ *Tips are introduced by this vertical symbol, and they appear in italic type. They provide program- or process-specific hints to save you time and effort in developing your expertise in PostScript illustration.*

Following the project chapters is the "Gallery," with works from several other PostScript artists. Altogether, over 100 outstanding examples of PostScript illustration are showcased throughout the book. After the "Gallery," an "Appendix" tells how to find products and services useful to PostScript illustrators. "Production Notes" gives a straightforward description of how we produced the book itself, from word processing to digital color separations. The "Index" will provide the direction you need to go straight to the specific information you want.

What is Verbum?

Verbum, the Journal of Personal Computer Aesthetics, is a magazine dedicated to exploring the aesthetic and human aspects of using microcomputers. *Verbum* is created by a group of editors, writers and artists, most of whom had the good fortune to be involved in the emergence of desktop publishing, and, more specifically, the refined electronic art and design tools that followed. There is magic in the synergy of science and art: top programmers and

engineers become passionate artists, composing their code, while successful graphic designers and illustrators, as they always have, combine impressive technical skills with ample "right-brained" creativity.

The first issue of *Verbum* was published in the summer of 1986. It was a 24-page, 1000-copy edition produced with PageMaker 1.0 on a Macintosh Plus computer. The response to this pc art journal was positive, and the quarterly magazine was formally launched in 1987. Issue 1.1 was produced with the Mac and LaserWriter, and subsequent issues have used increasingly sophisicated desktop publishing output, reflecting the state of the art of microcomputer-based electronic production as the technology has evolved. In design, production and even in its editorial content, *Verbum* is an ongoing experiment, exploring the cutting edge of electronic art and design.

Thanks to many

The *Verbum* book series is the result of many people's efforts. Our core team owes thanks to the contributing artists who have taken the time to share their experiences with us; William Gladstone, our agent; our service bureaus in San Diego, Central Graphics, Thompson Type and Laser Express; the many software companies who made sure we had up-to-date products and information; and our *Verbum* readers, who keep us on our toes!

The electronic art revolution

As we begin the 1990s, the pc-based design and illustration technology has matured: standards have been established, and all the elements of a new industry are in place — the major DTP software and hardware environments, scanners, printers, imagesetters, service bureaus, links to the prepress world — and a critical mass of users has developed. The graphic design industry is being transformed. Studios and art departments are being retooled. The traditional ways of doing things, although not completely obsolete, are in many aspects giving way to more efficient, and more exciting methods. Computers save graphic artists time and money. But artists tell us that by far the most important benefit of the pc tools is that they *enhance creativity,* giving them the freedom they need to explore design options, to see the results of their experiments immediately.

Beyond these benefits to established designers and illustrators, the digital revolution has allowed a sigificant expansion of the graphic arts field as thousands are given the opportunity to design pages, produce illustrations, even create typefaces, with the personal computer. Whether you're an established illustrator or a novice, we wish you the best possible results using the *Verbum Book of PostScript Illustration.* May you push the envelope a little further!

C H A P T E R   1

An Overview

f you love technical illustration but hate inking, PostScript illustration is for you. PostScript illustration software is a very powerful graphics medium: As an imitative tool, it lets the artist achieve and even surpass the mechanical quality of artwork rendered by hand; the smoothness of the lines and the density of the solid areas and screens can be virtually indistinguishable from hand-inking or continuous-tone work. And as a medium in its own right, it lets the artist produce effects that would be virtually impossible without the computer (Figure 1). PostScript illustration software lets the artist:

- Draw smooth, easily adjustable curves.
- "Ink" a rough drawing, with the ink provided in any color or in a fountain of colors, or in any of a series of predetermined patterns, or an original one.
- Instantly achieve effects such as shadowing, airbrushing, rotating, skewing and flipping across any axis.
- Space elements of a drawing by uniform distances, align them with each other or copy them.
- Trace around images.
- Automatically draw a specified number of intermediate steps in a transformation of one drawn object into another.
- "Cut" masks.
- Fit type to a curved baseline or modify the outlines of individual characters.
- Change parts of an illustration in progress without starting over.
- Print or display illustrations at the best resolution a display or output device can produce.

Figure 1. Doing the impossible. Designer/ illustrator David Smith produced this set of fluid curves in the Adobe Illustrator 88 PostScript drawing program in color. The top curve was drawn and assigned a color. Then it was copied, modified slightly, rotated and assigned another color to form the bottom curve. The curves in between, intermediate in shape, position and color, were created automatically with the program's blend function. To draw these curves in any other way would have been technically too difficult to be practical.

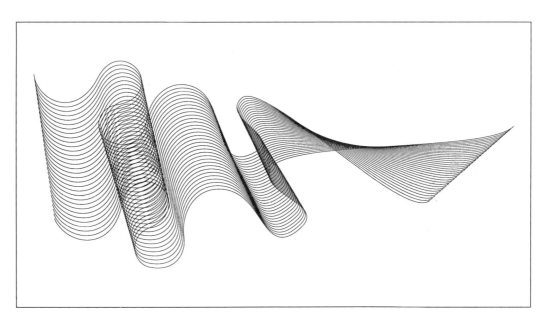

• Choose part or all of a completed illustration and reuse it, changing its size, color or other attributes.

The PostScript language

PostScript is a *page-description language* — a computer programming language that provides a way to represent the lines, curves and solid areas that make up the text and graphic images on a computer "page." A PostScript illustration document is actually a computer program that tells a printer how to render the images (see "The invisible language of PostScript illustration" on page 3). Since its introduction in 1985, the PostScript language has been endorsed and used by both Apple and IBM and has gained acceptance as the computer industry standard for page-description (see "The early history of PostScript" on page 5).

Paint, draw, PostScript To the illustrator, PostScript offers some big improvements over the other computerized art-making possibilities — bitmapped "paint" programs and object-oriented "draw" programs. Printed output from paint programs is dogged by the appearance of jagged, stair-stepped "bits" on any edge that's not horizontal or vertical. Draw programs can create smoothed objects, but they offer limited drawing tools and manipulations. PostScript has vastly expanded the range of possibilities.

Bitmapped images Paint programs like MacPaint, PC Paint, PixelPaint, Studio 8 and the paint functions of SuperPaint and Canvas create *bitmapped* images — arrays of small rectangular dots that make up on-screen or printed images. In effect, computer painting is like trying to paint curves and swirls using small, square tiles (Figure 2). Bitmaps are usually keyed to the computer's screen resolution (expressed as the number of dots per linear inch [dpi] that make up the image; for the Macintosh, for example, this resolution is 72 dpi). And they won't improve in resolution even when printed at higher than screen resolution, on a laser printer, for instance.

Figure 2. Stacking pixels. Bitmapped illustration (or *paint*) programs create drawings constructed of black-and-white square pixels, often at the same low resolution as the computer screen. While horizontal and vertical lines appear perfectly smooth, angled and curved lines suffer from the "jaggies" (see inset).

The invisible language of PostScript illustration

by John Ivory

Imagine yourself creating an art project at the beach with two friends. You want to make two large, identical drawings in the sand by standing on a lifeguard chair and shouting commands to your friends, who will shuffle their feet through the sand to create separate drawings.

Once you've raked the sand to start with a "clean slate," the first step is to figure out how to instruct your friends. Your first thought is to give commands in a "Simon Says" fashion. "Take three giant shuffles forward," you yell.

Your friends shuffle according to your commands, but you quickly realize that the two lines they've created are pretty different — one person's line is 6 feet long and the other's is 9. One look at your friends' heights (5'6" and 6'4") and shoe sizes (7 and 13) and you realize that giving the same commands to both is not going to produce the same result.

Instead, you calculate in your head how much farther the taller friend will go than the smaller, given their sizes. To produce a 12-foot line, you tell the taller friend to shuffle four steps and you tell the smaller friend to shuffle six.

A new set of commands

After half an hour of shouting two sets of commands for the same actions, and plenty of mental calculations, especially when you get to circles and other curved shapes, you've got a headache. You begin to wonder if there might not be a better way. Then you remember something — not only are both people great judges of distances, but each got an A+ in geometry. You decide to try describing what you want the final result to be instead of telling them how to do it with their particular bodies. For instance, you tell them to "draw a box 5 feet square, starting 1 foot north and 1 foot east of the southwest corner" of the sand patch. It works! And for the rest of the afternoon, your job's a lot easier. You end up with two identical drawings in the sand.

The computer in the printer

Like your friends, PostScript printers can "think" for themselves. Receiving only a description of the end result desired (draw a box with *x,y* dimensions, for example), they figure out how to make their mechanisms produce the appropriate marks on the page. For the application program sending the information to the printer (and for the programmer who designed it), it's like a graphic designer's dream come true: the applica-

tion has only to describe the idea; the printer handles all the production.

PostScript is the computer programming language that communicates this information. It's called a *page description language* — it describes the results it wants on the page rather than concerning itself with the details of how each printer must work to produce that image. For the printer to "be a good judge of distance and have an A+ in geometry," it must contain a computer of its own. When you print on a PostScript printer, your microcomputer sends a computer program — a set of instructions describing how the page should look — to the printer's computer. This computer contains a PostScript *interpreter,* which is able to take any PostScript description and translate it into commands for that printing mechanism.

You can send the same PostScript program, or description, to *any* PostScript printer, and it will produce the same result, depending on the qualities of that printer. In other words, PostScript is *device-independent.* So if you send the PostScript description of how to make a 2-inch circle to both a LaserWriter printer and a Linotronic imagesetter, both will produce a 2-inch circle. The only difference will be that the circle will look a little jagged when printed on the LaserWriter at 300 dots per inch, while it will look perfectly smooth on the Linotronic at 2540 dots per inch.

It's all relative

"Big deal," you say. "I have only one computer hooked up to only one printer, and I'm not interested in art projects on the beach. What can PostScript do for me?" While PostScript was a revolution in the way computers communicate with printers, it's also revolutionary in the flexibility it allows the graphics professional. For instance, on many printers, if you want to print a certain size type, say 20 points, you have to first check to make sure the printer has that particular size stored in its memory or has access to it through a cartridge or through software. Often it won't be possible, since 20 is a nonstandard size. So you'll have to make a different design decision to accommodate the limitations of the printer. With PostScript, you can print type from very small (4 or 5 points) to very large (well over 100 points), because PostScript stores type as geometric descriptions of the characters. It can then substitute the appropriate numbers in the description to size the characters as you choose. The same is true

for lines. And beyond this, PostScript can print text and objects in any shade of gray from black to white (the number of shades depends on the resolution of the printer) or even in different colors on a color printer.

When you want to get still fancier, PostScript can rotate text and graphics to any angle, reduce and enlarge them to any size proportionally or disproportionally, and even run text along a squiggly line. Further, it can work with scanned images, generate halftones, and work in spot color and process color. It's designed to handle any image that can be printed on paper.

The silent partner

While PostScript is a computer language, it's different from other computer languages in two ways. First, the PostScript program is processed by the computer in the printer rather than by the computer on your desk. Second, most PostScript programs are written automatically by other computer programs rather than by humans. For instance, when you use the mouse to arrange text and graphics on the screen using PageMaker, the PageMaker software actually writes a PostScript program that describes what you've put on the page and sends that program to the laser printer. Here's an example: **/Times-Roman findfont 24 scalefont setfont 72 100 moveto (ADEPT) show** tells the printer to find the mathematical formula for the Times font in its memory, scale it to 24 points, set it as the current font, and print "ADEPT" at 72 points, starting from a point 72 points from the bottom of the page and 100 points from the left side of the page. To get the type to print sideways, the instructions might say **90 rotate** before the other commands. (If you're interested in learning how to use PostScript yourself, an excellent book for beginners is the *PostScript Language Tutorial and Cookbook,* written by Adobe Systems (the creators of PostScript) and published by Addison-Wesley. Although the book expects the reader to understand programming, it gives sample programs and their results, which you can try yourself and modify, even if you don't understand them fully. — *Adapted from "PostScript: A Look at the Invisible Language of Desktop Publishing," ADEPTations, No. 6, Spring 1989, with the permission of John Ivory and ADEPT (the Association for the Development of Electronic Publishing Technique).*

Bitmap programs are easy to use. Of all the computer graphics techniques, "painting" with the mouse feels most like drawing with a pencil or painting with a brush or airbrush. But paint programs limit artists in two ways: First, once an image is painted, it can't be easily changed or manipulated (Figure 3); and second, printed output is jagged.

Object-oriented drawings Draw programs like MacDraw, MacDraft and the draw functions of SuperPaint and Canvas describe objects as sets of mathematical parameters, rather than as arrays of fixed dots. Most draw objects improve in resolution when printed on high-resolution printers and can be manipulated in a variety of ways without disturbing other elements in a picture

Figure 3. Removing the paint. Typically, in a paint program a foreground figure can't be selected cleanly or moved without leaving a "hole" in the background.

Figure 4. Drawing on grids. Non-PostScript illustration (or *draw*) programs provide tools that operate with the "feel" of the traditional drafting environment. They create objects that can be enlarged, reduced, or stretched or compressed uniformly or disproportionately. The rounded shapes in this rooster were created with an arc tool, which automatically closes open paths when a fill color is assigned.

The early history of PostScript

The Macintosh computer, introduced by Apple in 1984, was based on a 72 dpi matrix keyed to standard font sizes (a 12-point letter is 12 pixels high on the screen). As the Macintosh was gaining in popularity, John Warnock and Charles Geschke were working to develop a page-description language for graphics printing. In December 1982 they formed Adobe Systems Corporation to promote and license the use of PostScript for computer systems.

At the same time, Steve Jobs, a cofounder of Apple, was working on the development of Apple's first laser printer. Through an agreement with Adobe, the laser printer was equipped with a PostScript interpreter that translates images in QuickDraw (the Macintosh graphics programming language) into descriptions that take advantage of the printer's 300 dpi resolution. Another new product added to the impact of PostScript's debut. Aldus Company developed PageMaker, the first sophisticated page layout program to support PostScript output. The release of these three products in January 1985 — Apple's LaserWriter, Adobe's PostScript language, and Aldus's PageMaker software boosted PostScript and high-quality desktop publishing into the marketplace.

For two years, PageMaker dominated the field of PostScript output. Publication designers could make good use of the Macintosh's PostScript capabilities, but illustrators were still limited to non-PostScript programs like MacPaint and MacDraw. Enterprising artists who wanted to use PostScript capabilities had to write their own PostScript code. Cricket Draw was the first drawing application to make use of PostScript, but it suffered from slow running and printing times. In March 1987, Adobe introduced Adobe Illustrator, the first high-quality PostScript illustration software. Other illustration software soon followed, including Aldus's FreeHand and software for IBM systems including Micrografx Designer and Corel Draw.

(Figure 4). But computer languages that serve as the basis for draw programs are not as sophisticated in their representational ability as PostScript is. For example, Macintosh draw programs, which are based on a language called QuickDraw, are limited in the fineness of the dots and lines they can produce; they draw no lines lighter in weight than 1 point, no matter how high the printer's resolution is.

PostScript illustrations Like draw programs, PostScript illustration programs are object-oriented. But they're truly resolution-independent. As the artist draws in a PostScript application, the mouse movements are converted into a PostScript text file of programming instructions (equations) whose results can be printed, displayed or otherwise output at the best resolution the output hardware is capable of. Both draw and PostScript illustration programs make it possible to move, resize and otherwise change both text and graphics easily and quickly, without having to retype or redraw. And, in general, both kinds of object-oriented files are smaller and more compact than bitmaps. (It's easy to understand why when you realize that an equation can describe a curve with far fewer characters than can a plot that has to account for the location of every single dot along that curve. The files take up less space on a computer disk and will print more quickly.) But the sophistication of PostScript makes it possible to specify and print a much wider range of graphic effects and manipulations than are available with draw programs. The savings in time, effort and cost are tremendous.

Working with PostScript illustration software

Users of PostScript-based illustration software have to get used to drawing tools that look and operate a little differently than traditional artists' tools (Figure 5). And there are also some basic differences between the way PostScript creates an image and the way a similar image would be drawn on paper.

Opaque layers In many traditional media, underlying colors and patterns can be blended with those applied on top of them. But in PostScript this isn't the case. PostScript illustration works in opaque layers, from back to front. That is, each object acts as if it's drawn on a separate layer, in front of or behind each of the other objects in the drawing. When an illustration is printed, all objects are opaque. So an object on top completely obscures whatever lies beneath it (Figure 6). Designers need to think in terms of layers of opaque paint to visualize how an illustration should be constructed. It's also helpful to understand the basic elements of a PostScript illustration: paths, imported images (or templates) and type.

Paths PostScript paths are lines and curves that can be open (having two endpoints) or closed (forming a complete circuit, with no exposed ends), stroked or filled with color or pattern, or used for masking (Figure 7). Paths are created by drawing with a *freehand* drawing tool, which operates like a pencil or paintbrush, or by using other tools to plot individual anchor points that allow the software to draw straight lines or curves connecting them. Paths are defined as *Bezier curves,* named for the Frenchman who created the set of curving templates we call "French curves." The characteristics of a Bezier curve path can be modified after it's drawn either by relocating individual anchor points, or by manipulating the Bezier "handles" attached to each point, which bends the curve segment between that point and adjacent points on each side (Figure 8).

Imported images Paint images and scans (a kind of digitized photo) can be brought into PostScript illustration programs and used as temporary on-screen templates that can be traced with the PostScript tools (Figure 9). Some PostScript illustration programs can also incorporate the imported images as permanent elements of the final illustration. Imported images retain their original resolution.

Type Text characters are generated via the keyboard from a PostScript font (alphabetic, numeric and symbol characters of the same typeface). In general, their outlines can be treated graphically as paths, and they're subject to the same sorts of manipulations as other graphic objects (Figure 10).

Advantages of PostScript A major difference between PostScript illustration and hand-drawing is that the elements of a PostScript composition can be moved or modified without having to erase or disturb other parts of the picture. A well-drawn face can be resized to fit an overly large body, for instance, without having to lose the line work done on either element. The computer separates the art-making process into both on-screen and printer images.

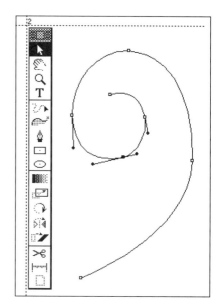

Figure 5. Using new tools. PostScript illustration programs such as Adobe Illustrator include tools whose operation is not intuitive. For example, the pen tool defines curves by placing points, and then the pointer tool (the arrow at the top of the tool palette) can be used to adjust the shape of the line segments between points by moving the "handles."

Figure 6. "Building" illustrations of layers. In PostScript illustration, opaque shapes are layered on top of one another to form a finished drawing. For example, the oval and the rectangle shown on the right (in the program's keyline mode) are filled with the primary flesh tone of the face and neck and layered behind the shapes that define highlights, shadows and hair.

In a sense, drawings made by hand are "printed" as they go. This immediacy is both a benefit and a drawback — on the one hand, a final inked drawing that's acceptable aesthetically is ready to be used as camera-ready art. But on the other hand, having to start over to redraw unsatisfactory art can be quite time-consuming. By contrast, a computer drawing has no fixed form until it's printed. It can be modified on-screen at any point. This allows tremendous flexibility for making changes and corrections. But without a final print that faithfully reproduces the designer's intentions, the most elegant on-screen image is of no practical use. So the process of printing is crucial.

PostScript output

For PostScript illustration, the process of generating hard copy (an illustration in a form you can hold in your hands rather than only view on the screen) is

Figure 7. Closing and filling paths. The drawing at top left is an open path drawn in PostScript and assigned a line weight. At top right, the path has been closed and filled with black. In the illustration at the bottom, the image of a panda has emerged, as white filled shapes have been layered on top of the black to indicate changes in fur color and space between the arm and the leg.

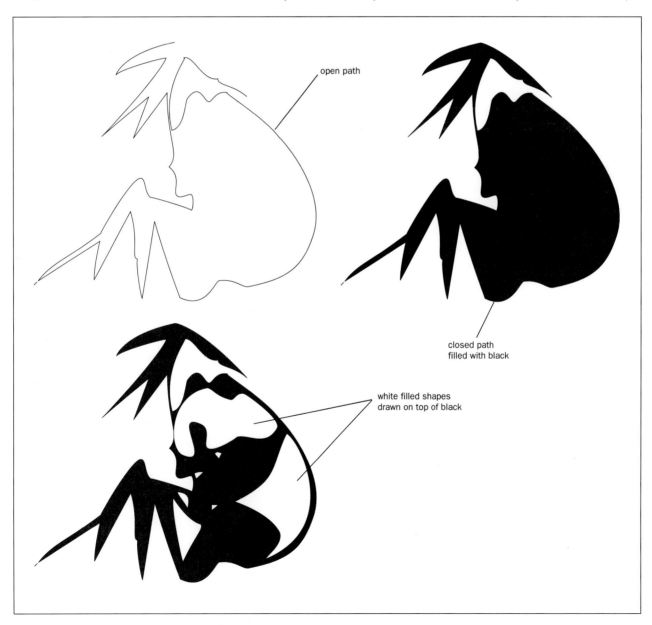

open path

closed path
filled with black

white filled shapes
drawn on top of black

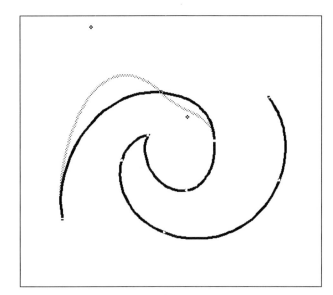

Figure 8. Reshaping Bezier curves. In this PostScript illustration program, moving the handles (each formed of four tiny squares surrounding a white center) changes the position of the curve on both sides of the point those two handles control.

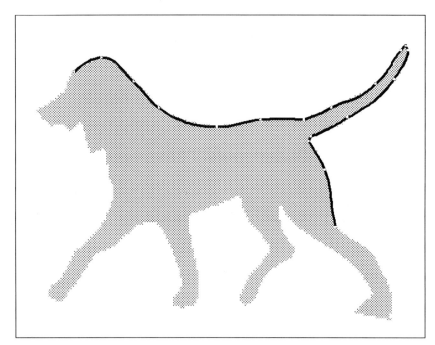

Figure 9. Tracing templates. Paintings, drawings or scanned images can be imported into many PostScript illustration programs and traced by placing Bezier curve points. Some programs also have autotrace functions that place the points automatically. Typically, some points have to be removed and curves adjusted after autotracing to get a smooth, accurate drawing.

Encapsulation

Drawings made in most PostScript illustration programs can be saved in three formats: in the format particular to that program, as pure PostScript code, or in an encapsulated format. Pure PostScript files include only the PostScript text instructions that tell an output device how to generate the printed illustration. Encapsulated PostScript files contain two kinds of instructions: the pure PostScript code, and a set of instructions to the computer for displaying the illustration on a monitor screen that is not a PostScript-driven device.

The encapsulated formats are referred to as EPS (encapsulated PostScript) or EPSF (encapsulated PostScript format). Some programs, like Illustrator, for example, can encapsulate drawings in either Macintosh or IBM PC format.

A pure PostScript file can be interpreted by any PostScript-based program or output device. An EPS file, on the other hand, is less available. For example, Illustrator can open and modify its own EPS files. FreeHand can open and modify Illustrator 1.1 EPS files, but not those of Illustrator 88. FreeHand EPS files can be placed (imported into a file) in FreeHand and in page layout programs, but they can't be modified at all — not even by FreeHand itself.

usually fast and easy. Typical output devices are laser printers, imagesetters, film recorders and color thermal and ink-jet printers.

Laser printers The Apple LaserWriter was the first PostScript printer designed for the Macintosh. It prints images at a resolution of 300 dots per inch, which became the first standard for laser printers. For some illustrations, particularly line art, this resolution is good enough to use as a final printed piece, or as camera-ready copy for making photo-offset plates. But for more complex illustrations, especially those containing shades of gray or color, many artists use a laser printer only as an intermediate step, for proofing PostScript illustrations before sending them to a high-resolution imagesetter at a typesetting service bureau (Figure 11).

Figure 10.
Manipulating type.
Many PostScript effects can be applied to type that you enter from the keyboard or to letters that are drawn as objects in PostScript illustration programs, such as this ampersand from Adobe's Collector's Edition of clip art.

| Service
bureaus

Because imagesetters are expensive, most designers rely on service bureaus for output. As the imagesetter technology was evolving, jobs sometimes took many hours to run or refused to print at all. Because of the problems encountered on the journey from floppy disk to final output, some designers became hesitant to attempt printing complex graphics. The Linotype company, as well as the service bureaus that buy and operate their machines, have worked with designers to resolve many disk-to-print problems. It's important to develop a close working relationship with an experienced service bureau dedicated to improving quality and responding to designers' needs.

The Professional PostScript Alliance, a national group of service bureaus, was formed to share information and improve quality in this new and rapidly changing field. One of the first projects of the Alliance was *The PPA System of Adobe Fonts*, developed to eliminate the font ID number conflicts (more than one font with the same identification number used by the computer to call it up for printing) that have plagued the transfer of documents from computer systems to imagesetters.

Imagesetters

To take full advantage of the capabilities of PostScript illustration, files should be printed by an imagesetter, which is a photo-imaging device. Imagesetters can print at resolutions of 635, 1270 and 2540 dpi, for example. They make it possible to enjoy the ease of art production with a computer without sacrificing clean, high-quality output. At high resolution, imagesetters can also be used for producing halftones and color separations.

For computer input, an imagesetter is used with a *raster image processor,* or RIP, which interprets PostScript code sent by the computer, converting the code into a rasterized image, a series of dots best suited to the specified resolution. The speed and success of rasterization depends on the size and complexity of the illustration, the resolution desired and the capabilities of the RIP. RIP units have been upgraded over the past 5 years to provide more memory, speed and storage capacity, so they can print complex PostScript illustrations, with more paths, color gradations and typefaces per file than used to be possible.

Imagesetters can print on photomedia paper (as a positive, black-on-white image) or on film (as a negative or a positive). Some can also print on plain paper or directly on a printing plate. Maximum printing media widths and lengths vary with the type of imagesetter. Imagesetter paper or film output is typically used as camera-ready copy for plate-making.

The high cost of imagesetters, combined with the necessity for highly experienced staff and time to run them (see "Service bureaus" on this page), means that high-resolution output is relatively expensive. As greater competition improves performance and lowers prices of imagesetters, illustrators will be able to afford to experiment more with high-resolution output.

PostScript color

With the advent of the Macintosh II computer with on-screen color, PostScript illustration programs have been improved to include sophisticated color

Figure 11. Increasing output resolution. Printing an illustration at 72 dots per inch (dpi), which is the resolution of the Macintosh screen or the Apple ImageWriter printer, for example, gives a different result (top left) than printing it at 300 dpi (top right) or 2540 dpi (bottom). Three hundred dpi is the standard first established for laser printers, and 2540 dpi represents high resolution on Linotronic imagesetters, for instance.

capabilities. Most support the Pantone Matching System (PMS) and also allow users to specify custom colors using several models, including spot color formulas like RGB (red, green, blue) and process colors based on the CMYK formula (cyan, magenta, yellow, black). Full-color illustrations can be created and viewed on-screen, and then separated for both flat color and four-color process printing. High-resolution imagesetters can be used to print the separations on paper or negative film. This technology is relatively new and problems do arise, particularly with trapping, screen angles and color matching.

Flat color Traditionally, flat (or spot) color printing is used for illustrations that contain one or more premixed ink colors. A completed illustration is *separated* so that all the images of each ink color appear in position on that color's piece of negative film; then a printing plate is made for each. The elements of a PostScript illustration can be specified in different colors and separated automatically (Figure 12). Colors and color separations can be specified even when the artist is working with a black-and-white system. PostScript programs are especially good at producing flat color separations for illustrations in which the color areas are not contiguous.

Trapping When colored objects are butted together in an illustration and then the illustration is separated as flat colors, gaps can appear between objects if the paper shifts slightly during the printing process. To avoid gaps, printers have traditionally used a technique called *trapping,* in which color areas printed next to each other are allowed to overlap slightly. This is done by overexposing

Figure 12. Separating spot colors. The six colors that make up this logo (see the front cover of the book for the color version) were defined as spot colors and automatically separated by the FreeHand PostScript illustration program to provide elements of output, one for each pass through a printer with a different ink color.

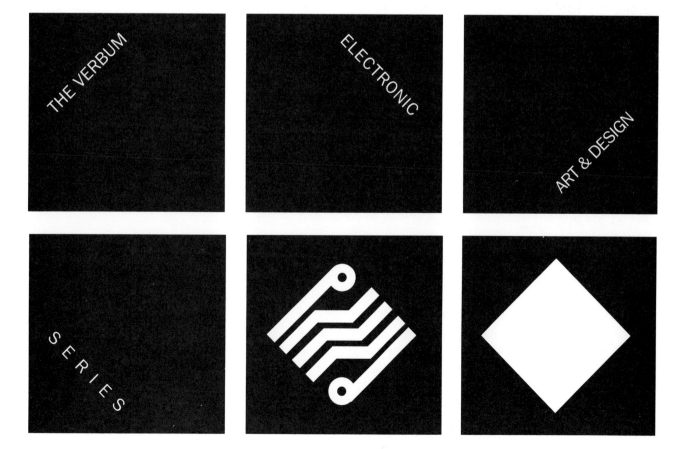

the film when plates are made. Illustrators producing film with PostScript software must create their own traps, if they're needed, by slightly increasing the size of an object or by "fattening" it with a same-color stroke (Figure 13).

Four-color process Four-color process printing is traditionally used for the reproduction of full-color, continuous-tone images such as color photographs and paintings. The image is photographed four times using special filters to produce four separate halftoned images. These are printed in four specific colors — cyan, yellow, magenta and black — on top of one another (Figure 14). The overlapping of the many colored dots of ink produces the effect of a full-color image.

In conventional color separations the halftone dots vary in size and shape. In the PostScript model for four-color process, an array of "cells" is created, with each cell able to contain a dot (actually a tilted square) of varying size. The array remains fixed, depending upon the resolution specified. Traditionally each color in a four-color separation is photographed at a different halftone screen angle to prevent the appearance of moiré patterns (the interaction of dot screens to form unintended patterns) when the screened colors are printed on top of one another. Screen angles can be specified in PostScript illustration programs, but use of the angles commonly used in commercial printing have not always proved satisfactory. Service bureaus have had to develop their own practical combinations of screen angles.

Color matching While printed color is formed additively from cyan, yellow, magenta and black ink, color on the computer screen is formed by subtractive mixing of red, green and blue light. So on-screen colors typically won't exactly match those in a color proof or in a final printed piece. In fact, some of the colors that can be displayed by some monitors can't be duplicated by certain printers, and vice versa. Designers must learn to predict and compensate for color changes from system to system. Some recommend exclusive use of Pantone Matching System colors, which are supported by most PostScript illustration programs. Hardware and software manufacturers (such Barco, Radius and Tektronix are developing methods for calibrating color display and printing systems (see "Matching screen to printer" on page 55).

Prepress proofs There are a number of ways to proof color illustrations before going to press. Both thermal transfer printers such as the QMS ColorScript and inkjet printers such as the Hewlett-Packard PaintJet provide color but are limited to 300 dpi resolution or less, so not all the PostScript effects are rendered as well on proofs as they will be in final high-res film separations. Film recorders can print computer graphics files as 35mm full-color slides. These can be projected for presentations or used to print color output by traditional photographic methods. It's also possible to make color slides and prints by photographing the computer screen.

Figure 13. Trapping. When PostScript illustrations are output as negative film, the illustrator takes responsibility for *trapping,* making sure that gaps don't occur between areas of different colors. Traditionally, trapping has been done by the printer, who makes negatives by photographing reflective art.

Figure 14. Using process colors. This poster by John Odam, with a rainbow of colors going from red at the top right, through the spectrum to orange at the bottom left, is separated here into four "plates," one for each of the four process ink colors (cyan, magenta, yellow and black). After printing on a press, dots of these four colors, printed on top of one another, will create all the colors needed for the poster.

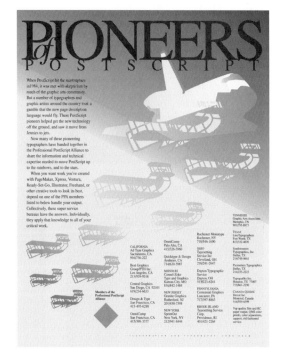

CYAN

MAGENTA

YELLLOW

When PostScript hit the marketplace in1984, it was met with skepticism by much of the graphic arts community. But a number of typographers and graphic artists around the country took a gamble that the new page description language would fly. These PostScript pioneers helped get the new technology off the ground, and saw it move from Jennies to jets.

Now many of these pioneering typographers have banded together in the Professional PostScript Alliance to share the information and technical expertise needed to move PostScript up to the rainbows, and to the stars.

When you want work you've created with PageMaker, Xpress, Ventura, Ready-Set-Go, Illustrator, Freehand, or other creative tools to look its best, depend on one of the PPA members listed to below handle your output. Collectively, these super service bureaus have the answers. Individually, they apply that knowledge to all of your critical work.

Members of the Professional PostScript Alliance

CALIFORNIA
Ad Type Graphics
Sacramento, CA
916/736-222

Best Graphics
Group/PTH Inc.
Los Angeles, CA
213/939-9518

Central Graphics
San Diego, CA 92101
619/234-0633

Design & Type
San Francisco, CA
415-495-6280

OmniComp
San Francisco, CA
415/398-3377

OmniComp
Palo Alto, CA
415/326-5960

Quicktype & Design
Anaheim, CA
714/630-5987

MISSOURI
Comtel-Zeko
Type and Graphics
Kansas City, MO
816/842-1484

NEW JERSEY
Granite Graphics
Rutherford, NJ
201/438-7398

NEW YORK
SprintOut
New York, NY
212/941-8444

Rochester Monotype
Rochester, NY
718/546-1690

OHIO
Typesetting
Service Inc
Cleveland, OH
216/241-2647

Dayton Typographic
Service
Dayton, OH
515/223-6241

PENNSYLVANIA
Centennial Graphics
Lancaster, PA
717/397-8863

RHODE ISLAND
Typesetting Service
Corp.
Providence, RI
401/421-2264

TENNESSEE
Graphic Arts Associates
Memphis, TN
901/795-8973

TEXAS
Line/Typographics
Fort Worth, TX
817/332-4070

Southwestern
Typographics, Inc.
Dallas, TX
214/748-0661

Pacesetters Typographics
Dallas, TX
214/235-2222

Typografics Inc.
Houston, TX 77007
713/861-1290

CANADA-QUEBEC
Droste Inc.
Montreal, Canada
514/939-6399

Top quality film and RC paper output, QMS color proofs, color separations, support, old fashioned service.

BLACK

Color separations generated by the computer can also be used to produce the types of pre-press color proofs already standard in the printing industry. These include acetate overlay "color keys" and printed proofs based on a transfer system (such as Cromalin prints).

The sophistication of computer technology for color printing is increasing, but at present designers using color need to have a good relationship with their service bureau and a willingness to pay for experimentation. The computer offers its users more power and creativity with color, but the designer must learn, and sometimes take on, tasks previously done by the stripper and printer.

Programming in PostScript

Most designers are not programmers and could not tap PostScript's power without the user-friendly interface of a PostScript illustration program. But illustration programs don't use the full power of the language. So for some

Figure 15. Programming in PostScript. These spiralling shapes were produced by 76 lines of PostScript code written by Tony Smith of Sydney, Australia. Some of the code is shown here. The PostScript commands tell the output device how to produce the illustration. For those who don't care to learn to program, PostScript illustration applications automatically translate the drawings created on-screen into code like this.

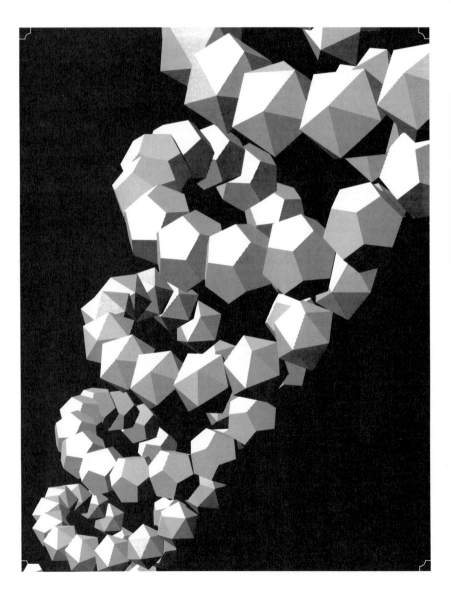

```
{inHard  Disk:Full  Polys}
{ps}
/TurnXYZ
    { ax /mat1 mat0 store mat1
    rotate transform 3 -1
    roll
     ay /mat1 mat0 store mat1
    rotate transform 3 -1
    roll
     az /mat1 mat0 store mat1
    rotate transform 3 -1
    roll
    } def

/DrawFace
    { Vertex face 3 get get
       aload pop TurnXYZ pop
     moveto
      4 1 face length 1 sub
        {Vertex face 3 -1 roll
       get get aload pop
          TurnXYZ pop lineto}
     for
     closepath
     /angcos x px mul y py
       mul z pz mul add add
        size psize mul sqrt div
     def
     angcos
     1 add 2 div
     dup 0 1t {pop 0} if
     dup gsave setgray fill
     grestore
     2 exp setgray stroke
     /n n 1 add def
    } def
```

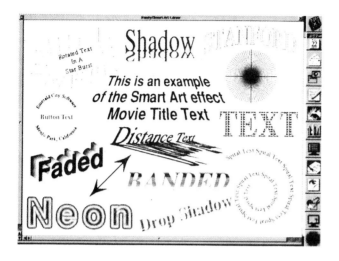

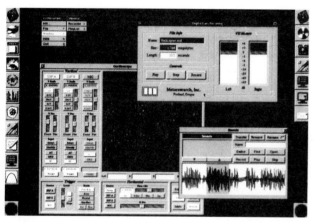

Figure 16. Coming closer to WYSIWYG. The NeXT computer uses Display Post-Script to define its on-screen images, which makes them more like the output that results from printing them. Post-Script illustration programs are among the applications developed for this new computer.

special effects it's necessary to look through the application interface to the programming language underneath.

One way to do this is by modifying the code that's written by a PostScript illustration program to create a graphic image on-screen. Some applications let users type in PostScript code directly to create special effects like fill and line patterns not available through the regular interface. PostScript code can also be saved as a text file and edited with a word processing program.

Some illustrators have also learned to program in Post-Script directly, bypassing or supplementing the use of an illustration program (Figure 15). At present, only a few people are both artists and PostScript programmers, but this combination of skills should lead to important discoveries.

Future directions

Computer illustration and the products that support it are changing fast. Designers keep pushing at the limits of the technology, forcing service bureaus, developers and vendors to scramble to provide new products and capabilities.

Improvements in WYSIWYG The WYSIWYG (what you see is what you get) mode of operation of PostScript illustration programs is undergoing substantial improvement, as designers press for the efficiency of seeing on-screen type and pattern images that more closely match the hard copy they get from output devices.

NeXT The NeXT is a UNIX-based personal computer system released in October 1989 (Figure 16). It uses Display PostScript to create its screen display. Because both screen and printer use the same (PostScript) imaging model, WYSIWYG comes closer to WYSIRWYG ("what you see is *really* what you get"). On-screen and hard-copy imaging are futher enhanced by the NeXT's 92 dpi MegaPixel Display and its 400 dpi laser printer. A variety of PostScript-based illustration programs have been developed for the NeXT, including Adobe Illustrator, Smart Art, ARtisan, TopDraw, TextArt and Flash Graphics.

C H A P T E R   2

Applications

Each PostScript illustration program is unique — with particular capabilities and a "look and feel" of its own. But all PostScript illustration programs have many features in common. For example, all the programs mentioned here make it possible to precisely specify line width. Line width (or weight) is automatically sized up or down when a drawing is rescaled, or it can be preserved so that lines stay the same weight, regardless of the rescaling.

• The color, pattern and percent intensity of lines and fills can be specified precisely.

• Tool palettes provide a selection of specific tools for generating text, basic shapes, straight and curved lines and freehand lines.

• Objects can be selected and grouped together and ungrouped.

• Transformations — scaling, rotating, reflecting and skewing — can be performed on both grouped and ungrouped objects. The parameters assigned to transformations can be specified by dragging objects into their new alignments with the mouse or by typing numbers into a dialog box.

• The drawing area can be viewed in enlarged and reduced views.

• Rulers at the edge of the drawing area enable precise positioning of objects in the illustration.

• Discretionary "snap-to" functions automatically pull elements toward a guideline or underlying grid as the mouse drags them.

• Programs allow users to import computer paintings, drawings or digitized scanned objects as templates for tracing, with the freehand tool or automatically (Figure 1).

• Paths can be used to "clip" a background element, creating the effect of a mask.

• All PostScript applications offer a WYSIWYG ("what you see is what you get") viewing mode that shows the art as

Figure 1. Tracing over a template. Art that has been scanned or created in another program can be opened in a PostScript illustration program and used as a template for tracing by hand (as shown here) or for autotracing.

it will be printed (or as close to printed form as screen characteristics will allow). All the programs allow drawing and editing in a "keyline" mode that shows only the paths (no line weights or fills) that make up the drawn objects.

• Most PostScript applications provide a way to "constrain" drawn objects to regular parameters. For instance, holding down the Shift key while creating a rectangle will constrain it to a perfect square.

The following product descriptions provide an overview of each application's capabilities. More detailed information about using the programs is provided in the tips and text of the chapters on individual artists' projects.

Adobe Illustrator

Adobe Illustrator was the first high-quality illustration program designed to take advantage of PostScript's advanced graphics capabilities. Illustrator provides the ability to draw and modify straight lines and curves in a very precise way, using Bezier points. Another primary use of this program is to produce smoothed line art using a bitmapped template as a base (Figure 2). Illustrator incorporates all of the features already mentioned for PostScript illustration programs in general plus some additional capabilities.

• Illustrations previously created in MacDraw can be automatically converted to Illustrator format using the DrawOver feature.

• Illustrator allows access to the PostScript code so that users can edit illustration text files.

• Color illustrations can be created and previewed on screen. The program allows use of user-mixed colors or the Pantone Matching System. Color separations can be made through a separate utility, Adobe Separator.

Figure 2. Creating smooth lines. Adobe Illustrator's packaging uses the well-known image of Botticelli's Venus overlaid with cleanly traced, PostScript lines.

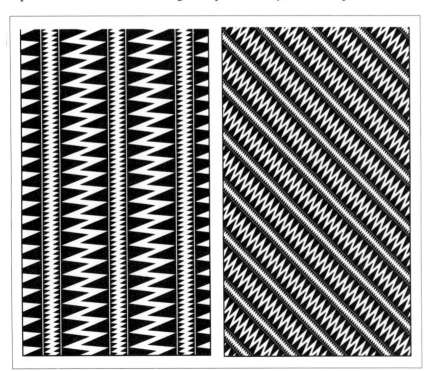

Figure 3. Transforming a PostScript pattern. A pattern from the Adobe Collector's Edition can be used as is (at left) or transformed using the move, scale, rotate or shear tools. The pattern at right has been rotated 45 degrees and scaled 50 percent.

Figure 4. Creating a blend. Illustrator's Blend function can be used to create the effect of a graduated fill. In this figure a black rectangle was blended to a white rectangle in 50 steps. The intermediate steps are drawn as grouped objects. See "Producing smooth gradations" on page 69 for more information about determining the optimal number of steps in a blend.

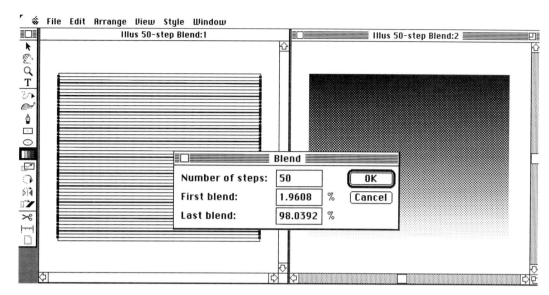

A library of additional materials (sold separately) adds to the power of Illustrator. The Adobe Collector's Edition provides patterns and textures, symbols, borders and letterforms that can be used as is, or modified using Illustrator's tools (Figure 3). Illustrator's built-in autotrace function works well to convert most bitmapped line art to PostScript, but a separate autotrace utility, Adobe Streamline, provides even greater accuracy. Both Illustrator and FreeHand (see below) can be used with the complete library of PostScript fonts produced by Adobe.

Some drawbacks of versions through Illustrator 88 include the lack of alignment grids and rules and the absence of "layers" for organizing complex illustrations. The elements of a drawing can be "stacked" using the Bring To Front and Send To Back commands, but only within the single drawing layer. Another problem is the program's inability to create graduated fills (fountains) in a one-step function. Illustrator's Blend function can be used to create linear or radial fills, but the process requires several steps (Figure 4). Illustrator does not allow editing in preview mode, so to see the effects of editing changes one must view the keyline illustration and its preview in a split screen.

Illustrator was created to be used on a Macintosh computer. Recently an IBM version has been developed, but it doesn't include all the capabilities of the Macintosh version. Missing are the Blend function, the ability to use clipping paths for masking, the ability to create custom PostScript patterns, the Pantone Matching System, and on-screen color preview.

Aldus FreeHand

Aldus FreeHand provides virtually all the capabilities of Illustrator and adds a few special functions. Graduated fills can be created easily in one step without using the "blend" function (Figure 5). Also, it's possible to draw and edit in "preview" mode, which enables the artist to see the final art at all times. Bitmapped images (saved in computer file formats called PICTs and TIFFs) can be used as templates (as in Illustrator and other programs) and also incorporated directly into an illustration (Figure 6). FreeHand can also open and edit illustrations created or saved in Illustrator's version 1.1 format.

FreeHand provides 200 drawing layers to help in the organization of complex illustrations. A background element can be placed in layer 90, for example, and rendered "inactive." Complex foreground objects can be drawn on top (in default drawing layer 100) without disturbing the background.

FreeHand provides many levels of "Undo" (the exact number can be user-specified), so artists can work backwards if editing changes are not to their liking. Guidelines can be pulled into the image area from the rulers, and a grid system allows "snap-to" alignment of objects. Text can be joined to a path of any shape, a feature especially useful for labeling features on maps or for fitting type around a circle in a logo (Figure 7).

In addition to ready-made palettes of fill and line styles, FreeHand allows users to specify custom PostScript fills and lines by entering PostScript code

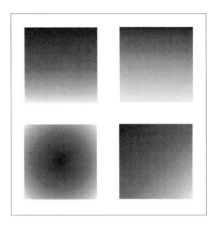

Figure 5. Creating a graduated fill. FreeHand allows the creation of graduated fills that are linear (top left), logarithmic (top right) or radial (bottom left). The angle of a fill can also be specified (bottom right). Gradations can blend between any two colors or any two shades of gray (tints of black). All the examples shown in this figure go from 90 percent black to 10 percent black.

Figure 6. Incorporating a TIFF image. "Palm Evening" by Janet Ashford incorporates a TIFF image into a FreeHand illustration. The TIFF was created by scanning a black-and-white photograph with a flatbed scanner. The figure was silhouetted using ImageStudio and placed in FreeHand. The TIFF image is opaque and obscures the background on which it's placed. Colored elements were drawn over portions of the clothing. This TIFF was used in black-and-white, but FreeHand does allow color to be applied to a grayscale image.

Figure 7. Setting text along a path. In FreeHand text can be made to flow along a path. To keep text upright around an ellipse (or curve), the circle must be ungrouped, the bottom must be cut off, the top cloned and reflected, and the text blocks joined to the two arcs.

in a dialog box. Code for several fills is included in the manual and programmers can also create original fills. FreeHand also allows users to add "comments" to the PostScript code as an illustration is created. When the code is printed as a text file, comments appear immediately before the code for the object to which they were attached. This allows easy identification of graphic elements within the code.

FreeHand supports spot and four-color process color and the Pantone Matching System. Color separations can be made directly from the program.

The method of creating masks is different in FreeHand than in Illustrator. In Illustrator the clipping path is placed behind the object to be masked and the two elements are grouped. In FreeHand, the clipping path is positioned in front and the background is "pasted inside" (see "Creating a mask" below).

Corel Draw

Corel Draw is the first illustration program to provide PostScript's capabilities to users of IBM and compatible systems. Its screen interface is simple, with few tools in the toolbox, as each one can perform multiple tasks. The mouse clicks and drags used to activate the options can be tricky to learn but ultimately save time (Figure 8).

Corel Draw incorporates most of the features common to PostScript illustration programs, including the ability to create graduated fills, an auto-

Creating a mask

Masks are created differently in FreeHand and Illustrator. In this example for a stylized drawing of a speaker grille, the following steps were taken in FreeHand:
1. Create the artwork to be masked or "clipped."
2. Create a path to serve as a "clipping path."
3. Position the clipping path over the artwork.

4. Select the art to be masked and choose Cut from the Edit menu. The art will disappear from the screen.
5. Select the clipping path and choose Paste Inside from the Edit menu. The art will reappear inside the shape of the clipping path.

To create a mask in Illustrator, follow these steps:
1. Create the artwork to be masked (such as a patterned fill).
2. Draw the masking path and select it.

3. Choose Paint from the Style menu.
4. Set the Fill and Stroke options.
5. Click in the Mask checkbox to define the path as a masking path.
6. Position the masking path over the artwork to be masked.
7. Select the path and choose Send To Back from the Edit menu.
8. Select both masking path and art and choose Group from the Arrange menu. The background art will be masked so that it shows only through the shape of the masking path.

Step 1

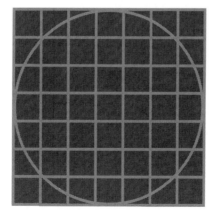

Step 3

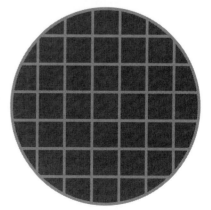

Step 5

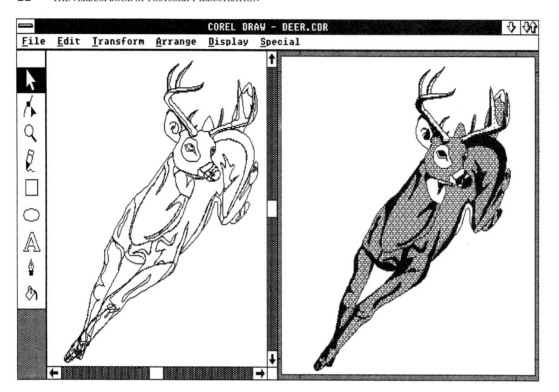

Figure 8. The Corel Draw interface. A screen shot shows the menu bar, the tool icons and a drawing in keyline (left) and preview modes.

trace function, fitting text along a path, the use of bitmaps as templates, Pantone and process color options, and custom PostScript fills.

Like Illustrator, Corel Draw works in keyline mode, providing a separate or split-screen preview mode. A freehand tool is used for drawing and for tracing templates. It automatically assigns Bezier points to curves. The point-to-point drawing tools used in Illustrator and FreeHand are not available. Calligraphic pen shapes provide some thick-and-thin variation to the PostScript line.

Corel Draw is the first program for PostScript illustration to include "macros." A macro is a series of commands or specifications assigned to a single key combination, and therefore can be applied to objects quickly and easily.

Corel Draw allows precise text handling and custom kerning (adjusting the space between pairs of letters), but only with its own set of about 50 fonts. An upgrade allows conversion of fonts from other companies. Corel Draw runs under Microsoft Windows, which must be purchased separately.

Micrografx Designer

Micrografx Designer, another program available for IBM and compatible systems, includes a freehand tool and also pen tools for generating curves point-by-point (Figure 9). Designer can create linear and radial graduated fills, and its autotrace function is particularly clean and accurate. Designer's text-handling ability is limited, but it does work with any PostScript font. Display type cannot be stroked or filled, but Designer can import large blocks of body text. There are 64 drawing layers for the organization of complex graphics. The layers can be printed together to produce a composite print, or

Figure 9. The Micrografx Designer interface. This screen shot shows the menu bar and tool icons. Designer features a freehand tool, a tool for drawing point by point, and tools for generating ellipses and rectangles.

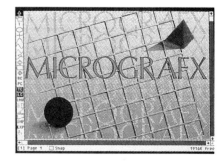

Figure 10. Starting from clip art. Arts & Letters comes with thousands of predrawn images. Additional libraries of compatible clip art (on anatomy, zoology, holidays, vehicles, maps, agriculture, computers and space) can be purchased separately. Illustrations can be created by combining clip art images.

printed individually to produce spot color separations. Designer comes with 39 standard patterns for use as fills. Custom patterns can also be created.

Designer is packaged with a version of Microsoft Windows, which imitates the Macintosh user interface. It can import and export documents in many formats, including DXF, a common format used by computer-aided design (CAD) programs. The toolbox can be customized, and the workspace accommodates about 50 pages. Fifteen different line endings are available as well as a symbol library and a large collection of compatible clip art.

Designer allows programming of the second button on the mouse and provides an on-line "context-sensitive" help system. Designer supports spot and process color and separations and provides the Pantone Matching System at an additional cost. A special "Array" feature makes it possible to copy an object a multiple of times and at the same time specify that each copy be scaled, moved or rotated in 5-degree increments.

Arts & Letters

Arts & Letters, for the IBM, is designed to be used with clip art (Figure 10). It comes with over 1000 illustrations, and users can buy up to 15,000 more. The images can be altered and will print with PostScript's clarity. Fifteen fonts come with the program; 23 more are available at $25 each. Type can be rotated and filled.

Arts & Letters comes in two packages. The Graphics Composer places and rescales clip art. The Graphics Editor manipulates clip art and allows creation of new art. Text can be used with either package. The features common to most PostScript applications are included: a freehand tool, tracing from templates, autotrace, text along a path, shape blending, clipping masks and four-color separations. Also included are calligraphic pen tools, enhanced line styles, and a "hole-cutting" function.

GEM Artline

GEM Artline is designed to work with Ventura Publisher, a page-layout program that also runs under GEM (an interface like Windows). Artline includes a symbol library and uses PostScript fonts available from the Bitstream company. It saves illustrations in the GEM line-art format and the EPS (encapsulated PostScript) format (see "Encapsulation" on page 8). Illustrations can be printed on any printer used by GEM or Ventura. The program is fast-running and features an easy-to-learn, intuitive interface.

GEM Artline can use only 14 colors at a time and cannot create graduated fills. It's not possible to rescale objects with the mouse — only through the menu. There is no "undo" capability. Artline comes with only four fonts.

Figure 11. Cricket Stylist. This logo features rotated polygons, patterned fills, and text with a drop shadow effect.

Other PostScript illustration products

Cricket Stylist A new version of Cricket Draw, the first PostScript draw program. Cricket Stylist features an easy-to-use object-oriented draw interface with additional PostScript features including Bezier curves, fountains, shadows and manipulation of type (Figure 11). Cricket Stylist is compatible with 32-bit as well as 8-bit color systems, and colors can be specified by RGB, CMYK, HLS or grayscale methods. Text can be stretched, skewed, rotated and bound to a path. Manual kerning is also available. Cricket Stylist can import PICT, PICT2, EPS and MacPaint files.

Streamline Streamline is an autotrace program designed to be used with Adobe Illustrator. Bitmapped black-and-white line art can be automatically traced and saved as a document that can be placed "as is" in a page layout program or edited further in Illustrator (Figure 12). Streamline documents that have been opened and saved as Illustrator 1.1-compatible documents can also be opened and edited in FreeHand. Streamline traces documents in TIFF, PICT and MacPaint formats. Because it's dedicated to a single purpose, Streamline produces finer, more detailed results than the autotrace functions built into many PostScript illustration programs.

Smart Art I, II and III The three Smart Art packages each contain 15 PostScript effects that are designed to be easily used by those who are not familiar with illustration. Packages I and III focus on text effects. Package II provides a series of two- and three-dimensional shapes that can be customized by changing angles, shading and rotation, and by inserting text. Smart Art must be used with a PostScript printer in order to generate its WYSIWYG screen display.

Smart Art also includes a desk accessory that can be used to create a bitmapped image from a PostScript illustration. The bitmap can then be traced (automatically or by hand) to produce a new PostScript file that can be edited. This process is sometimes desirable when working with fonts or other PostScript images that are saved in an EPS format. Such documents cannot be edited and will open without their original anchor points. When converted to bitmap, then back to PostScript, an image is equipped with points and can be further modified.

Clip art

Electronic "clip art" in PostScript format is available from many sources. Clip art collections include a variety of ready-to-use images found useful in business communications, education and other areas. Images can be used "as is" (to enliven a newsletter, for example), or incorporated into logos or other artwork. Some can be modified using the same methods used to create original art (see "Using clip art" on page 25).

Figure 12. Using autotrace. At top is a close-up of a bitmapped line drawing, at center is the PostScript autotraced version produced by Streamline, and at bottom is the complete image, saved as an Illustrator 1.1 file and then opened and enhanced in FreeHand.

Using clip art

Electronic clip art serves the same purposes as standard clip art and stock photos — for many projects it can save the time and expense of generating new art. In general, it's more versatile than the nonelectronic variety because it can be modified and combined with other clip art or with "hand-drawn" electronic artwork.

Two pieces of PostScript clip art from different files, or even different manufacturers, can be modified and successfully combined, as shown here (1).

Elements of a PostScript clip art file can be filled with flat or graduated color (2).

Clip art, "as is" or modified, can be incorporated into a PostScript illustration. Here it serves to show scale in a comprehensive drawing for signage (3).

Bitmapped clip art can be imported into a PostScript illustration program and used as a template for tracing (4). The resulting illustration has the advantage of PostScript's smooth lines and fill effects.

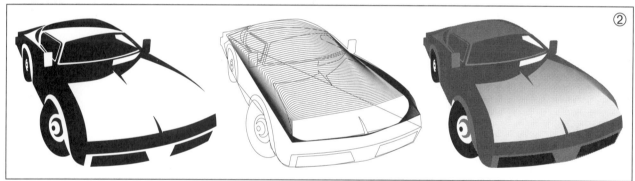

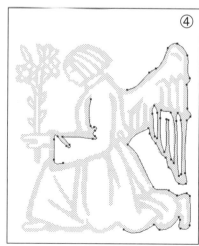

Creating a Corporate Mark

Artist

Susan Merritt has worked as a graphic designer and photographer for the past 15 years. She has a B.A. in art from Queens College in Charlotte, North Carolina and studied for five years at the Basel School of Design in Switzerland, where she specialized in graphic design. She especially enjoys designing publications, posters and symbols. Susan teaches graphic design at San Diego State University and a computer graphics workshop at Platt College in San Diego. She is a principal in Calvin Woo Associates (CWA, Inc.), a marketing communications and design firm.

Project

The assignment was to create a new corporate mark and identity package for a large East Coast seafood commodity company. The new mark was to be used on letterhead, envelopes and business cards.

Rough designs were produced using conventional methods and the final production employed a Macintosh Plus, a Sharp scanner and Chromascan software to create a bitmap template for art reference, Adobe Illustrator 1.1 for drawing and PageMaker for adding type. Proofs were printed on a LaserWriter Plus and final output was repro, produced with a Linotronic L-300 imagesetter at 2540 dpi.

Pasternak Seafood

**PROJECT
OVERVIEW**

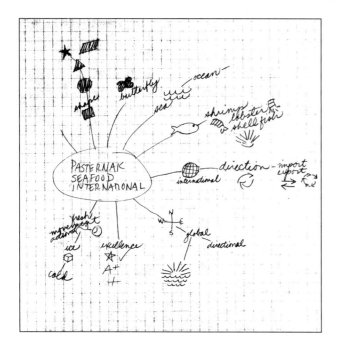

I used a "mind map" to stimulate my creative process in thinking of symbol ideas. The map begins with a central concept, in this case *Pasternak,* which is surrounded by a stream-of-consciousness network of related ideas and images.

Once I decided to use the images of sun and ocean in the symbol I made many preliminary sketches combining these elements. Shown here are three examples of the design combination that eventually evolved into the final symbol.

Design process

The client wanted a new graphic image that would convey the idea of ocean, or seafood, or freshness, but otherwise he had no particular image in mind. I began the project by creating a "mind map" of ideas associated with seafood. Mind mapping is a technique I learned while taking photographs for a brochure we did for an accelerated learning camp for teenagers. A mind map begins with a single idea or image, in this case the word *Pasternak,* the name of the company. I placed the word in the center of a page and built a network of other images and words around it as they came to mind. The map helps to connect the right and left hemispheres of the brain — your imaginative and literal sides. The process helped me to generate a number of symbol and logotype ideas, which were roughed out in marker. Three symbols were selected and prepared as color cut-paper composites and sent to the client for approval. The client chose one of these designs, which was developed into the final symbol.

Working with a consultant

Around the time we took on this project, we had become aware of the Macintosh computer and its use in graphic design. We thought the seafood symbol might be a good project to use in learning this new technology. We hired Jack Davis, a designer who had established and was director of the computer graphics and design department at Platt College in San Diego. Jack worked with us to generate our design with Adobe Illustrator and also trained us at the same time. Since then we've found the computer to be an invaluable design tool.

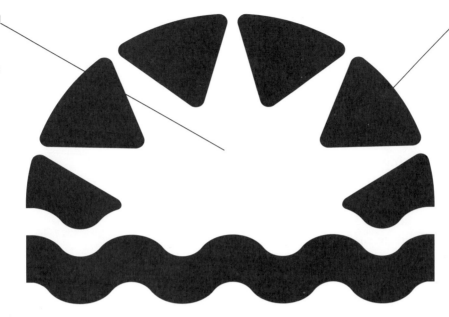

Our symbol design makes use of negative space to create the image of a sun over water. The design is composed of simple geometric shapes that are easily rendered and manipulated in Illustrator.

Each triangle shape contains two straight sides and one slightly curved side. The curved sides are fitted against an invisible arch. Bezier curve control in Illustrator allows for precise fitting of curves.

The finished corporate mark is printed in three PMS colors: the triangle shapes are printed in turquoise (PMS 313) and the wave shape in a medium blue (PMS 285). The type is gray (PMS 424).

Pasternak Seafood

Pasternak Seafood International, Inc.

777 West Putnam Avenue
Greenwich, Connecticut
06830

(203) 531-3400

TLX: ITT 475-0030
FAX: (203) 531-3429

Pasternak Seafood International, Inc.

777 West Putnam Avenue
Greenwich, Connecticut
06830

Vincent F. Arfuso
Int'l Sales Manager

Pasternak Seafood International, Inc.

777 West Putnam Avenue   (203) 531-3400
Greenwich, Connecticut   TLX: ITT 475-0030
06830   FAX: (203) 531-3429

Using the computer to generate our symbol allowed us to easily resize it for use on letterhead, envelope and business cards. The mechanicals for these were produced using PageMaker 1.2 and conventional art production. We also generated repro sheets of the symbol and logotype for the client to use.

The initial symbol design combines an image of the sun with an image of ocean waves. The symbol is constructed of separate inked elements, spaced so that the sun and some of the wave image are created by white space. It would have been extremely tedious and time-consuming to produce by hand, requiring the use of a compass and drawing templates. But its execution in Illustrator was fairly simple.

Copying and reflecting

Jack scanned a copy of our symbol comp to use as a template in Illustrator. First we drew a circle and a vertical rule (Figure 1). These were painted with no stroke and no fill so they would not print in the final image. The template was positioned to align with the circle and rule guides. Then we drew our basic triangle shape with the pen tool (Figure 2), using as few points as possible to define the shape. ▮ *It's most efficient to use as few anchor points as possible when drawing lines and curves (see "Reducing the number of points" on page 145). Curves can be adjusted by dragging the direction lines that are displayed with each anchor point. If needed, new points can be added later using the scissors tool.* We copied the triangle, rotated the copies and aligned them against the inside of the left half of the circle (Figure 3). Once aligned, these three triangles were grouped, copied and flipped across the vertical axis to create an arch of triangles (Figure 4).

Figure 1. Setting up guides. We drew a nonprinting (no stroke, no fill) circle and vertical line to act as on-screen guides for our drawing.

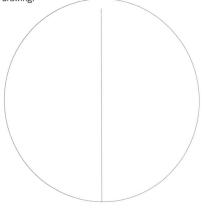

Figure 2. Drawing the triangle. The basic triangle shape was created using Illustrator's pen tool, using the minimum number of anchor points needed to define the shape.

Figure 3. Aligning the triangles. The triangle was copied twice and each copy was moved and rotated slightly to fit in position around the inside of a circle. Objects can be rotated in two ways: manually, by dragging the object with the mouse, or by typing a numerical angle of rotation in a dialog box. We used the manual method to align the PostScript triangles with those in the bitmap template.

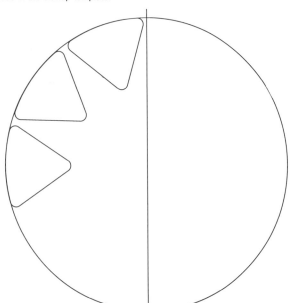

Figure 4. Completing the arch. The three triangles were selected and copied as a group and reflected across the vertical diameter of the circle.

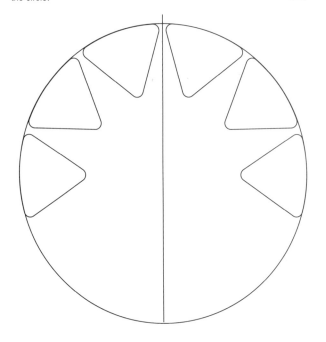

Figure 5. Drawing the wave top. Jack used an ingenious method to create the wave shape. First he used the pen tool to plot points defining an undulating line segment. To make the line more interesting than a simple sine wave, he tweaked the curves so that the wave peaks are slightly wider than the wave troughs.

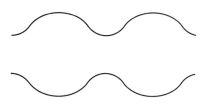

Figure 6. Duplicating the line. The first line segment was copied and the copy was reflected across a horizontal axis and positioned to serve as the bottom line of the wave.

Figure 7. Aligning peaks and troughs. The copy was offset to the right by one-half wave length, so that the wave peaks and troughs were lined up over each other.

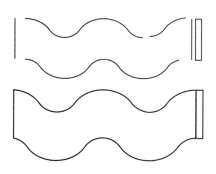

Figure 8. Completing the wave segment. The overhang at the left of the top line was cut using the scissors tool and this small line segment was repositioned and joined at the right of the line. The top and bottom lines were joined at the ends with vertical rules to create a closed path that could be filled with solid color. A narrow rectangle was also added to cap the end of the curve shape.

Next we created a shape to represent the ocean waves. A curve was drawn, with some careful tweaking of the Bezier curves to get the line just right (Figure 5). The curve was duplicated and the copy was flipped horizontally (Figure 6) and slid to the right (Figure 7). Original and copy were joined (Figure 8) and copied, and the copy was flipped across the vertical axis (Figure 9).

Using opaque layers

If we had executed this design traditionally, we would have had to outline and ink the special shapes that occur where the bottom pair of triangles meet the wave shape. Using Illustrator offered the opportunity for a quicker, easier solution. One copy of the wave shape was filled with white and used to mask off the bottom triangles. Then another copy was filled with black and set just below. Layering to partially obscure elements of a design is possible because of the opacity of filled objects created in PostScript illustration (Figure 10).

■ *When planning an illustration, keep in mind that PostScript objects are always opaque. Layering opaque objects over each other can produce unique design solutions. Some PostScript designs would need to be planned and executed differently if they were to be done using conventional art media.*

Fine-tuning the image

After we saw how the finished symbol construction looked, we noticed a slight difficulty with the look of the inside corners of the lower pair of triangles, where these were overlaid by the opaque white wave. To make the curved corner look more pleasing, Jack edited the anchor points to better fit the area of overlap (Figure 11).

Choosing the type

The finished symbol was saved as an EPS file and imported into PageMaker, where we added the type. We made the switch because PageMaker allowed us to individually kern character pairs in the type, a feature that Illustrator didn't have.

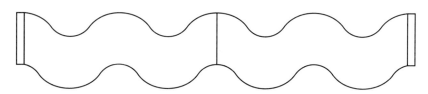

Figure 9. Finishing the shape. The wave shape was copied and reflected across the vertical axis at the center of the design. The two halves were grouped so that they could be moved together as one shape.

We chose a serif face for the type because the contrast between thick and thin lines in the letters complemented the thick and thin interplay in the symbol. We also wanted a classical face to convey stability, reliability and a sense of quality and excellence. We wanted to give a feeling of warmth and friendliness to the mark and felt that a sans serif face would be inappropriate. The Garamond typeface fit all our requirements.

Final output

The final imagesetter output was pasted up mechanically, and the colors were designated for the printer. Illustrator did not support color separations at that time, but because our color elements did not touch, the design allowed easy specification of spot color.

The computer turned out to be a big advantage for this job. It would have been difficult to match the precision and accuracy of Illustrator using traditional methods. Masking, duplicating and repeating elements is much harder to do by hand, and it requires much more time. Another real advantage was the computer's ability to rescale images. We were able to put together a repro sheet for the client, with the corporate mark in various sizes for photo reproduction.

In retrospect

When we began the Pasternak project we had no idea it would ultimately be produced using the computer. The particular strengths and capabilities of Illustrator were not a factor in the design process. Later it turned out that the Pasternak symbol was a perfect candidate for computer illustration, and we were fascinated to observe how Jack constructed it on-screen.

Figure 10. Creating shapes with opaque overlay. One copy of the wave shape was filled with white and used to obscure the lower portion of the bottom pair of triangles. It's shown here with a black outline, but in the final design it was stroked with None. By partly obscuring one solid object with another we created the illusion of a single shape with a complex outline. The anchor points that define the inside curved corner of the lower pair of triangles were adjusted to better fit the shape of the white wave element that partially obscures them. Another wave shape was filled with black and positioned slightly below and in front of the white wave shape. This completed the graphic elements of our logo design.

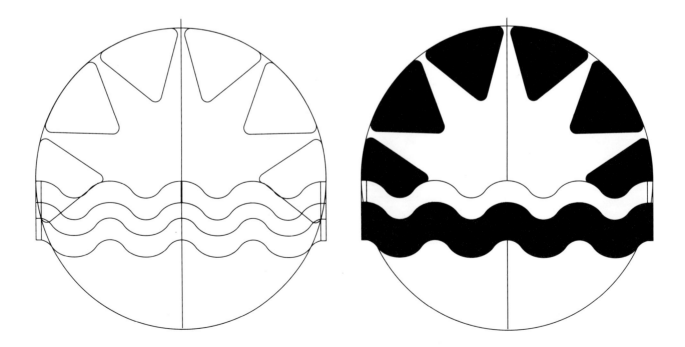

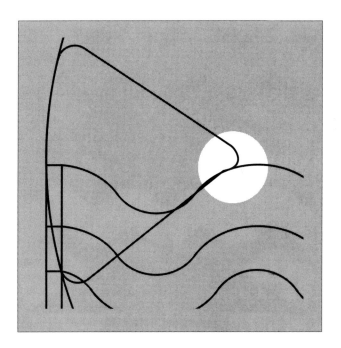

Figure 11. Fine-tuning the lower triangles. The curved corners that face inward on the two bottom triangles were clipped by the white wave element in a slightly unpleasing way. To resolve this, the anchor points defining the inside point of each triangle were tweaked to make them better fit the curve of the wave shape.

Our design firm has changed drastically since we started using the computer. Probably 90 percent of our design work now involves the computer. I have a hard time finding a non-repro blue pencil around the studio anymore.

Using the computer was neither an advantage nor a disadvantage with our seafood client. I don't think the client was even aware that a computer was being used. But now we find that designers who've been in business for 15 or 20 years are losing jobs if they can't handle computer input. For instance, clients, especially institutional clients, often bring their text copy on a computer disk and expect the designer to be able to handle that. People tend to expect that the computer can get a job done faster, which is often true — but not always. The computer has the potential to save time, because you don't have to duplicate your efforts, especially with typesetting. I think the industry has lost some quality with type, though, as designers take on the tasks previously done by the typesetter and proofreader. Designers typically haven't been expected to watch out for typographic mistakes. To ensure absolute satisfaction, we usually hold the client responsible for final proofing of copy.

Another problem we've noticed is that people with a computer but without design training sometimes feel they can create or duplicate artwork, but they don't pay attention to the details that make a design effective. For instance, one of our client's employees wanted to use our new logo design but didn't have a repro available, so she scanned the image using a fax transmission as an original and re-created the logo on the computer. The final result was distorted, and it was used with the wrong typeface. We quickly sent the company a repro sheet of logos. We feel it's very important for designers to oversee jobs done with the computer. Nondesigners often produce work that's unacceptable from a design standpoint, but that has impressed them because it's cleanly printed with finished-looking type. Good results require both design skills and computer skills.

Susan Merritt

"I still like to use a mix of methods in creating artwork. It seems more comfortable to begin with a drawing or sketch. But there's no doubt that I now prefer using the computer for the final execution of a piece. I've tried not to fall into the trap of designing for the computer and its particular limitations. Before the advent of the Bezier curve, you were quite limited in what could be executed. But now virtually anything you can imagine can be accomplished. I find I make more use of elements like graduated fills, which were harder to manage before the computer. Wrapping type or placing type along a curve is also much easier and can be done within a small budget. And it's wonderful to see the final design effects right on the screen, without having to wait for typesetting or a press proof."

I used Illustrator to create the graphic elements and vertical type for this calendar for SOS Printing. The layout was done in PageMaker.

This symbol for the Printing Industries Association of San Diego was created in Illustrator 88.

The symbol and logotype for Palmier Bistro (*palmier* means "palm" in French) were finalized using Illustrator 88. To create a template, hand-rendered sketches were scanned using a Thunderscan and an ImageWriter.

The symbol for Modular Building Concepts was created with Illustrator. The letterhead features the symbol in large and small sizes, with the larger size bled off the top to emphasize the M shape within it.

For a brochure describing San Diego State University's Creative Arts Showcase, I used Illustrator 88 to create tilted squares filled with letterforms and other rotated type elements. These were imported into a PageMaker layout.

C H A P T E R   4

A Technical Tour de Force

Artist

Bert Monroy, illustrator, designer and native New Yorker, has worked in advertising for 20 years, first for several large agencies and more recently as owner of his own shop. He is also a principal of Incredible Interactivity, a firm specializing in the production of interactive and multimedia presentations. In 1984, Bert produced HumanForms. One of the first graphics packages for the Mac, Human-Forms is a collection of over one thousand body parts that when assembled, can create human figures in any possible position.

Bert's illustrations have been published in *MacWorld*, *MacUser*, *MacWeek*, *Personal Publishing*, *Verbum* and *Byte*. His images have also been used to introduce and advertise several major graphics software programs including ImageStudio and PixelPaint. Bert currently serves as a consultant to various advertising agencies and financial institutions as well as major corporations in the New York area and is also on the faculty of both the School of Visual Arts and the Dynamic Graphics Educational Foundation.

Project

A friend at a local service and training bureau asked if I would do a quick illustration of a loupe to include in a brochure for classes on prepress techniques. The illustration was created in Adobe Illustrator 88 on a Macintosh II. A LaserWriter IINT was used for proofing, with final output on a Linotronic L-300 imagesetter.

Design goals

No photograph was available to scan as a template, nor did I have one to look at for reference, so the loupe had to be drawn from "life." The overall shape of the magnifying glass is quite simple and could be rendered with a series of ellipses. But careful attention had to be paid to the textures of plastic and glass to give it a realistic look. Shading and highlights were necessary to give a feeling of depth and to make the illustration pop off the page.

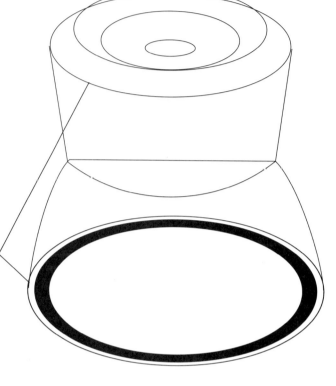

A series of ellipses formed the basis of the loupe.

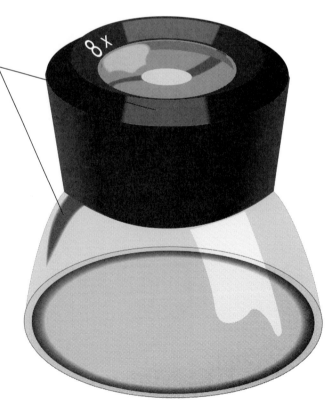

The ellipses were filled with black and shades of gray and both hard- and soft-edged highlights were added to suggest the reflective surfaces of black plastic and clear glass.

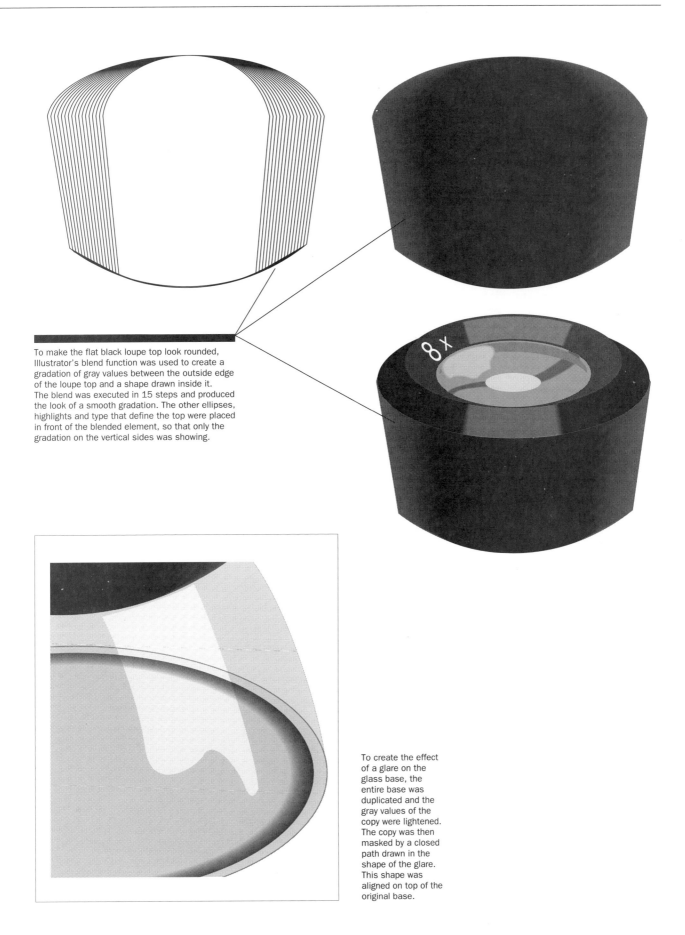

To make the flat black loupe top look rounded,
Illustrator's blend function was used to create a
gradation of gray values between the outside edge
of the loupe top and a shape drawn inside it.
The blend was executed in 15 steps and produced
the look of a smooth gradation. The other ellipses,
highlights and type that define the top were placed
in front of the blended element, so that only the
gradation on the vertical sides was showing.

To create the effect
of a glare on the
glass base, the
entire base was
duplicated and the
gray values of the
copy were lightened.
The copy was then
masked by a closed
path drawn in the
shape of the glare.
This shape was
aligned on top of the
original base.

llustrator 88 is one of the most powerful drawing tools available for the Macintosh. It may not have fancy type effects built-in, but it has perfected the art of object-oriented graphics. With high-resolution output devices, the line quality is perfect. Even with a magnifying glass you can't detect the stair-stepping synonymous with bitmapped computer art. Using Illustrator is like having the most elaborate set of French curves and one of every Rapidograph pen imaginable (even the ones too fine to allow ink to flow). A designer's magnifying glass (loupe) is a good example to demonstrate the capabilities of Illustrator 88. The basic shape of the magnifier was achieved by creating a series of ellipses (Figure 1). Tones were added to each, with the color saturation being determined by the light source above the loupe (lighter tones toward the top, darker toward the bottom).

To create the straight-sided shape that defines the black top of the magnifier, I made a duplicate of the ellipse that makes up the outside rim. The duplicate was brought directly below to form the bottom of the plastic eyepiece. The duplicate was then reduced in size by 10 percent because the eyepiece narrows toward the bottom. The ellipse was then ungrouped. With the scissors tool, I cut the bottom ellipse at the left and right anchor points and discarded the top portion of the ellipse. Using the pen tool, I constructed the rest of the shape from the edges (Figure 2). Since the new polygon for the base fell behind all the ellipses that form the top of the eyepiece, the base could be squared off thus eliminating the need to follow the contour of the top.

Figure 1. Using ellipses. Construction of the magnifier began with a series of ellipses.

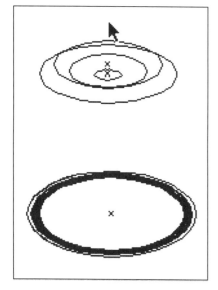

Figure 2. Constructing the top. To create the loupe's plastic top, the bottom ellipse was cut and joined to the top ellipse with slightly flaring straight lines.

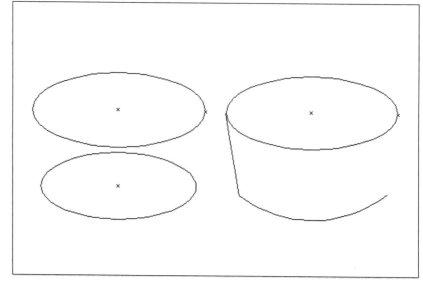

Simulating roundness

To create the shading at the right and left sides of the top, a narrow version of the outside shape was created. This new shape was centered within the eyepiece and assigned a black fill. The outside edge was assigned a 65 percent black fill. With the blend tool, the two shapes were then interpolated to create a smooth gradation, giving the effect of roundness to the eyepiece (see page 39).

Tilting the type

The tilted lettering on the top of the loupe was easy to create. The "8" and the "x" were typed in Helvetica. Each character was typed separately, since each is distorted differently. Each character was skewed and rotated by eye to follow the contour and direction of the eyepiece's curved top (Figure 3).

Soft-edged highlights

Highlights were added as polygons within the ellipses. Highlights in most cases have soft edges, so I created a polygon with the same tone as the ellipse, and then placed a duplicate polygon within the original and reduced it slightly in size. The duplicate was assigned the color of the highlight. The original and the duplicate were then interpolated using the blend tool (Figure 4). The soft shadow at the base of the glass was obtained in the same manner.

Using masking to create a glare

To simulate the look of a glare on the right side of the glass base, I needed to create a highlight that also contained a section of the curved lines that define the edge of the base. I did this by using Illustrator's ability to mask objects. (For more about masking to create highlights, see "A blue-eyed tutorial" on page 42.) I duplicated the base and made the copy a percentage lighter in tone

Figure 3. Distorting the type. The "8" and the "x" at the top of the magnifier were skewed and rotated to fit the inside curve of the top.

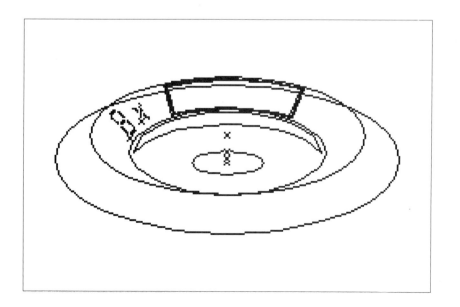

A blue-eyed tutorial

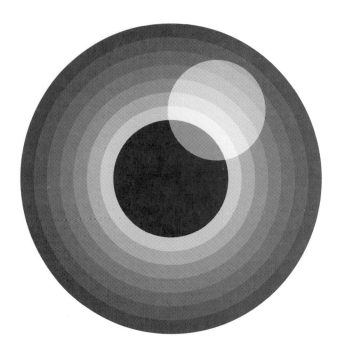

The following is an exercise I developed for an Illustrator class I teach for Dynamic Graphics. It's simple and easy to follow as you sit at your Macintosh, and it teaches the use of the blend tool, masking and color.

1. To start, go to the Open option under the File menu. In the Illustrator folder select the file called "Pantone colors." Now select New from the File menu. ▌ *When the Pantone file is opened in the background it allows selection of Pantone colors in the Paint dialog box under Custom Color.*

2. With a new, blank Illustrator document now open, select the circle tool, hold down the Shift key to constrain the object and drag the mouse to draw a circle large enough to almost reach the top of the window. Don't deselect the circle.

3. Go to the Paint dialog box by pressing Command-I on the keyboard or by selecting Paint from the Style menu.

4. Select Custom Color in the Fill portion of the dialog box and then scroll down and select Pantone 273 CV, a shade of blue. Click OK to close the dialog box.

5. Still using the circle tool, place the cursor directly on top of the center point of the first circle. Holding down the Option and Shift keys, draw another circle about one-third the radius of the original. Don't deselect the new circle. ▌ *Using the Option key with the circle or the rectangle tool allows you to draw from the center outward as opposed to drawing from the corner. The Shift key constrains these tools to draw perfect circles and squares as opposed to ovals and rectangles.*

6. With the smaller circle still selected, go to the Paint dialog box again by pressing Command-I on the keyboard or selecting Paint from the Style menu.

7. Select Custom Color in the Fill portion of the dialog box, scroll down and this time select Pantone 277 CV. Notice that this is a lighter version of the blue we previously selected. Click OK to close the box.

8. Now select all the points of the two circles by pressing Command-A on the keyboard or choosing Select All from the Edit menu. With all the points selected, ungroup the objects by pressing Command-U or choose Ungroup from the Arrange menu.

9. While the objects are still selected, choose the pointer tool, hold down the Option key and click and drag the circles to the right to create a copy of them.

10. With the new set of circles still selected, go to the Paint dialog box. Just below the Colors box within the Fill box you'll notice a Tint option. Type "40" into the percent box.

11. While the circles are still selected, choose the blend tool. Position the cursor, which has become a cross-hair, over the top point on the large circle and click. Notice that the right side of the cursor has extended.

Now click on the top point of the smaller circle. A dialog box will appear requesting the number of steps you desire. The computer will create this many steps to blend one object into the other, both in shape and color.

12. Type "6" and click OK. You have now created a blend between the circles of the duplicate pair.

13. Choose the pointer tool. Holding down the Option key, click on the original large circle. Now, holding down the Option and Shift keys, click on the original small circle. ▌ *Holding down the Option key when selecting an object will select all the points of the object as if it were grouped. The Shift-and-Option combination selects multiple objects in the same fashion.*

14. Repeat the same process with the blend tool on the original circles as you did with the duplicates. Now you have two pairs of blended circles.

15. With the pointer tool, select the center circle only of the original set of circles on the left and go to the Paint dialog box. Select Black, leave "100" in the percent box and click OK.

16. Select the center circle only of the duplicate pair of circles and go to the Paint dialog box. Select Black, type "40" into the percent box and click OK.

17. Now go back to the circle tool and draw a circle about two inches in diameter or just a bit smaller than the center circle of the originals.

18. With the new circle still selected, select Ungroup from the Arrange menu or type Command-U.

19. With the circle still selected go to the Paint dialog box and select None in the Fill box and in the Stroke box. Then select the Mask option. Click OK.

20. Choose the pointer tool and deselect the circle by clicking elsewhere in the window. Now click the center point of the new circle and hit the Delete key to discard it. Holding down the Option key to select all the points together, select the new circle and drag it over the blended set of duplicate circles on the right so that it covers part of the center circle. While it's still selected, send it to the back by choosing Send To Back from the Edit menu.

21. Select this masking circle and all of the duplicate blended circles (not the originals on the left) and group them together by pressing Command-G or choosing Group from the Arrange menu. The mask and large circles are now one. Drag them over the original circles on the left so that the two sets are centered over each other.

22. Center the drawing on your screen with the scroll bars and press Command-Y or select Preview Illustration from the View menu. Sit back and see the eyeball you've just created, complete with a glowing reflection.

Figure 4. Softening a highlight. To soften the edges, the inner and outer outlines of the highlight were blended using four intermediate steps.

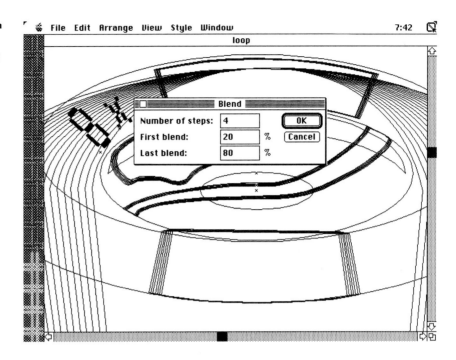

than the original. The shape of the glare was then designated as a Mask with No Fill and No Stroke in the Paint dialog box. This mask was placed behind the lighter-colored base and grouped with it to form one object. The glare shape was then placed over the original base and the result is the look of light hitting glass (Figure 5).

In retrospect

The magnifier was created from scratch as a life drawing without a template. However, when I first started experimenting with Illustrator, I would pencil out ideas, scan them and trace them in the program. The scan appears on the screen as a grayed-out image, a template for easy tracing. This process is exactly like the Old World process of placing a sheet of velum or tracing paper over a piece of art to be traced with a pen. PICT files can also be converted to the PostScript format, which can give new life to some of those old Draw files that have been stored away.

Figure 5. Creating a glare. A clipping path in the shape of a glare highlight was used to mask a lighter version of the magnifier's base.

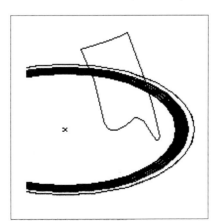

PORTFOLIO

Bert Monroy

"The flexibility of the computer and the fact that it allows us to create and preview various alternatives to a single idea greatly assists the creative process. The computer also puts all the tools of a traditional design studio, plus tools never before dreamed of, within one box. There are virtually no limitations on bringing the stuff of imagination to reality."

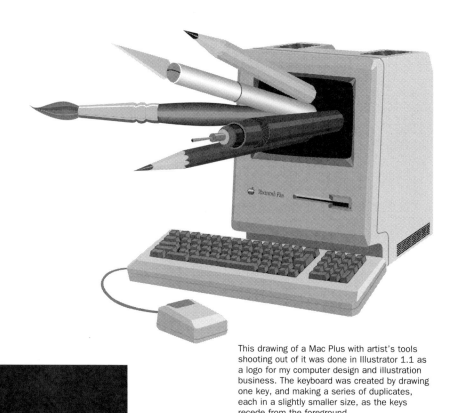

This drawing of a Mac Plus with artist's tools shooting out of it was done in Illustrator 1.1 as a logo for my computer design and illustration business. The keyboard was created by drawing one key, and making a series of duplicates, each in a slightly smaller size, as the keys recede from the foreground.

Illustrator 1.1 was used to create this illustration of a drawing board for *Computer Graphics* magazine. The Mac Plus and keyboard already created for my self-promotion logo (above) were copied, rotated and positioned in the trash can.

"Ol' 4:47" was drawn in Illustrator 1.1 for *Computer Graphics* magazine. I used a photo reference, but did not scan it for use as a template. The drawing was made by eye.

This illustration of an Olympus Pearlcorder was made in Illustrator 1.1 for *Verbum* magazine. I drew nonprinting guidelines for aligning the grid of dots that represents the speaker. The dots were duplicated and made smaller each time as they go from top left to lower right.

This drawing of a Mac II was made in Illustrator 1.1 for a service bureau's corporate identity package. After drawing the computer from "life" I exaggerated the perspective. The keyboard was created in the same way as for the Mac Plus (see opposite page).

CHAPTER 5

Birth of an Athletic Shoe

Artist

Kate Bartelmes is a freelance graphic artist who lives in Issaquah, Washington. She has been designing and illustrating for 20 years, for clients ranging from small businesses to major department stores and manufacturers. Kate became involved in computer graphics in 1987. One of her major clients is a shoe manufacturer who finds that the computer process greatly facilitates designing, colorizing and making samples.

Project

The project is an on-going one to create new designs and color illustrations for athletic shoes. The illustrations are used by the factory as a guide for making patterns and sample shoes.

Original black-and-white line drawings are done on an unenhanced Macintosh SE with a 20 MB hard drive and 1 MB of RAM and printed on a General Business Laser-Printer. Aldus FreeHand 2.0 is used for the illustrations. No scanning is done; I do all the drawings "freehand" using a standard mouse. Colorization is done on a Macintosh II with a 40 MB hard drive and 1 MB of RAM. Color proofs are run at high resolution using a Tektronix Model 4693D thermal transfer printer with 8 MB of RAM.

**▌PROJECT
OVERVIEW**

Project background

For the past several years I've worked with a shoe manufacturer who subcontracts for a large Northwest maker of outdoor sportswear. In the past I used pens and paper to create our initial shoe designs and went through masses of tracing paper working out revisions. Final designs were photocopied and colored with felt pen on occasion. Usually a drawing would be taken to a factory in the Orient along with English instructions on design and colorization to be translated into the local language. Producing a sample was often a disaster and had to be redone more than once because of miscommunication or errors in translation. We needed a way to streamline the process and reduce the possibilities for error overseas.

I've been drawing shoes and other line art for retail ads for 20 years. Two years ago I became aware of the graphics capabilities of the Macintosh and began using FreeHand for illustration. I immediately saw that PostScript illustration could solve many of our production problems.

Working with the client

When I first talked with the manufacturer about using the computer for illustration, he couldn't believe the ease with which changes could be made. Adjusting shape, stitching or form could be done on-screen, and — ZAP — by using the Command-Z keyboard shortcut for Undo we could compare the variations instantly. Coloring a line of shoes was a dream. The basic design was cloned and recolored — that's all there was to it. Using Copy and Paste we could produce line sheets, salesmen's catalogs, order forms, anything we needed. I had him hooked.

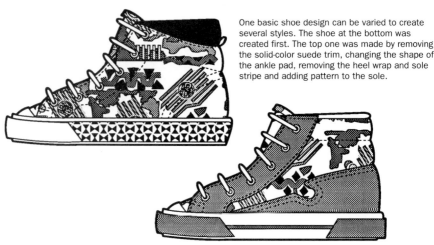

One basic shoe design can be varied to create several styles. The shoe at the bottom was created first. The top one was made by removing the solid-color suede trim, changing the shape of the ankle pad, removing the heel wrap and sole stripe and adding pattern to the sole.

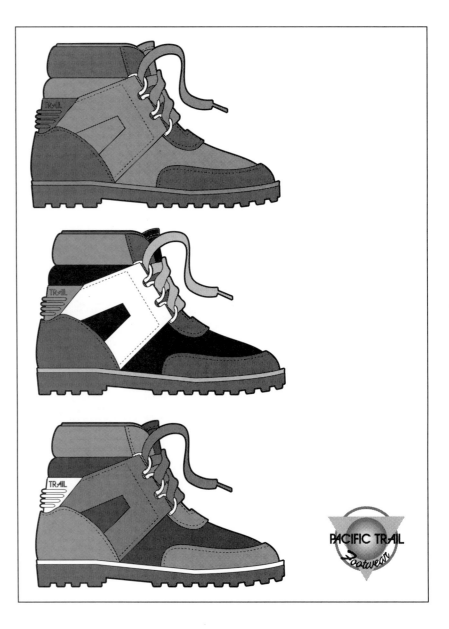

After approval of a design in black-and-white, the shoes are colorized and copies are printed on a color thermal transfer printer to be used as guides for making sample shoes.

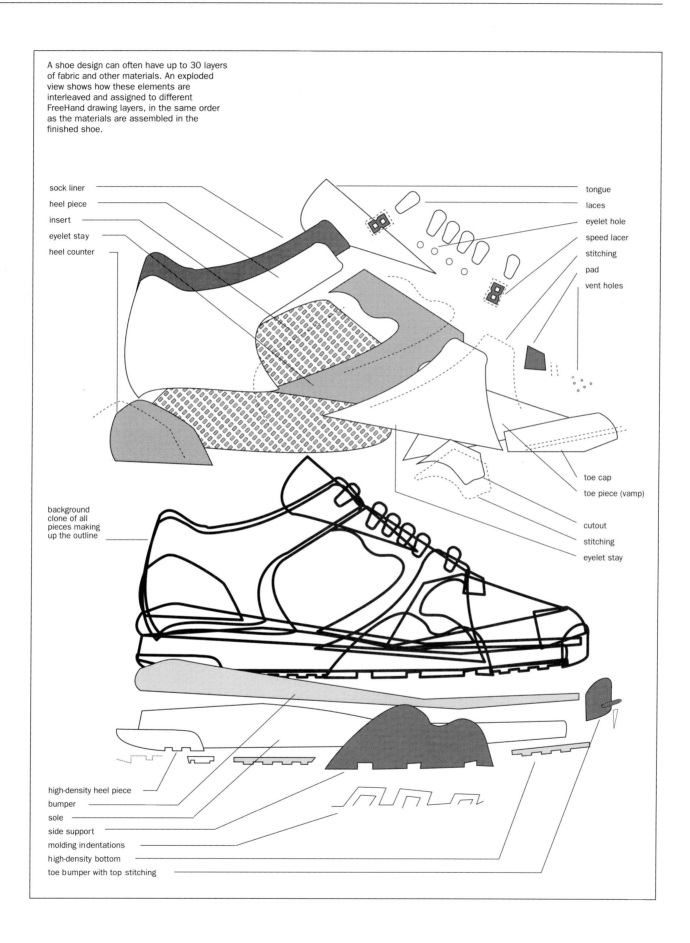

A shoe design can often have up to 30 layers of fabric and other materials. An exploded view shows how these elements are interleaved and assigned to different FreeHand drawing layers, in the same order as the materials are assembled in the finished shoe.

sock liner

heel piece

insert

eyelet stay

heel counter

tongue

laces

eyelet hole

speed lacer

stitching

pad

vent holes

background clone of all pieces making up the outline

toe cap

toe piece (vamp)

cutout

stitching

eyelet stay

high-density heel piece

bumper

sole

side support

molding indentations

high-density bottom

toe bumper with top stitching

To begin a shoe design I'm usually given a rough drawing showing what features are to be included. First I make an initial line drawing on my Mac SE and proof it on the laser printer. This first black-and-white drawing is used for working out the design. Do we like the sole? Should we try a different lacing system? Does the shape of the toe look right? What about heel height? The manufacturer and I used to work out the designs together at the computer. Now I do a first draft, he makes changes with a colored pen, and I do revisions. When changes have been made and approved, the design is colorized using a Mac II and printed on a thermal transfer printer. After approval the color proof, along with PMS color specifications, is sent to the Orient for use in creating shoe samples. After approval of the samples, the shoes are produced and distributed to stores.

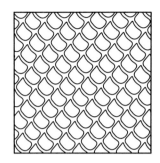

Templates

When creating designs for shoes, I use templates I've specially made with appropriate line attributes that will reproduce well on both the laser printer and the Tektronix. For instance nothing smaller than a half-point line comes out well on the Tektronix. One template is outfitted with precreated tiled fills (Figure 1), one without the fills to save memory, and another one is set up just for the color printer with all the colors premixed.

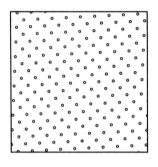

Making a tiled fill

To create a tiled fill, I draw a single element — the small rectangles, for example — and make a background box of whatever color or shape I want. The drawn element and the background box together make up a "tile" (Figure 2). This tile is cut or copied to the clipboard, and then pasted into the Tiled Fill dialog box found under the Fill menu. ∎ *A half-point line around the background in the same color as the fill eliminates the appearance of tiny white lines between the tiles.*

When the tile is created, I name it and the name appears in the Fill menu for use in any enclosed shape I wish. I find the tiled fills technique very useful for creating stripes, mesh, perforations in the leather, or any repeated pattern. I used to create fills using the cut-and-paste-inside method (FreeHand 1.0 didn't have the tiled fill option; it was a new feature with 2.0), but I found that this consumed too much memory. For instance, an illustration of a girl's tennis shoe with stripes took over an hour and 45 minutes to print on the Tektronix. Using tiled fills, the file was reduced in size by about a third and the printing time went to 20 minutes.

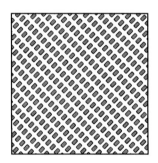

I've developed special lines to indicate outlines, stitching, basic shapes and detail. All the lines are selected from the Basic line option in the Line menu (Figure 3). Basically, these sets or templates of lines or fills are created by defining the characteristics and names in a FreeHand illustration document, and then always opening that document when I begin the design of a new shoe. I simply Save As and give the new shoe document a new name. The original document containing my lines and fills remains unchanged.

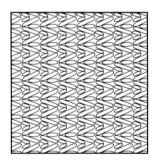

Figure 1. Creating a palette of fills. Sets of tiled fills are created and kept on hand in the Fill menu for use in new shoe designs. The fills shown here are called snake, holes, rectangles and rope.

Figure 2. Creating a tiled fill. Without a background box the drawn elements of a tile will be butted tightly together. Placing drawn elements in a box allows for more spacing between them. Other elements can also be used to create a tile, including type and imported bitmaps or TIFF images.

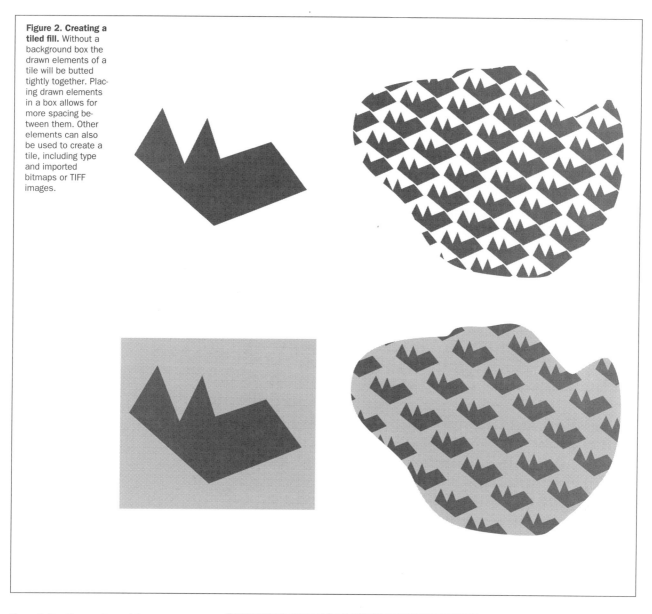

Figure 3. Creating a palette of lines. The lines preset in the shoe templates are quite straightforward. Patterned or custom PostScript lines are not used. Lines are selected for their ability to reproduce well on the color and black-and-white printers used. "Outline 2.5" is a 5-point line with rounded caps and joins to imitate the look of a mechanical pen. It's called a 2.5 outline because only half of the line width actually shows when other opaque shoe elements are placed on top of it. The "big stitch" line has a customized on-off pattern. To develop a custom line pattern, you choose Basic from the Line menu, hold down the Option key, choose a line from the pop-up Pattern series and edit it in the dialog box provided.

outline 2.5

blk 1

reg. line .7

blk .5

hairline .3

blk stitching .5

blk stitching .3

gray reg line .5

gray .7

gray stitching .5

big stitch

I don't often use custom PostScript fills or lines for the simple reason that they cannot as yet print on a Tektronix printer. PostScript is extremely important for graphics, and when I do get my own color printer, it will have to be PostScript-compatible. I've also had to scan many elements of type so that they would print on the Tek. An example is the "Footwear" type in script joined to a curve on the Pacific Trail logo (Figure 4). I had to create a graphic to make it print properly.

Using MacroMaker

System 6.02 with its macro recorder has been very useful for my outlining method. ▮ *MacroMaker is a feature of Apple's System 6.02 that allows the automatic recording of a custom series of commonly used procedures (a macro) which is then assigned a name or a function key.*

For instance, I used MacroMaker to create the macro for my shoe outline (note the fat black outline that holds the illustration together and gives it a lot of its individual style). I opened MacroMaker and recorded a set of commands that defined the outline as a 5-point black line (Figure 5). I assigned this to a key and saved it. Now whenever I need that procedure, I simply push one key.

Working in layers

FreeHand allows an illustration to be created on different "layers," up to a maximum of 200. I use a minimum of four layers, also employing front-to-back layering within each individual layer (Figure 6). Basically a shoe is drawn and its parts assigned to layers in the order that the layers of leather or fabric are put together and attached to the shoe. The sole is the final layer; it covers the bottom portion of the upper. The heavy black outline that surrounds the entire shoe goes behind on the lowest level. The use of multiple layers is essential for

Figure 4. Turning type into a graphic element. When a PostScript font is printed on a non-PostScript printer, the result is a poorly resolved image. PostScript fonts were used to create the Footwear logo, and then the type outlines were traced to create a graphic element that prints with better quality on the Tektronix printer.

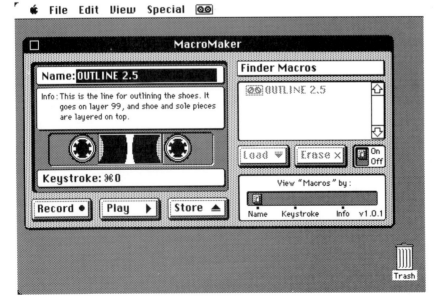

Figure 5. Using MacroMaker. To create the macro for the 5-point black shoe outline the following steps were recorded in MacroMaker:
1. *Command- =*, to clone the shoe outline.
2. Specification of no fill by choosing None from the Fill menu.
3. *Command- –*, to send the line to a layer.
4. *99*, to specify layer 99.
5. Specification of a 5-point black line with rounded caps and corners by choosing a pre-specified 5-point black line from the line menu. This sequence is assigned to a key combination (Command-o) and saved. Whenever the shoe outline is to be changed, all five steps can be accomplished by pressing one key combination. (MacroMaker is installed by moving the MacroMaker icon from the Utilities folder to the System folder and restarting the computer. The MacroMaker icon then appears at the right side of the menu bar with its own list of options.

organizing all the elements of an illustration. There can easily be over 30 shoe pieces layered on top of each other. "Bringing to front" or "Sending to back" can become confusing and is not time- and cost-effective. By organizing the parts into simpler layers of three or four items, I can control elements better and deactivate layers that are not in use.

Figure 6. Using layers. FreeHand's use of layers makes it easier to handle the elements of a complex shoe illustration. Three or four layers are used for each shoe, with related elements of the shoe's construction grouped together in each layer.

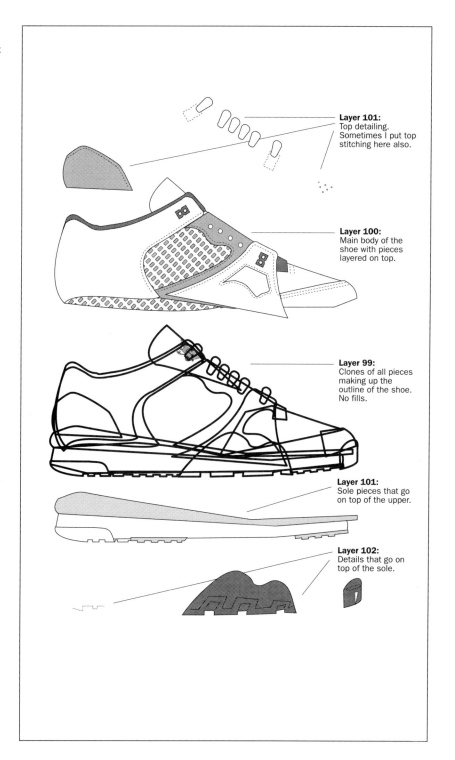

Layer 101:
Top detailing. Sometimes I put top stitching here also.

Layer 100:
Main body of the shoe with pieces layered on top.

Layer 99:
Clones of all pieces making up the outline of the shoe. No fills.

Layer 101:
Sole pieces that go on top of the upper.

Layer 102:
Details that go on top of the sole.

Adding color

When the design is right, the manufacturer and I take it to the color Mac II and work out the color variations we want. It really helps to be able to colorize several variations on the screen and change them with a click of the mouse. We work together for this stage of the design.

Improving the sample-making process

We print at least eight color copies of each finished design. One goes to the factory in Korea or Taiwan, and the others are used for regional sales books. When shoe boxes are printed or fabric dyed for shoes, our colors are transferred into Pantone equivalents. The Pantone Matching System (PMS), an international standard for reproducing color with a system of numbered colors with standard percentages of cyan, magenta, yellow and black, ensures exact matching of colors.

Since screen colors on a computer often don't match the printed colors, we've created our own color grids labeled with varying percentages of cyan, magenta, yellow and black (see "Matching screen to printer" on page 55 for an alternate solution). The grids were printed on the Tektronix printer we commonly use. When adding color to shoe designs, we pick colors we want from our grids and specify the CMYK values in the dialog box for creating new colors. We then attach a Pantone swatch to the illustration for reference when it's sent to the Orient. This has made it simpler to obtain accurate samples the first time through, though mostly it's the accuracy and detail of the illustration that have been most useful at the factory. At this time we don't produce computerized patterns for manufacturing the shoes. Many larger companies do this. And as Pacific Trail Footwear gets larger, this will definitely be considered.

Multiple uses

Black-and-white drawings of the finished shoe designs are transferred to the salesmen's line sheets and order forms (Figure 7). We hope that eventually some of these drawings will be used for retail advertising as well.

Creative expression

After the shoe and sales sheets have been created, the fun part begins for me. Often I get to create a new shoebox for a line of shoes, and that allows me more room for creative expression. In addition, I've used FreeHand to design several store-front signs, logos for awnings over entrances, logos for a health food store, a bakery and several sports stores, patterns for stencilling, newspaper ads, direct mail pieces, magazine ads, process-color catalog work and even items for the local PTA.

In retrospect

Using the computer has not greatly changed my graphic style. My FreeHand illustrations look very much like what I've done for almost 20 years with pen and

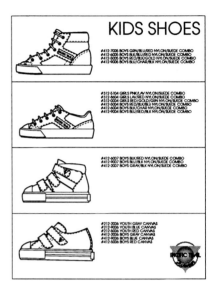

Figure 7. Using illustrations on other printed materials. The same FreeHand shoe illustrations used for sample-making are also placed on the line sheets and order forms used by the salespeople. These forms are printed from laser printer output.

Matching screen to printer

Making sure the color that prints on the page will look the same as the color on the screen is a complex task. First of all, monitors and printers can't produce every color that the human eye can see. Each model of monitor or printer is limited to a particular range of colors (its color gamut). Second, the programs that drive most monitors use RGB (subtractive) color mixing to generate the screen image, while the software for the printer or other color output device typically uses CMYK (additive) color mixing. And third, colors are seen in context. For example, "white" is different on-screen than on paper; reproducing screen white produces a bluish color on paper. So it's sometimes necessary to change the printed color to make it look the same as the screen.

TekColor is a program for color Macintoshes that helps users resolve these differences. Bundled with some Tektronix printers, TekColor is a color fidelity system that helps users pick screen colors that can be duplicated by their output devices. Installed in the System folder, TekColor includes device color databases for the leading Macintosh monitors. When TekColor was first released, the Tektronix ColorQuick inkjet printer was the only output device supported, but others have been and will continue to be added.

TekColor is accessed with the command in color graphics programs that lets you select or edit colors. The filled "leaf" shows which shades and intensities of the hue that's currently chosen can appear on the monitor. A second, unfilled leaf shows the range for the printer specified. A color that's inside both leaves can be both shown on-screen and printed by the printer, but a color that's inside the filled leaf but outside the unfilled leaf can be viewed but not printed. The third space in the window, defined by the left and top edges and the near-diagonal line, represents the *full color space*. It gives you a reference point, showing that other colors exist that neither your monitor nor your printer can produce.

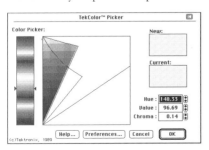

ink, only without the unsightly ink blobs and the frustration of white paint retouching. No longer must I repeatedly draw the same shoe. I can take a previously drawn shoe and simply change what is necessary to create something new. Essentially I'm free to draw or design without the limitations of traditional equipment.

I'd like to be able to get even more mileage from my computer drawings. The problem, at least in the Seattle area, is that the newspapers and larger department stores are not yet ready to utilize the new technology. The larger department stores are highly compartmentalized. There are copywriters for appliances, shoes, lingerie and so on. There are individual artists (often up to 30 or 40 for a store chain) with their own specialities. There are proofreaders, typesetters and production people. As an illustrator, being able to also set type or do paste-up is not an advantage. I once brought in a high-resolution Linotronic print with halftones and the store pasted it up with the type and made a velox. That made my illustration second generation and made all screen values under 50 percent wash out severely and all values over 50 percent darken and muddy drastically. They would not paste my output on the type and send it directly to the newspaper because the *Seattle Times* prefers camera-ready veloxes with no paste-up. Another major hang-up is size. Department stores think in terms of full-page and often double-truck ads. A Linotronic L-300 is not capable of output that large without tiling.

Desktop publishing works ideally for smaller stores, however. My other accounts love being able to call for a rush ad, give me the copy over the phone, get a proof the next day and have a complete camera-ready Lino positive or a negative that afternoon.

Because I'm now spending so much time doing PostScript illustration, my methods are constantly evolving. My most pressing need is to get my own state-of-the-art equipment and quit going blind using my SE. I'm looking into getting a fully decked-out Mac IIcx color system with a removable Syquest drive, an accelerator (*Speed!!!*), and a Pantone-certified QMS color printer.

There seems to be something new to learn or develop with each new project, and that makes computer graphics fun. It's a challenge and an adventure to transform myself into "Mutant-Ninja-Computer-Woman" as I solve various problems. I love it.

Kate Bartelmes

"My introduction to computer graphics was not initially connected to my work. I was organizing a parent-taught computer class for third-graders at my children's school. We were using Commodore 64s to create simple stories. One father who's a computer professional brought in a Macintosh user magazine with an article on computer graphics. It featured a wonderful illustration that had been done with PixelPaint and printed on a Tektronix. I went out of my mind! I had no idea that computer graphics could be so sophisticated.

I didn't sleep much that night. I decided then and there that I had found my new mission in life. I took the leap and bought my Mac. I began devouring Macintosh magazines and investigating software. When I found Aldus FreeHand, I knew that I had found my tool. When I first started using FreeHand, I couldn't drag myself away from the computer. I didn't sleep; I didn't eat. I lost 10 pounds in four days. My husband told everyone that buying the Mac was the best (and most expensive) diet I ever went on."

One of the things I like about FreeHand 2.0 is the ease of creating or customizing a typeface like the lettering for my business card. The typeface I wanted was not available at that time so I just drew it.

This graphic was created in FreeHand for a ski shop to advertise their children's ski school. We wanted a simple, bold image that would not get lost on a cluttered newspaper page. The semi-circle of text was created by joining the text element to the large circle with the Join command.

This color style sheet shows the ease with which color variations can be made for manufacturers of samples.

This logo design was created in FreeHand for a local ski and bike shop. I used FreeHand-drawn Koloss type.

When a line of shoes is created, designing the logos and shoeboxes is part of the "package" deal. I used FreeHand to draw the S.T.U.F.F. type in Koloss, a font that's not available in PostScript.

CHAPTER 6

At the Heart of Illustration

Artist

John Odam received a "straightforward British art school" education at the Leicester College of Art and Design. He designed book covers in London for three years before moving to the United States in 1967. He worked for several publishers and designed textbooks for CRM, publishers of *Psychology Today*, before becoming a freelance designer in 1975. He began working with a Macintosh in 1986 and has rapidly come to the forefront of designers working with electronic media. John is the art director of *Verbum* magazine and *Step-by-Step Electronic Design* newsletter.

Project

The project was to provide an illustration for an article describing heart pacemakers. The client was *HeartCorps*, an upbeat health magazine for people with heart disease. *HeartCorps* is art directed by my San Diego colleague Tom Lewis and is electronically produced. Tom wanted an illustration with a clinical look, that would simulate an airbrushed effect. The illustration was to show the different kinds of pacemakers available, without being specific to a particular manufacturer. We needed to clearly show how the pacemakers are put into the body, but without being too graphic in our depiction of veins and arteries. I used FreeHand 2.02 with a Macintosh II with 5 MB of RAM and an Apple Scanner. Proofs were made on a LaserWriter IINTX, and final output was separated film through a service bureau's Linotronic L-300.

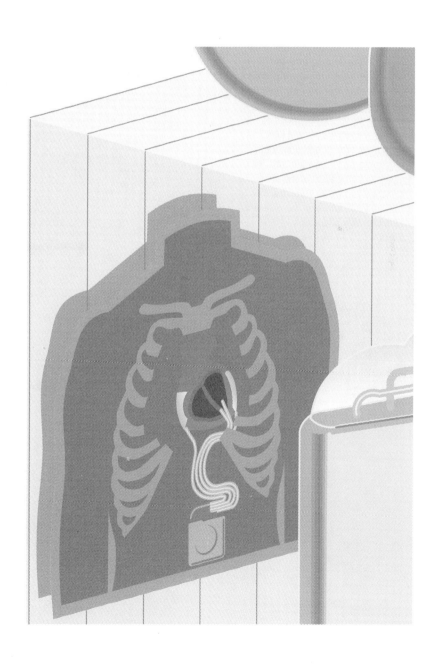

PROJECT OVERVIEW

Design process

Tom and I made a rough sketch of the design first, passing it back and forth across the table. *HeartCorps* is directed at heart patients and their families and contains high-quality articles and graphics on nutrition, exercise, medical procedures and so on. The illustration had to be clear and tasteful, but not very technical. We decided to use soft pastel colors and a schematic rendering of the pacemakers and body parts.

The illustration consists of a backdrop of Escher like stair steps with grid lines to make it look scientific. (The stair steps are actually an "impossible" construction, moving in and out of a literal space.) Seven elements are placed on this background: four pacemakers, two body diagrams and a wiring detail. Each element was drawn separately, and then all were combined on the final layout. Each object was drawn in a straight-on orientation, and then skewed within the final layout to match the spatial orientation of the background. I was provided with reference photographs of the pacemakers, but I didn't make literal tracings of these. Instead, I created more generalized pacemaker shapes.

The art director and I created a rough sketch while discussing how we wanted the illustration to look.

Body diagrams show the placement of the pacemaker. I chose a schematic rendering in order to soften the more realistic aspects of the anatomy.

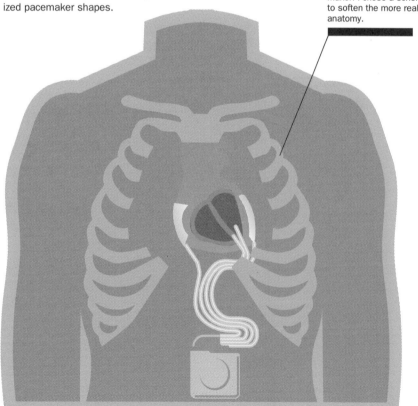

A combined heart-lightning symbol was created as a decorative element for the headline and succeeding pages of the article.

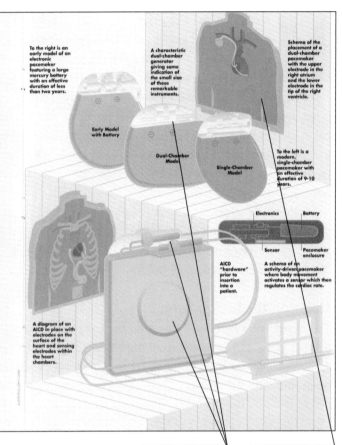

The illustration was used as one page of a two-page opening spread. The headline features Bodoni type in orange with a thick outline in pale gold.

The Blend function was used to create modeling and soft shadows on the pacemakers.

The pacemakers and body diagrams were created in separate FreeHand documents and then copied and pasted into the final layout. The body diagrams were skewed to fit the angle of the stair-step background. A drop shadow was added behind each.

Gray lines were used to indicate the wiring on the large pacemaker. A thinner, lighter line was laid on top to give the wires a rounded look.

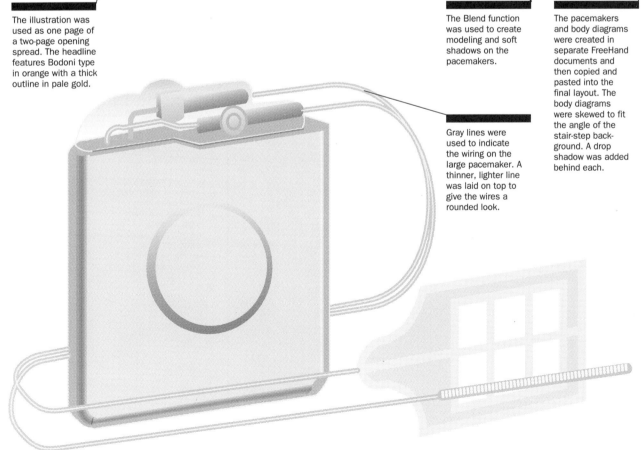

HeartCorps' art director and I discussed the overall color scheme for the illustration and agreed to use a yellow background. This would lend a feeling of warmth and friendliness to offset the metallic appearance of the pacemakers. We used a few highlights of hot pinks and deep green to add spark to the page. To make the colors relate to each other, I used all three process colors — cyan, magenta and yellow — in each color, but not black. Black was used only for the type describing and labeling the pacemakers (see "Black overprinting" on page 63). ▌ *Using black in mixed colors sometimes creates moiré patterns when printed, and it also seems to make the colors look muddy.*

I created the colors as I worked, beginning with the first pacemaker. Each subsequent pacemaker was begun as a "Save-As" of the previous one, so that I was able to retain the same color palette. As I went on to draw the body diagrams I added colors to the palette.

Creating the background

To create the background I first drew the trapezoidal shapes that define the treads and risers of the stair steps. I drew a single riser and a single tread, gave each a different shade of yellow, and then cloned and reflected these shapes to create the others (Figure 1). I used the blend tool to produce the vertical

Figure 1. Drawing the stair steps. To simplify the construction of the stair steps, the corner point tool was used to draw a skewed rectangle to represent a stair tread. This was cloned and reflected across the horizontal axis to create the next lower tread. Another shape was drawn to serve as the middle riser. This was cloned twice and the copies were reflected vertically to create the upper and lower risers. Then the upper and lower edges of these (respectively) were altered, to fit the rectangular frame of the illustration.

Black overprinting

When sending color Free-Hand files to the service bureau for separations it's important to remember to specify an overprint for black (top illustration). This should always be in the form of a written instruction on the job order form, but just to be on the safe side it's wise to send out the file properly configured by specifying a black overprint in the Print Option dialog box. (This window is reached by selecting Change at the bottom left of the Print menu.) To be sure you've set it up correctly run a test separation through your laser printer before sending out the file. If the Overprint Ink option is not selected for Black, then Free-Hand will automatically "knock out" all the colors that are on layers beneath the black, causing an unpredictable white halo around black areas (bottom illustration). The halo will vary in position and severity over the print run. For best results the black should overprint all the other colors, making a richer, glossier black and eliminating the trapping problem that would result from a knock-out.

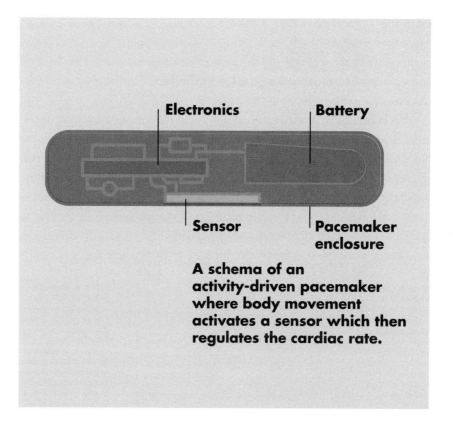

A schema of an activity-driven pacemaker where body movement activates a sensor which then regulates the cardiac rate.

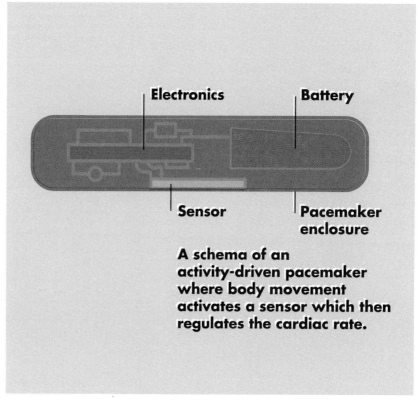

A schema of an activity-driven pacemaker where body movement activates a sensor which then regulates the cardiac rate.

pinstripes, a process that would probably have driven me crazy if I'd had to do it by conventional means. Using the computer, I drew a line at the right edge of a stair riser or tread, then drew a line at the left edge. I selected both lines, selected the top point of each line to serve as a reference point, then did a 10-step blend between them (Figure 2). The lines that are generated are equidistant from one another, and their length at top and bottom is adjusted automatically and perfectly to fit the shape of the stair step.

After I created the pinstripes, I realized it could have been done in an easier, more elegant way. I could have drawn a zigzagging line at the right edge of the stairs, another line at the left edge, and created the blend between just these two (Figure 3). I didn't see this solution at first, because I was caught up in designing the image on-screen at the same time I was executing it, a common situation in computer design. I've found that sometimes I can spend as much time trying to figure out the most efficient way to create an effect as I do in actually drawing it, so I usually work spontaneously. But if I have to do a whole series of similar

Figure 2. Creating pinstripes. To automate the drawing of pinstripes on the stairs, a line was drawn at the inner and outer edge of each tread or riser, and then the Blend function was used to generate 10 intermediate lines.

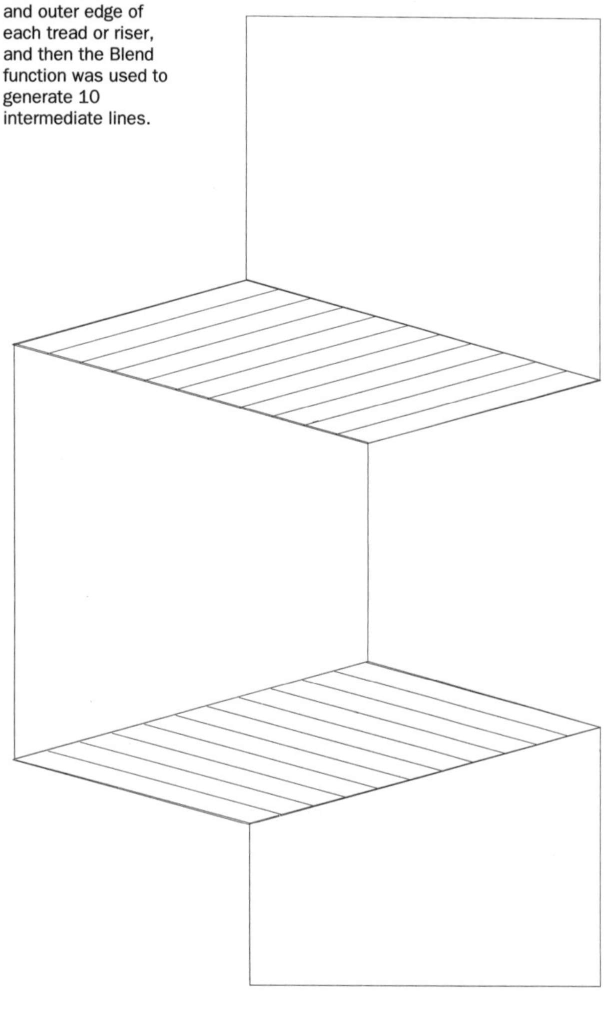

Figure 3. Finding a better method. The most economical solution is not always discovered first, especially when designing on-screen. An alternate approach to generating the pinstripes one stair step at a time, as shown in Figure 2, would have been to draw two zigzagging lines along the inner and outer edges of the stairs and then execute one blend to create all the pinstripes.

drawings, I might rough in the prototype first, getting from A to B however I can, and then go back and devise a more streamlined method of creating each effect. This process can often take several hours, but it's essential for large projects, especially if other people will be executing or correcting a series of drawings from my basic design. The opportunity FreeHand provides to work with finished artwork in view makes it easy to work in both ways — spontaneously and in a structured way that has been thought through in advance.

Once the background was created, I locked it down with the Lock function under the Element menu. This kept it from moving while I positioned the other elements on top of it. ∎ *Putting an element in the background so it can't be disturbed can also be achieved by sending it to a lower layer and rendering that layer inactive. But using the Lock option is quicker.*

Drawing a pacemaker

I drew the basic shape of the pacemaker, and then added a highlight and a shadow to give the appearance of a flat object with slightly rounded edges. The highlights were created with the blend tool. The shadow at the right was constructed of two blends. I drew a 2-point line and made it the same color as the pacemaker body. I cloned it, rotated it a few degrees to the left and brought the point at the upper end of the line up a few points to match the height of the original. To keep the bottom points aligned over each other I clicked on the common point with the rotation tool, so that my rotation would be about that spot. I did the rotation by dragging the mouse (Figure 4). ∎ *Rotation can also be done by typing numbers in the Rotation dialog box and specifying that the rotation take place about the mouse location.*

The clone was set to a darker color of beige. I selected the two lines and did a six-step blend between them, producing a subtly blended shadow. I then produced a second shadow shape blending back from the dark beige to the lighter background color (Figure 5).

Figure 4. Creating a subtle shadow. The Blend function was used to create a subtle shadow for the edge of the pacemaker. A single line was drawn, cloned, and then dragged into a new orientation with the mouse operating the rotation tool. Clicking with the rotation tool on the common bottom point of the lines made the rotation take place about that spot.

Figure 5. Drawing shadows back-to-back. A keyline view of the pacemaker shadow shows the multiple steps of the blend.

The area at the top of the pacemaker is filled with electrical wiring and tubes set in a translucent material. I carefully studied the photo references supplied by the author (Figure 6). But I didn't want to render the top exactly, since it varied from manufacturer to manufacturer, so I tried to achieve the general look of something transparent with objects embedded in it. I used a graduated fill for the shape of the top, and then drew smaller shapes within it that are also colored with the same dark-to-light fill (see "Producing smooth gradations" on page 67). This fairly simple device gave the appearance of a complex object (Figure 7).

Figure 6. Generalizing from a photo reference. The translucent top of the pacemaker varied slightly from manufacturer to manufacturer.

Figure 7. Creating an illusion of translucence. To create the impression of objects like wiring embedded in translucent plastic, small elements were drawn within a larger shape and most of them were colored with the same graduated fill, changing from a darker to a lighter shade of gold, from top to bottom. Two pieces of the larger shape were colored with radial fills in the same colors.

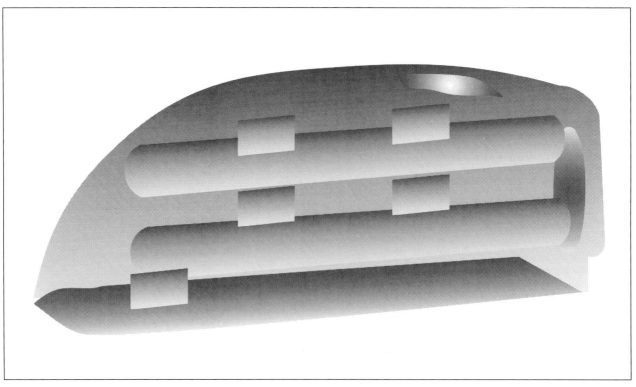

Producing smooth gradations

For many electronic illustrators, avoiding shade-stepping in graduated fills (also called *blends* in some programs) remains one of the most perplexing problems in PostScript illustration. The solution can be complex, because there are at least five variables that can affect the smoothness of a blend:

- Percent change in tint across the blend
- Distance across the blend
- Number of steps in the blend
- Resolution (dots per inch) of the output device
- Halftone screen frequency (lines per inch) of the printed piece

What you can do to get the smoothest possible blend depends on which of these five factors are within your control. Typically, one or more of the factors are set and not available to change. For example, some blend functions determine the number of steps automatically, and halftone screen frequency of the printed piece is often beyond the artist's control.

With blend functions (such as Illustrator 88's) that allow you to control the number of steps, you can calculate the optimal number using equations published in Adobe's *Colophon 6* (January, 1989):

$$A = [\text{printer resolution (dpi)} \div \text{screen frequency (lpi)}]^2$$
= number of tints available for a 0–100% color change

$$B = A \text{ x \% change in color}$$
= number of tints available for a color change of that %
= optimal number of steps to use in the blend

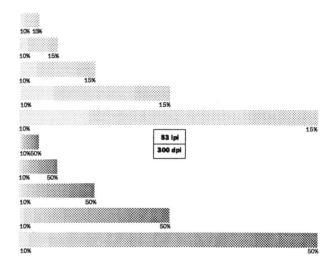

These equations lead to the following conclusions, which are demonstrated in the blends shown on this page:

- To take maximum advantage of the number of tints available, you have to use a step for each tint.
- Using more steps than there are tints available doesn't improve the look of the blend (but it does increase file size and printing time).

If you have more than one output resolution available:

- Increasing the printer resolution always increases the number of tints available and therefore increases the potential smoothness of the blend.

If you can specify screen frequency:

- Increasing the screen frequency always decreases the number of tints available and therefore decreases the potential smoothness of the blend.
- Decreasing the screen frequency isn't necessarily a good idea. Although it increases the number of tints available, it also increases the coarseness of the printed artwork.

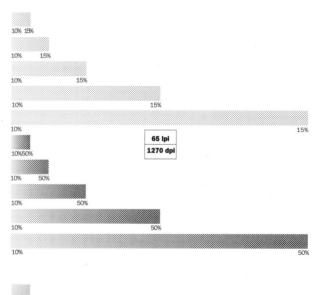

The illustrator can almost always control the percent change in color assigned to the blend.

- Increasing the percent change in color always increases the optimal number of steps in the blend and therefore improves the chances for smoothness.
- Sometimes, because of the size of the object to be filled, its better not to use a graduated fill at all. The measured distance a blend stretches plays no role in determining **A** or **B,** but it does affect how "banded" the blend looks. That means, for example, that a 20 percent change over 1 inch printed at 60 lpi will always look banded; there's just no way around it: $A = (300 \div 60)^2 = 25$; $B = 25 \text{ x } .20 = 5$ steps. Those 5 steps, spread over that 1 inch distance will give a banded look. If you're limited to 300 dpi and determined to blend over an inch, a bigger percentage change in color will help smooth things out. For example, a 100 percent change in color gives $(300 \div 60)^2 = 25$; $B = 25 \text{ x } 1.00 = 25$ steps.

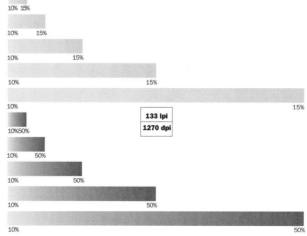

Anatomical schematics

The author of the article provided me with medical illustrations showing the placement of pacemakers in the body. I scanned these and used them as template guides for the placement and proportion of parts. But I created my own simple, stylized shapes to represent the ribs, heart, arteries and so forth.

My large pacemakers were too complex to be reduced and placed on the body diagrams. The detail would not have been visible, and even if it had been, the extra lines and fills would have slowed down the printing time. So I created new, simpler pacemakers, using some easy but effective techniques to create a sense of detail.

I've found it's often possible to imply detail that isn't really there, using minimal means. For instance, the tubes leading from the pacemaker are made to look round simply by cloning each and changing the clone into a thinner, lighter line on top (Figure 8). The roundness of the object on the front of the pacemaker was made by creating two circles, one with a graduated fill and another offset on top of it with a flat fill (Figure 9). To highlight the area of the heart and give it more solidity and dimension, I created a background shape with a graduated fill, using "sugary" pinks to make it stand out (Figure 10).

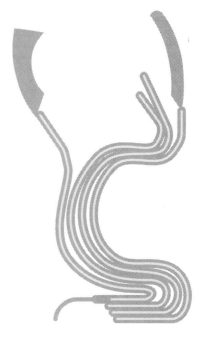

Figure 8. Adding roundness. To suggest the look of a rounded tube, each line in the wiring detail of the left body diagram was cloned and the copies were changed to thinner, lighter lines.

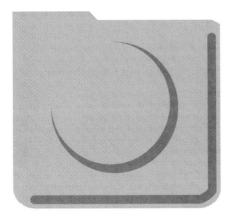

Figure 9. Creating a shadow. To add dimension to the raised round area on the front of the pacemaker in the left body diagram, a circle in the pacemaker color was slightly offset over a circle containing a graduated fill in a darker range of color.

Figure 10. Highlighting the heart. To make the heart stand out, a background fill of graduated pinks was added behind it.

Making a solid object translucent

One of the pieces of pacemaker apparatus has transparent windows, but these were created in FreeHand using opaque rectangles (Figure 11). When the piece was put in place against the background, it obscured the pinstripes underneath it. The obscured line segments were drawn back in by hand, though I could have used FreeHand's Paste Inside function to paste a copy of the obscured lines into the shape of the windows using the shapes as clipping paths (Figure 12).

Custom lettering

As a title for the article, I created a zigzagging lightning-bolt shape and surrounded it with type set in Bodoni. Using the Horizontal Scale option I scaled the lettering to 50 percent, as the art director wanted the text to be tight. To create the background outline, I cloned the type and then selected Stroke and Fill from the Effects submenu on the Type menu. I gave the type a stroke of a 12-point yellow line. This thick stroke plugged up the thin lines of the font. I sent this yellow clone to the back, which left the original type resting on top (Figure 13). ■ *Unfortunately, the stroke effect is not visible on-screen in FreeHand, but it can be seen on laser proofs.*

This stroking had the unexpected result of creating peaks that jut up above the A's. Because we were already using a jagged, lightning-bolt image, we decided to accept these unexpected peaks. But this is apparently a bug in the program.

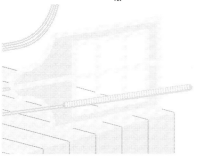

Figure 11. Drawing "windows." It's not possible to cut a "hole" in an opaque PostScript object, so to give the impression of windows in part of a pacemaker, a rectangle filled with the background color was placed on top of it.

Figure 12. Making the windows "transparent." The solid pacemaker piece obscured the pin stripes beneath it, so these were drawn back in, on top of the window rectangles, to give the impression of transparency.

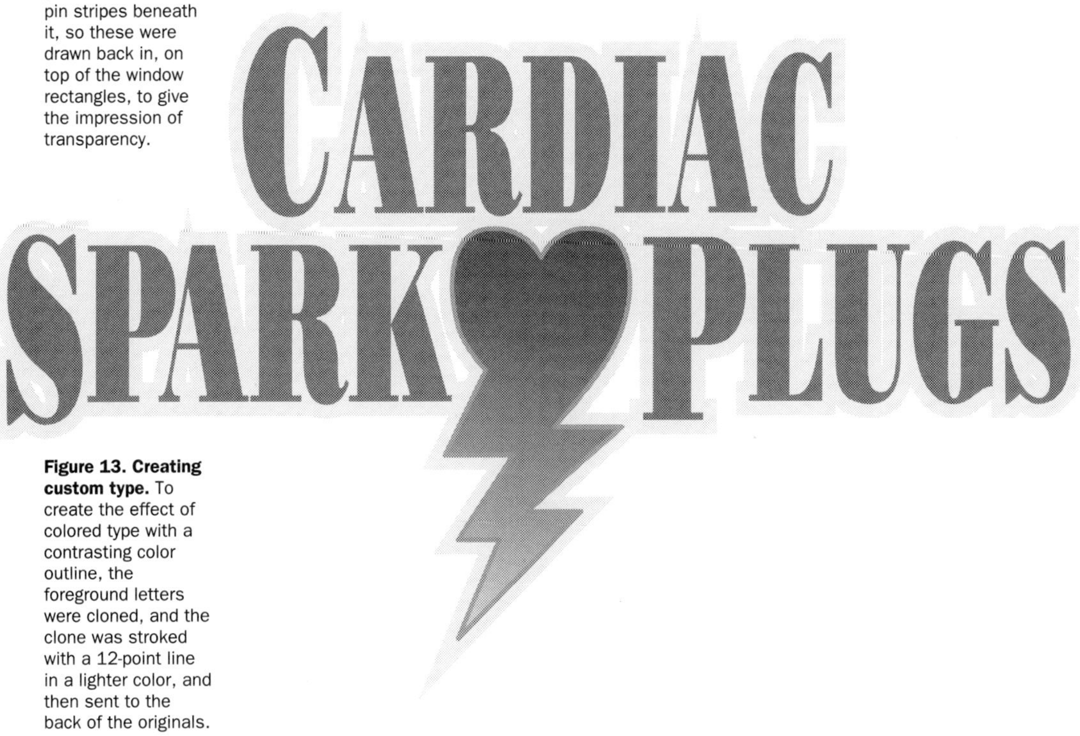

Figure 13. Creating custom type. To create the effect of colored type with a contrasting color outline, the foreground letters were cloned, and the clone was stroked with a 12-point line in a lighter color, and then sent to the back of the originals.

Looking at a keyline

Viewing the illustration in "wire-frame" or keyline mode reveals that it's actually much simpler than one would expect by looking at the finished piece (Figure 14). There are relatively few discrete objects, and the file size was accordingly a modest 71 kilobytes.

Sometimes objects that are partially obscured by other objects are hard to select, or may disappear from view behind overlying opaque layers. Toggling to the keyline viewing mode (Command-K) makes all objects transparent and easier to select. Scrolling to different parts of the drawing and moving elements is also quicker in keyline mode. I prefer working in Preview mode, because I can see exactly what I'm getting with color and line weight. But I switch to keyline mode on occasion to retrieve stray objects, to maneuver complex groupings or to manipulate things that have obstinately refused to be selected.

Overprinting, knock-outs and trapping

The color separations were made directly from FreeHand, with only one hitch. I was not responsible for the final output to the service bureau, and there was one slight mistake with the black type that overlays the illustration. Tom's staff forgot to specify that Black should Overprint, so the program automatically knocked out the background behind the type, creating the potential for misregistration on the final printed piece (see "Black overprinting" on page 63). We did see a slight misregistration when the magazine was printed.

In retrospect

I got into using FreeHand because for a time it was the only program I could run in color. I especially like FreeHand because it allows you to draw directly in color and see the results immediately on the screen. I soon saw that it was a very powerful program and had color separation capability built right into it. Right

Figure 14. Working in keyline. It's sometimes handy to switch from Preview to keyline view when trying to select and edit parts of an illustration that are partially obscured by others.

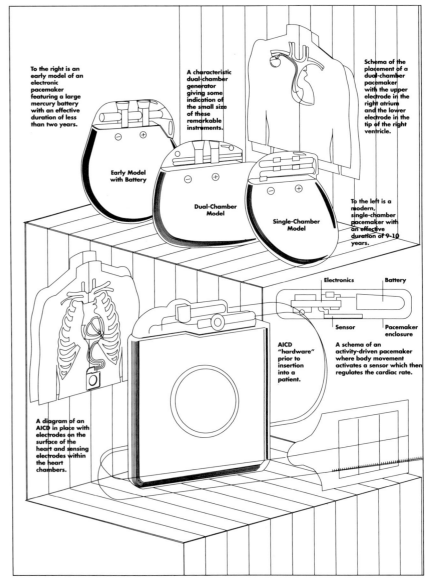

To the right is an early model of an electronic pacemaker featuring a large mercury battery with an effective duration of less than two years.

A characteristic dual-chamber generator giving some indication of the small size of these remarkable instruments.

Schema of the placement of a dual-chamber pacemaker with the upper electrode in the right atrium and the lower electrode in the tip of the right ventricle.

Early Model with Battery

Dual-Chamber Model

Single-Chamber Model

To the left is a modern, single-chamber pacemaker with an effective duration of 9-10 years.

Electronics   Battery

Sensor   Pacemaker enclosure

AICD "hardware" prior to insertion into a patient.

A schema of an activity-driven pacemaker where body movement activates a sensor which then regulates the cardiac rate.

A diagram of an AICD in place with electrodes on the surface of the heart and sensing electrodes within the heart chambers.

away I was able to use FreeHand on projects for clients, and I've now developed a specialty service of providing diagrams and technical illustrations like the pacemakers for textbooks and other publications.

Finding FreeHand was just one step in my search for ways to take the drudgery out of line art, diagrams and publication design. I hate to specify type, I hate to do inking and I hate to draw straight lines with mitered corners. Years ago I thought of using a CAD system. My son Seth had an interest in personal computers, and after watching his work I thought computers might be useful for mechanical tasks like copyfitting or making rough layouts. I never dreamed of the high-quality typography and layout capabilities we have today.

I wasn't very impressed with the first Macintosh I saw in 1984 or so. All it could do was draw rather funky, textured boxes. It was whimsical and cute, but I couldn't see how I could use it to produce work that clients would pay for. It wasn't until Apple came out with the laser printer and Aldus produced PageMaker that I got excited. So my first electronic studio consisted of a Macintosh Plus with 1 MB of RAM, a LaserWriter Plus and version 1 of PageMaker.

At first I underestimated the power of the computer. I expected to use it simply as a design aid, for previewing what set type would look like, for instance. A year or so later the Linotronic imagesetter came out and one of the service bureaus in San Diego bought one. They showed me a page of output that contained rules, boxes and reversed type as well as diagrams, flow charts and bar graphs. It had been done on a Macintosh. At this point I realized the Mac was a revolutionary tool, and I began to really explore and use its capabilities, beginning with PageMaker and moving on to the object-oriented and Post-Script illustration programs. I now find myself pushing at the technical limits of the system, trying to do color separations of complete pages, for instance. The technology has improved tremendously, and during the last three years I've learned to use a great deal of new software, including color paint programs, animation software, autotrace functions, flatbed and video scanning, digital photography, grayscale painting, optical character recognition, MIDI interfaces and on and on.

PORTFOLIO

John Odam

"I'm still in transition between electronic and traditional media. I still use a pencil to get design thoughts down quickly. But pencil sketches tend to be crude and schematic. With the computer I can go from a loosely rendered sketch fairly quickly to something that's rendered in exquisite detail.

The most interesting aspect of computer design is the thorough way that typography can be integrated into a design. Before the computer, setting type was a mechanical process separate from the design process. Now the availability of a variety of fonts within an illustration program makes it possible to fit type with graphic elements right from the beginning."

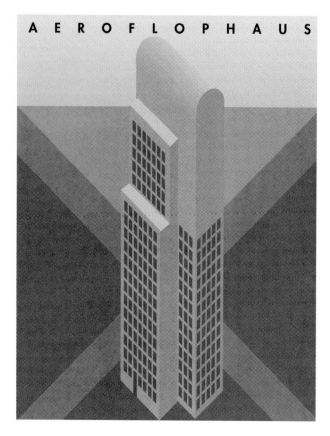

The Aeroflophaus poster is the tongue-in-cheek result of testing out FreeHand 2.0 at the Stanford Art Director's Mac-workshop in May 1989. Aeroflophaus would be the related hotel chain of a hypothetical airline, *Aeroflop*. FreeHand's Alignment command from the Element menu was used to line up the many skewed rectangles that make up the grids of windows.

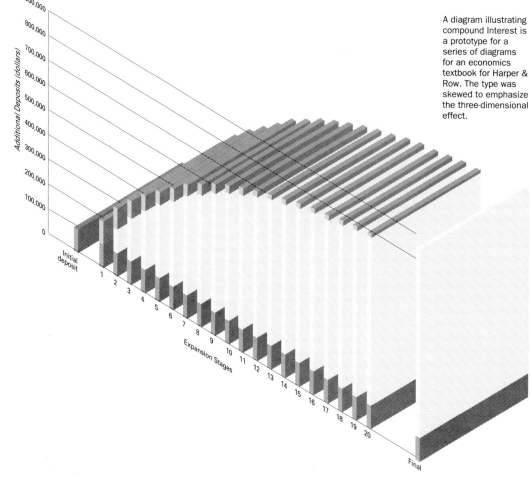

A diagram illustrating compound Interest is a prototype for a series of diagrams for an economics textbook for Harper & Row. The type was skewed to emphasize the three-dimensional effect.

A cover illustration for a children's science fair textbook was derived from one of the author's wife's sketches. To achieve a uniform, geometric look, the different elements were drawn using FreeHand's corner and curve point tools. The electronic production saved hours of overlay and keyline work.

A book cover for an adult education book employs a mock woodcut technique. This was achieved in FreeHand by autotracing a scan of a broad-tipped marker sketch, selecting a heavy gray line and placing broadly drawn polygonal shapes behind the outlines.

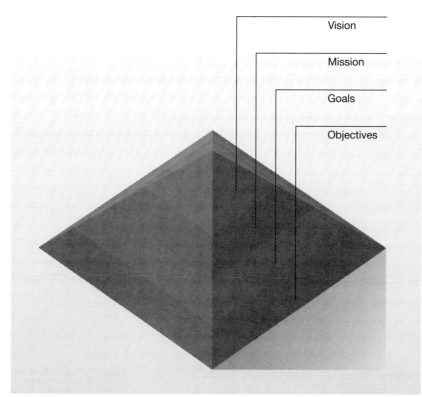

A hierarchical diagram, developed for a business text for Macmillan, shows some of the subtle shading and delicate gradations possible with FreeHand.

C H A P T E R   7

Converting a Map to PostScript

Artist

Doug Alexander received a Bachelor of Fine Arts degree from the University of Houston in 1985. He has worked for the past year and a half with The Hill Group, a marketing and design group in Houston. Hill's cliets include Champion International, Dai Nippon, Fujitsu, Ringling Bros. Barnum & Bailey and Southland Corporation. Doug has lectured to the Dallas Society of Visual Communicators and CASA, the art director's club of San Antonio. He was a panel speaker for the Stanford Art Director's Conference and the Creative Summit at Southwest Texas State University. In addition to his work in PostScript illustration and design, Doug has created computer animation and hypermedia presentations.

Project

The project was to update a series of color maps already produced by the Hill group by conventional art methods. The maps had been made for Champion Realty, a subsidiary of Champion International, to show the locations of property sites for sale in Florida and Texas. We believed that by converting the maps to PostScript illustration we could more easily update and reprint them.

We used Adobe Illustrator 88 running on a Macintosh II computer with a 100 MB internal hard drive and 5 MB of RAM. A Microtek MSF400G scanner running VersaScan was used for scans. Black-and-white proofs were made on an Apple LaserWriter IINTX, and Cromalin and color key proofs were produced as well. Final output was color-separated film processed through Adobe Separator to a Linotronic L-300.

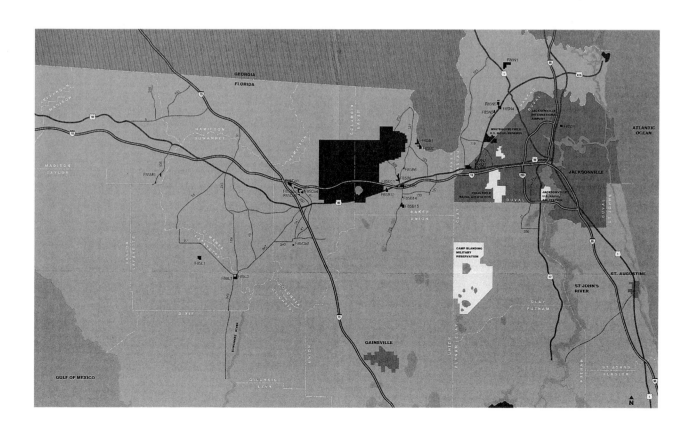

PROJECT OVERVIEW

Design approach

We had previously made several maps using Illustrator (directions to shopping malls and so forth), but the Champion maps were our first attempt at large-scale output. The particular map presented here is of the northern part of Florida, around Jacksonville. It was designed to show the location of, access to and amenities associated with Champion's properties. We decided to retain most of our original design solutions for the maps and focus on reproducing the same format with the computer. However we did choose new colors to differentiate the important elements (municipal areas, parks, properties and so on) and created new styles for the roads and county lines.

Our plan was to produce and preview the map on-screen and output the entire file on a Linotronic as color separations. We assumed that the proofing process would be sped up, mechanical production would be nil, and the whole procedure would be more efficient. In general, we've noticed a great improvement in speed and accuracy when using the computer to generate maps. The Champion maps presented some difficulties, however, from which we learned a great deal.

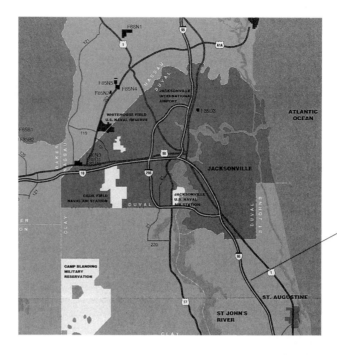

Major highways were styled by drawing a dark gray line, and then cloning it and making the clone thinner and white. The clone sits directly on top of the original line.

The river was created by drawing a squiggly closed path, using a scanned map as a template. The shape was filled with light blue and placed in front of the solid land mass.

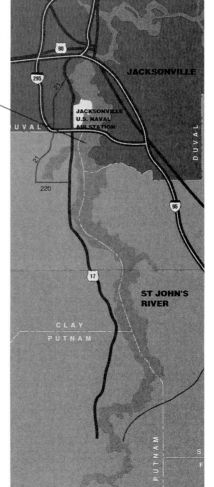

A custom dashed line was created to indicate county lines. Some of the county names were rotated to follow the direction of the county boundaries.

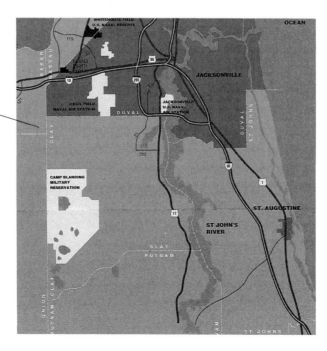

A close-up of the map for Lake Livingston in East Texas shows the many complex closed paths created to represent the lake and property sites.

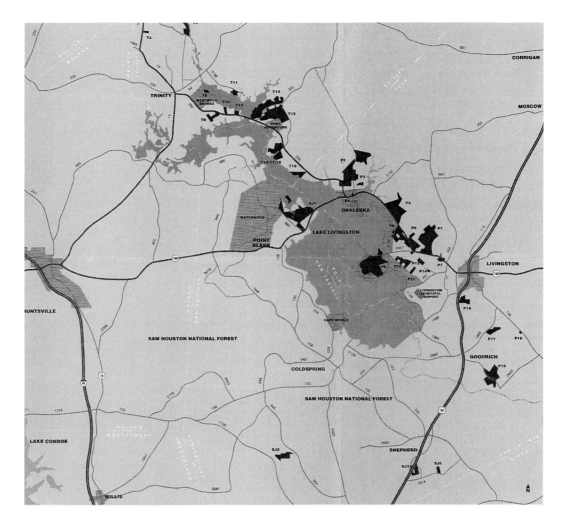

Another map in the Champion series shows the area around Pensacola, Florida, employing the same techniques and colors as in the Jacksonville map. The long stretch of major highway from east to west across the middle of the map required careful registration of the center white line.

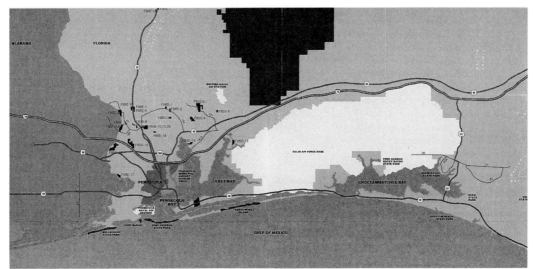

The production process began with a tracing of the existing map. Using tracing paper and a pen, I drew the center of the roads and the outlines of the properties, lakes, rivers and municipal areas. To make it possible to fit this tracing onto our scanner, it was reduced on a copier, pieced together and reduced again until it fit on a letter-sized sheet of paper, a reduction to about 25 percent of the original (Figure 1). The final reduced version was scanned and saved in a PICT format, then used in Illustrator 88 as a template.

Problems with scale

At this point I realized that the process of reducing a large map (12 x 20 inches) for use in the computer would present some problems. The bitmap scan had a coarse resolution of 72 dpi. Of the property outlines that survived the copier reduction process, some were degraded to single pixels. Using the scan as a template meant I had to refer back to the original map and create some of the outlines by guesswork. We were able to get a good representation of the contours of the roads though, and we depended on the scan for that purpose.

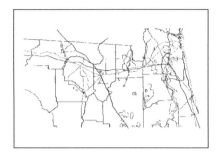

Figure 1. Creating a template. The original map was traced by hand. Then the tracing was reduced with a copier and scanned to serve as a template in Illustrator.

Using color in Illustrator

There are three ways to specify color in Illustrator: four-color process, Pantone Matching System (PMS), and custom color. All three options are accessed via the Paint dialog box under the Style menu. Adobe Separator, a separate color utility, is used to print four-color and spot-color separations.

To create a four-color process color, click on Process Color in the Fill or Stroke option group, and then enter percentage values in the fields that appear for cyan, magenta, yellow and black (see below). A color preview box shows an approximation of the specified color as it is created. The color will be assigned to whatever object or objects are currently selected, but it's not given a name. To use the color again, select an object that contains it, choose Paint from the Style menu and click OK in the Paint dialog box. This sets the current Paint specifications to those of the selected object. Now select or create a new object. It will automatically be painted with the current Paint specs.

Spot color and spot-color separations are produced using the Custom Color option, which provides access to both PMS and custom-mixed colors (see below). Illustrator comes with two PMS documents, one each for coated and uncoated paper. To choose a PMS color, open one of these documents, then open the illustration document. When Custom Color is selected in the Paint dialog box the PMS colors will appear in a scrolling menu box.

When no Pantone document is open, the Custom Color option in the Paint dialog box is grayed back. To create your own custom color, choose Custom Color from the Style menu to view the Custom Color dialog box. With New selected, per-centage values can be entered into CMYK fields and the color can be given a name that then appears in a scrolling menu box whenever Custom Color is selected in the Paint dialog box (see below). When an illustration containing custom color is separated through Adobe Separator, one negative is produced for each color that has been created or chosen from the Pantone documents.

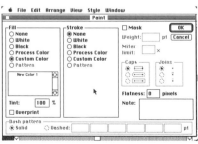

Defining line styles

Before drawing the map, I defined line styles for the three different types of roads and for the county lines. Major highways were represented by an 8-point dark gray line with a white stripe down the middle. Primary roads were made slightly thinner with no white stripe. Secondary roads were made thinner still and in a lighter shade of gray. County lines were made white and dashed. I used the Dash Pattern field in the Paint dialog box to create a line style with alternating long and short dashes (Figure 2). ■ *To create a custom dashed line, open the Paint dialog box by choosing Paint from the Style menu and click on Dashed in the Dash Pattern options. In the first dash field enter a value (in points) for the length of the first dash, then press the Tab key to go to the next field. Enter the length in points of the first gap. Repeat this process until all six fields are filled.*

Figure 2. Making a dashed line. A custom dashed line was created by entering values for the dashes and spaces between them in the Dash Pattern fields.

Figure 3. Using custom color. Custom colors were created so that their names would appear in a menu in the Paint dialog box.

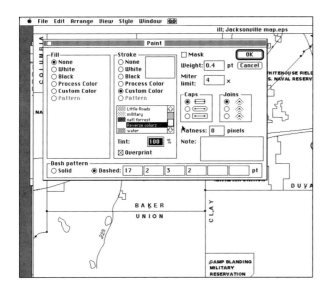

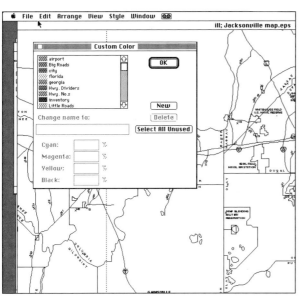

Creating custom colors

The design specifications called for the use of seven spot colors on the printed map. This was a generous palette, but even so I had to be frugal in its use. In addition to the two states of Florida and Georgia, six elements needed to be differentiated. These included Champion's properties, parks and wildlife preserves, military installations, airports, municipal areas and water. I decided to assign a distinctive color to the four major subjects that needed to stand out: the properties are colored a dark blue that's already used in Champion's corporate mark; parks are dark green, military installations are a mustard yellow, and airports are rust. Municipal areas are indicated with a screen of black over the gray ink used to define the state of Florida. The small portion of Georgia that shows along Florida's northern border is indicated in the same way except with a lighter screen. The ocean and rivers are colored with a light blue ink.

Having determined how many and which colors to use, I specified each one as a custom color in Illustrator and gave it a name. The color names then appeared in a menu when Custom Color was checked in the Paint dialog box (Figure 3). I've found it helpful to create a palette like this even when I plan to specify PMS colors for the printer because I can change the specs of all objects that have been assigned a named color by editing it from the dialog box. By contrast, when colors are created using the four-color option, the specifications apply to a particular object and cannot be globally edited via a specific color name (see "Using color in Illustrator" on page 78).

Drawing the map elements

Having defined the line styles and color palette, I began drawing the map. I created a rectangle the size of the map border, to provide a frame of reference and later act as a mask or cropping path for the final art. Next I drew the squiggly curves of the coastline and river's edges and Joined these to straight lines to create a closed land mass shape that was filled with gray (Figure 4). I drew the ocean and river areas by duplicating the outlines of the land masses and Joining these to straight lines that extend beyond the boundaries of the map outline (Figure 5).

The lakes, properties, parks and so on were drawn next and filled with the appropriate colors. The paths used to create the roads and county lines were drawn and assigned the appropriate line styles. To create the two-tone highway line I stroked each highway as an 8-point gray line and then chose Copy and Paste In Front from the Edit menu. This created a duplicate that sat directly on top of the original line. With the copy still selected, I stroked it as a 2-point white line, to create the highway's center stripe.

Adding text

Finally the text was added and positioned in the appropriate places. We used Helvetica for the county names and property numbers and Helvetica Black for the city, river and ocean names. The names of the color-coded amenities were done in Helvetica Black. We used all caps and standard letter spacing for all the names except those of the counties, which were spread. ■ *Specifying a positive number in the Spacing field in the Type dialog box inserts a uniform space between the letters of a word.*

Some of the type was rotated to fit along the diagonal lines of rivers or county lines. (Illustrator 88 does not create text along a curving path, so we designed our maps to minimize the need for this function).

Managing the object order

When drawing a map with many elements, I use the grouping feature of Illustrator to cluster together those objects that share the same characteristics. For example, the individual properties were grouped so that by selecting one I selected them all. Grouping items makes the task of managing the object order a bit easier. ■ *Illustrator has only one drawing layer. Objects are interleaved within this layer by using the Bring To Front, Send To Back, Paste In Front and Paste In Back commands. In all PostScript programs the most recently created object is at the top or "front" of the illustration. When filled with paint, it obscures whatever objects lie in back of it. In Illustrator, when several objects are grouped they retain their order relative to each other, but the group is placed in the front-most layer of the illustration.*

Figure 4. Drawing the land mass. The curving lines of the coastline were combined with straight lines to create a closed path to represent the land mass. This was filled with gray.

Figure 5. Duplicating the coastlines. To create the ocean shapes, the land mass shape was copied and split with the scissors tool so that the noncoastal lines could be deleted. The coastlines were joined to straight lines to create closed paths that could be filled with light blue to form water body shapes. The river and lake shapes were drawn as separate closed paths.

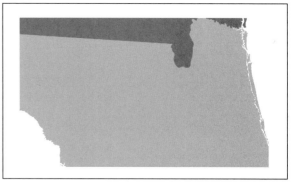

Working with a printer

Our first big color job using Illustrator and a printer with an in-house service bureau was stressful, but we learned a lot about how to avoid costly mistakes.

Communicate with your printer. Call your printshop before you begin production and let them know what you're planning. If you're lucky, the printer may already have some experience in dealing with digital art and will be able to advise you about trapping, overprinting and how best to prepare your work for printing. Keep your printer informed of what you're doing as you go along for the same reasons. The technology of computer illustration and production is new to all of us and has produced a set of yet-to-be-defined rules about who's responsible for what. You may believe the printer is responsible for registration and trapping. But when you complain about poor results and he points to the lino-generated negatives you provided, you find that you're stuck with the responsibility.

Keep digital files up-to-date. If your printer has an in-house service bureau, be sure to keep track of who's making revisions and whose version of a job is the latest. Also note that if changes are stripped in by hand on the negative film, they aren't going to appear on the digital file. If you subsequently run out new film without adding the appropriate changes to the file, they won't appear on your next proof. This very thing happened to us and it was not a cheap mistake. Again, communication with your printer is paramount.

Using a clipping path

When all the elements of the map were drawn, painted and positioned correctly, I selected the large rectangle I had originally drawn as a boundary reference and checked Mask in the Paint dialog box to specify it as a masking object. ■ *When a rectangle or circle is used as a masking object it must be ungrouped first, and its center anchor point must be deleted.*

I then sent the rectangle to the bottom of the object order by choosing Send To Back from the Edit menu. I selected the mask and all the other map elements by choosing Select All from the Edit menu and then chose Group from the Arrange menu. Once the mask was grouped with the rest of the map it functioned as a clipping path to mask off any elements that fell outside its boundaries (see Figure 8, "Creating a mask," on page 21).

Proofing the map

Our first color proof, an expensive Cromalin, was a disappointment. The registration was poor, especially with the white lines on the major highways. Some of the art was overprinted by other art. On a later proof the long barrier islands on Florida's eastern shore were simply gone! Ultimately three Cromalins and one color key had to be produced before we resolved all the problems. This didn't bode well for the bottom line.

Many of our output problems were caused by poor communication with the printer, who had an in-house service bureau. For example, we originally requested that the color separations be printed to 11 x 17-inch film (the largest size the Lino can handle) and then shot up to finished-size film of 12 x 20 inches. Instead, the printer's lino department output the seps on paper, which is a less stable medium and stretches during the developing process. This caused many of the registration problems we saw on the proofs.

After the proofs were made, we learned that the printer's lino department had not provided the strippers with a composite proof of the finished map, making it difficult for them to correctly strip and compile the film. The map was successfully printed eventually but not without a lot of anxiety along the way. Our design group held a meeting with the printer to determine who should absorb the cost of the mistakes (see "Working with a printer" on this page).

In retrospect

The computer has done more to change the way we do our work than any other medium we've used. The production process is usually faster, proofing is easier and revisions are quicker. But these gains have come only with a lot of agonizing and learning. We hope that someday our use of the computer will be second nature and the software will take care of the technical concerns while we concentrate on design. But for now we're learning — and learning.

PORTFOLIO

Doug Alexander (right)

"Possibly the most difficult thing for a person new to computer illustration to grasp is the idea of opaque layers. My contention is that once you learn how to work in layers you've just about arrived. I use layering extensively when I create a map or just about anything else. Done correctly, layering allows you to create a railroad track, a single-lane road, or a multilane highway, simply by drawing a single path once and copying and pasting it on top of itself, changing the stroke characteristics as you go along. The trick is to think about what you want to do before you do it."

Chris Hill (left)

"My first hands-on experience with a computer was at the Stanford Art Directors Invitational MacWorkshop in March 1988. I was interested in bringing desktop publishing to my firm, yet hesitant about the monetary investment. At first the computer confused me and excited me but the bottom line is that it opened my eyes. Within a year we have become so committed to the computer and its power that all design and typography and much illustration is now done on our two Macintosh II systems."

The illustrations and cover of this brochure for the Wilson Company were produced in Illustrator. We made extensive use of custom patterned fills to show the geological layers of earth. The brochure was laid out in PageMaker.

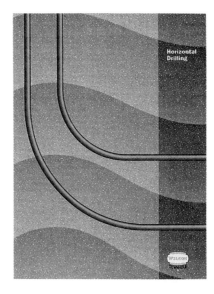

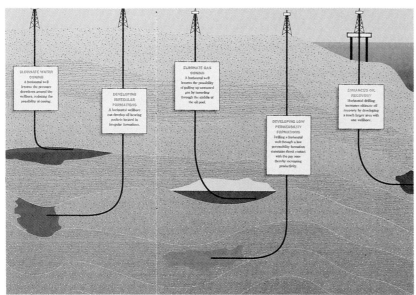

The four logos above were produced in Illustrator. The clients included the Hotel Okura in Kobe, Japan, the Fujitsu computer company, the Intersect international design conference, and New Territory, a residential development outside Houston. For the Hotel Okura symbol I drew a single leaf shape, and then duplicated it and rotated the copies to fit around a circle. This, with the addition of a black dot, created the shape of a flower in the center of the symbol.

This color poster advertising a tree-lighting ceremony used Illustrator's blend function to create the arrays of dots that vary from small to large to define the tree and the sky area.

The large type for this Father's Day poster was drawn in Illustrator and filled with pinstripes created as a patterned fill. The three posters on this page were screen-printed from film enlargements made from Linotronic color separations.

A color poster for the Good Eats restaurant features type drawn in Illustrator, in front of a rectangle of patterned fill. The alternating stripes in the background were created by drawing triangle shapes and filling them alternately with two patterned fills. The fills are clones of each other, except that the color values in the stripes are reversed. Because the tiles used to create the fills have the same zero point, the patterns line up perfectly when used to fill objects that are next to each other.

C H A P T E R   8

A Self-Portrait in Black-and-White

Artist

Janet Ashford studied music at USC and then received a B.A. in psychology from UCLA in 1974. After graduation she painted and studied silk-screen at the School of the Art Institute of Chicago, creating a line of political posters. The home birth of her first child in 1976 curtailed the poster business, and led to ten years as a writer, publisher and lecturer on alternative childbirth. Janet purchased her first Macintosh computer in 1986, ostensibly to aid production of her childbirth newsletter. But she became so fascinated by electronic media that her interest shifted from childbirth back to design. She now works as a freelance graphic designer and illustrator. Janet is a co-author of *The Verbum Book of Post-Script Illustration.*

Project

The project was to create an illustration that would highlight particular features of PostScript illustration software not yet fully explored in this book — specifically, the use of TIFFs as part of a PostScript design, the process of tracing over a TIFF used as a template, the use of the blend function, the use of Streamline for autotracing and the use of illustration programs for page layout. Since the number of color pages was limited, the project would be black-and-white.

I created the illustration in FreeHand 2.02 using a Macintosh IIcx with 4 MB of RAM and an 80 MB internal hard drive, and a 13-inch color Apple monitor. I used an AppleScanner to create TIFF scans and ImageStudio to edit them. Streamline was used for autotracing. Proofs were printed on a LaserWriter IINT and at low, medium and high resolutions on a Linotronic L-300. Final output was on paper and film at 1270 dpi through a Linotronic.

You MUST ADJUST...

this is the motto inscribed on the walls of every nursery, and the process that breaks the spirit is initiated there ... Slowly and subtly, the infant is shaped to the prevailing pattern, her needs for love and care turned against her as weapons to enforce submission. Uniqueness, individuality, difference — these are viewed with horror, even shame, at the very least they are treated like diseases, and a regiment of specialists are available today to "cure" the child who will not or cannot conform.

Robert Lindner, *Must You Conform?*, 1956

Design process

I knew which features my illustration should include — the use of TIFFs, the Blend function, autotrace, page layout with text — and I knew that it needed to look good in black-and-white. But I had no particular image in mind. For inspiration I leafed through the *Print Regional Design Annual* which had recently come in the mail. I was struck by a gallery poster that featured a tightly cropped black-and-white close-up of a woman's face, with a vertical black band running down the right side. I had been working with self-portraits for some time, both in PixelPaint and through manipulating flatbed and video scans of myself. I also have a long-standing interest in posters and the use of text to create anti-establishment propaganda. I decided to use my self-portrait material along with a provocative quote culled from the file I keep for poster material. The quote, from a 1956 book on child-rearing, speaks strongly against society's practice of forcing children to conform to external standards, at the expense of their own uniqueness. My goal was to convey this oppression graphically.

I began by making a rough sketch in pen on lined paper. The sketch and my notes about it helped to clarify my thinking about which graphic elements would be assigned to which PostScript features. I next made a rough composition in FreeHand, using TIFFs already on hand. This gave me an idea of how the finished design would look and encouraged me to continue with my idea. The next step was to gather together the finished material I would need to create my final design. I selected photographs of myself as a baby, child and adult and made TIFF scans of these. I also found a suitable architectural detail to autotrace and use as a graphic element. I used these materials to create a final design, changing the composition somewhat to fit the characteristics of the new elements.

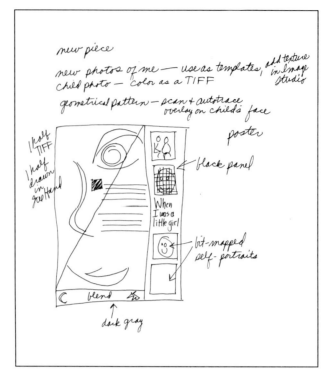

A rough sketch shows my idea for an image of my face divided into two parts. One part would contain elements drawn in FreeHand using a TIFF as a template. The other half would be the TIFF itself. I wanted to create the feeling of a persona overlaid with abstract standards, but irrepressibly emerging through these constraints.

A black vertical band along the right would contain other picture elements — a TIFF of myself as a child, as a baby and so forth. An architectural detail of some kind would serve as material for autotracing and would be superimposed on one of the TIFFs, also to convey the sense of superimposed ideals. The poster would incorporate a block of type, perhaps positioned over a light area of the large face.

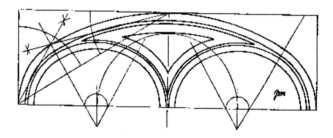
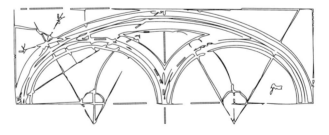
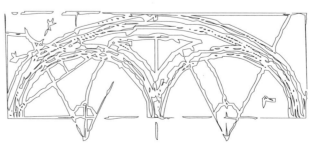

A black-and-white line drawing from the *Handbook of Ornament* was scanned as a line TIFF (top) and converted to PostScript using Streamline, a dedicated autotrace program. The scanned element was slightly askew, so it was rotated in Illustrator 1.1 (center). It was autotraced again in FreeHand to create an airy rendering (bottom).

FreeHand's Paste Inside masking function was used to create a reversed copy of the black line architectural detail, for placement over the dark area at the top of the TIFF portrait.

Three TIFF scans were incorporated as part of the PostScript illustration. These were scanned from black-and-white photographs, and then edited for contrast and cropping in ImageStudio before placement in FreeHand.

A high-contrast drawing was made over part of the large TIFF image, using the TIFF itself as a template.

The blend tool was used to create a series of white design elements for placement in the vertical black border.

The Paste Inside function was used to create a reversed top half of the large capital Y that begins the text. The type was positioned in a blank area at the bottom of the poster.

YOU MUST ADJUST...

this is the motto inscribed on the walls of every nursery, and the process that breaks the spirit is initiated there ... Slowly and subtly, the infant is shaped to the prevailing pattern, her needs for love and care turned against her as weapons to enforce submission. Uniqueness, individuality, difference — these are viewed with horror, even shame, at the very least they are treated like diseases, and a regiment of specialists are available today to "cure" the child who will not or cannot conform.

Robert Lindner, *Must You Conform?*, 1956

K nowing that I could use only black-and-white seemed like a constraint at first. But I remembered, as a teenager, catching a glimpse of Igor Stravinsky back stage at a Los Angeles premiere of one of his later, beautifully spare chamber works. Stravinsky believed that the opportunities for creativity are inversely proportional to the number of materials available. So being "confined" to black-and-white can sometimes provide a special challenge to the imagination. The use of black-and-white, and the limitations it imposes (or transcends), also seemed appropriate to the poster text I had chosen, which speaks of society's attempts to make children conform to conventional standards of behavior.

A rough layout

My first FreeHand rough was assembled from materials already at hand — TIFF scans of myself and my baby daughter and a PixelPaint self-portrait. These served as placeholders and material for experimentation (Figure 1). But the large self-portrait lacked sufficient contrast or interest. So once I had created a rough layout, I gathered a set of better quality photographs to scan and prepare as TIFFs for the final composition.

Preparing TIFFs using ImageStudio

I knew I would want to crop the TIFF images, but wondered how best to do this. I tried placing each TIFF in FreeHand and cropping it by pasting it inside a smaller rectangle. This did the job visually, but I was concerned that the use of three elements incorporating clipping paths might create a document that would be difficult to print. After fiddling with cropping and positioning in FreeHand, I opened each TIFF in ImageStudio, a program designed for editing grayscale photographic images.

I first used ImageStudio's contrast and brightness controls to darken each TIFF slightly. Then I tried cropping the photos by progressively selecting and deleting portions of the image, working from the outside edges toward the center. But when these were saved as TIFFs and placed back in FreeHand, they appeared with a large opaque white bounding box around the image. I consulted with a colleague, who advised me to crop the TIFFs by using ImageStudio's marquee tool to select the portion of each image I wanted to use. When I placed these new TIFFs in FreeHand they came in with their bounding boxes neatly at the edge of the image itself (Figure 2). ∎ *To save a selected portion of an image in ImageStudio, use the lasso or marquee tool to select the desired section, choose Save As or Save As Other from the File menu and make sure the Save Selection box is checked.*

The photo of myself as a little girl contained some distracting dark elements in the foreground and background. These were edited in ImageStudio. I used white to paint out part of the black chair that falls across the little girl's white blouse. Then I used a brush loaded with black to silhouette the figure by painting out light-colored elements in the background. I could have used the

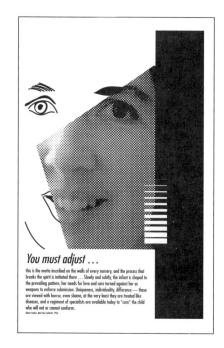

Figure 1. Creating a rough comp. The first FreeHand "rough" was composed with TIFFs on hand. But the large portrait was too bland to serve well as a template for tracing over.

marquee and lasso tools to select and delete the background. But it would have been difficult to use these coarse tools near the delicate areas where the edges of the little girl's hair are highlighted against the background. Because I knew that this image would be placed on a solid black background in Free-Hand, I chose the black paint-out method of silhouetting the figure, leaving the boundaries between hair and background untouched (Figure 3).

Drawing on top of a TIFF

I began my composition by positioning the cropped scan of a recent photo of myself next to a vertical black bar (Figure 4.) I used the corner point tool to draw a polygon shape on top of the TIFF, outlining the portion that would be rendered as a high-contrast drawing. I gave the shape a half-point line and no fill for the time being, to serve as a guideline. I sent the TIFF to layer 0 so that it would be grayed back for use as a template (Figure 5). Using the freehand tool, I drew over the shapes of the eyes, mouth and hair in the area

Figure 2. Cropping in ImageStudio. Using ImageStudio, I first attempted to crop a TIFF by selecting and deleting the unwanted areas of the image. But when placed in FreeHand, the TIFF came in with a large, opaque white bounding box (left). A better method was to crop the image by selecting the desired portion with the marquee tool and save the TIFF with the Save Selection box checked in the Save As Other dialog box. The TIFF saved in this way appeared without a bounding box when placed (right).

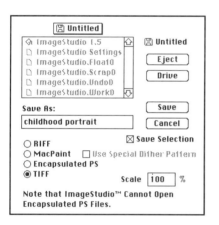

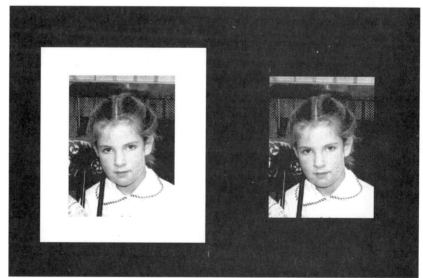

Figure 3. Silhouetting the figure. To silhouette the figure and remove distracting elements from the background, I painted over the background with black in ImageStudio (below left), knowing that the image edges would disappear when placed on a black background in FreeHand (right).

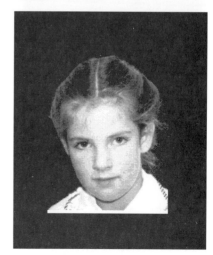

defined by the polygon. These shapes were filled with solid black and two different shades of gray, using the gray densities of the TIFF as a guide (Figure 6). When these drawn elements were finished, I brought the TIFF back to the drawing layer of 100 so that it appeared with its original gray values. I selected the polygon and gave it a white fill and no line so that it obscured part of the TIFF. The drawn elements sat on top of the white polygon, giving the effect of a high-contrast posterized overlay on a photograph (Figure 7).

I next positioned the TIFFs of myself as a child and as a baby in the black vertical band. I scaled the TIFFs by dragging their corner handles with the mouse, trying different sizes and positions until the composition seemed right.

Creating type elements

I created the type for the "You must adjust…" quote by selecting the text tool, clicking with its icon, and typing into the type dialog box that appeared. I clicked OK to close the box, and then adjusted the size of the text block element by dragging its lower right corner handle with the mouse (see "Working with text " on page 91). Once I saw roughly how much room was available, I went back into the type dialog box and adjusted the point sizes of

Figure 4. Positioning the elements. The first two elements positioned were an edited TIFF scan and a vertical rectangle filled with black.

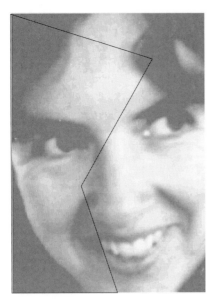

Figure 5. Drawing guidelines over the template. So that the TIFF image could be used as a template for tracing over, it was sent to FreeHand's nonprinting layer 0, where its gray values were automatically lightened. The corner point tool was used to draw a polygon over the TIFF.

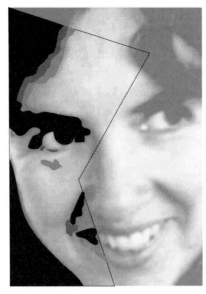

Figure 6. Drawing over the TIFF. The freehand tool was used to draw over the shapes of mouth, eyes and hair in the area defined by the polygon.

Figure 7. Creating the drawing. When the drawn elements were completed, the TIFF was brought back from layer 0 and the polygon was filled with white.

▌Working with text

Using the pointer tool to manipulate the type element box changes the type in several ways. To change the column width (but not the type size), drag a corner handle. To resize the type proportionally, hold down the Shift and Option keys while dragging a corner handle. To stretch or compress type, hold down the Option key while dragging a corner handle. To change the leading between lines, drag a middle handle from the top or bottom of the box. To change the space between letters, drag a middle handle from the left or right side. To adjust only the spacing between words, hold down the Option key while dragging a side handle.

the heading, body text and credit line. I chose Futura Condensed because it seems very hard-edged and unforgiving, like the process of socialization described in the text (Figure 8).

I decided to position a large initial capital partly over the black area in the lower left of the large portrait image. To reverse the upper half of the Y, I selected the letter, colored it white, and then pasted it inside a small rectangle drawn over the top half of the Y (Figure 9). The rectangle was given no fill and no line, so it serves simply as a clipping path for the Y. I positioned the reversed Y half over the black background, and then used the rectangle tool to draw in a stem filled with black (Figure 10).

Using the Blend function

I wanted to create a white graphic element for the vertical black bar that would convey my sense of the text. I used the Blend function to create a series of white bars that vary from light to heavy as they move downward (Figure 11). These were placed on top of the photo of myself as a baby, where they acquire a dual meaning of both oppression as they move down, and lightening as they move up (Figure 12).

Y**OU MUST ADJUST...**

this is the motto inscribed on the walls of every nursery, and the process that breaks the spirit is initiated there … Slowly and subtly, the infant is shaped to the prevailing pattern, her needs for love and care turned against her as weapons to enforce submission. Uniqueness, individuality, difference — these are viewed with horror, even shame, at the very least they are treated like diseases, and a regiment of specialists are available today to "cure" the child who will not or cannot conform.
Robert Lindner, *Must You Conform?*, 1956

Figure 8. Creating the type. The text was typed into the text dialog box and specified as Futura Condensed with justified margins. Type sizes were adjusted after the text block was viewed in place on the poster.

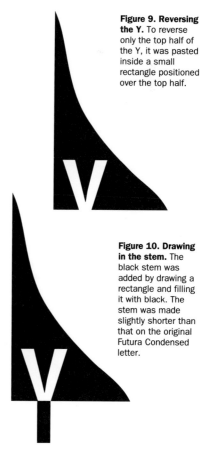

Figure 9. Reversing the Y. To reverse only the top half of the Y, it was pasted inside a small rectangle positioned over the top half.

Figure 10. Drawing in the stem. The black stem was added by drawing a rectangle and filling it with black. The stem was made slightly shorter than that on the original Futura Condensed letter.

Using autotrace, not once, but twice

Having got this far with the composition, I quit FreeHand for a while in order to create the autotraced element I needed to complete the design. I opened Streamline and created an autotrace of a TIFF scan I'd made of a line drawing from a book on the history of ornament. I used the default conversion options for outline rather than centerline tracing, and normal settings for the curve vs. straight line scale and the tight vs. loose bitmap match tolerance. Streamline is an Adobe product designed to be used with Adobe Illustrator; its documents can be placed but not edited in FreeHand. To get around this, I opened the Streamline tracing in Illustrator 1.1 and saved the document in this format because Illustrator 1.1 (but not Illustrator 88) documents can be edited in FreeHand. Before saving, I defined the graphic as having half-point lines and

Figure 11. Creating a blend. A white, half-point line was drawn and duplicated, and the copy was changed to 24 points. The two lines were aligned against a vertical guideline. Each line was selected, the right end points of both lines were selected, and then Blend was chosen from the Special submenu under the Element menu. An eight-step blend was specified, which created eight lines between the original starting and ending lines.

Figure 12. Positioning the blend and TIFF. All the lines were grouped together and positioned above the TIFF of the baby's face. The mouse was used to adjust the TIFF and the lines to be the same width.

Coloring TIFFs in FreeHand

Unlike Illustrator 88, FreeHand allows the use of TIFFs not only as templates but as elements incorporated into the finished illustration. For the self-portrait poster featured in this chapter I worked only in black and white, but TIFFs can be colored in FreeHand. This is done simply by selecting the TIFF and assigning it a color from the color menu. This results in a monochrome rendering in the chosen color. Figures 4 and 5 on page 88 were colored with 40 percent gray to simulate the way a TIFF looks when placed in layer 0 as a template. When a TIFF is colored, all the black areas of the original become the specified color, while the lighter areas are rendered as tints of this color.

Different parts of the TIFF cannot be rendered in different colors. However, TIFFs can be selectively colored in a program like PhotoMac and incorporated in color back into FreeHand.

no fill. Because the scan, and hence the autotracing, was slightly askew, I rotated the image slightly using Illustrator's rotation tool (Figure 13). I reopened the FreeHand poster document and brought the autotrace element into it by choosing Place from the File menu. I tried positioning the element in different parts of the poster but was unhappy with the heaviness of the lines. Rather than go back to Illustrator, I used FreeHand's trace tool to create a new version of the arch element, specifying tight curve fit and sharp corners (Figure 14). ∎ *FreeHand's trace tool functions like a marquee to surround the object or portion of it to be traced. All lines that fall within the selection box are traced in one step. It's best to send the object to be traced to an inactive layer while tracing, so the new lines don't interfere with the original.* ∎ *Double-clicking on the trace tool brings up a dialog box in which you can specify curve fit (from tight to loose) and corners (from sharp to round.)*

The autotrace function traced around the lines of the original Streamline tracing, creating a more airy and open feeling when these new lines were defined as hairlines with no fill. Again, the element had a dual meaning — the geometry of the lines was idealized and confining but the rendering was loose, organic and open. I positioned the ornament in the space above the large face, where it seemed to suggest the top of the head.

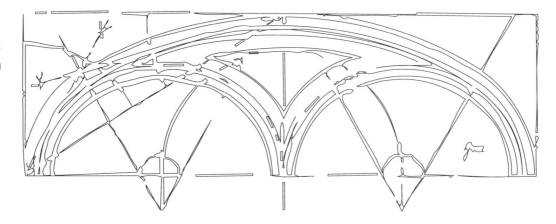

Figure 13. Autotracing with Streamline. A TIFF scan of a line drawing was autotraced in Streamline and edited in Illustrator 1.1.

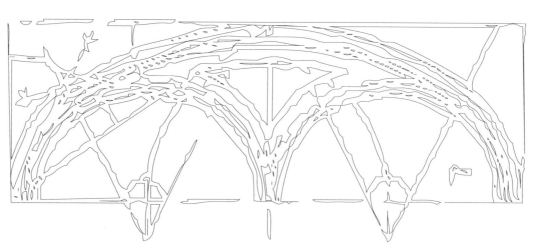

Figure 14. Autotracing in FreeHand. The Illustrator version of the ornament was placed into FreeHand and autotraced again, resulting in an open, airy texture of lines.

Clipping paths with Paste Inside

The black lines of the arch were not visible where they overlaid the dark area at the top of the portrait TIFF, so I created a reverse clone of the arched element to sit over the black areas. With the black autotraced element in place (Figure 15), I cloned it, ungrouped it so that each line would be selected, and then specified the lines as half-point, white. This clone sat directly on top of the black arch, obscuring the black lines (Figure 16). (Though the black lines of the arches were hairlines, I used a slightly thicker white line for the reverse, so the white wouldn't get lost on the black background.) I regrouped the white clone and then used the corner point tool to draw a polygon shape outlining the area in which I wanted the white lines to appear. I drew this shape with the same half-point white line, so that it would be visible while I worked (Figure 17). I then selected the white clone and used the keyboard shortcut of Command-X to cut it. I selected the white polygon, gave it no line and no fill, and then chose Paste Inside from the Edit menu. This created a masked section of the white line detail, which sat right where I wanted it, without obscuring the black arch lines above (Figure 18).

Making test proofs

At this point I sent my poster file to a service bureau for Linotronic proofs at 635, 1270 and 2540 dpi. I specified that the 11 x 17-inch poster be printed with FreeHand's Fit On Paper option to save output costs by printing on 8½ x 11-inch paper. My LaserWriter II proofs at 300 dpi worked well for rendering the solid black areas of the poster, but left blotchy areas in some parts of the TIFFs. The appearance of the TIFFs was improved at higher resolution, but because a TIFF is a bitmap, it can't improve beyond the resolution at which it was created. The use of TIFFs did add to the size of the

Figure 15. Positioning the black ornament. The black line tracing was lost where it fell against the dark areas at the top of the TIFF image.

Figure 16. Creating a reversed clone. To create a reversed element the ornament was cloned and grouped, and the lines were specified as half-point white. The clone sat directly on top of the black ornament.

Figure 17. Using Paste Inside to mask the clone. The white ornament clone was pasted inside a polygon drawn around the part of the image that falls over the black background.

Figure 18. Combining black and white. The completed ornament is black over the white background and white over the black, with perfect alignment of the lines.

Fig. 15

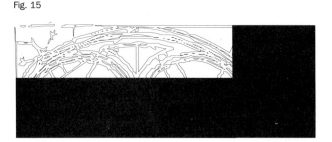

Fig. 17

Fig. 16

Fig. 18

PostScript file and slowed the printing time. The high-resolution proof took 17 minutes to print and the service bureau billed me extra for each minute beyond 10.

The most noticeable differences between the prints at different resolutions were in the rendering of the hairlines and the gray fill areas. At 300 dpi the hairlines looked more like one-point lines. At 635 and above they looked truly like hairlines. At 300 and 635 dpi the dots composing the gray fills were clearly visible, but not at the higher resolutions. The fineness of the higher resolutions helped me to pick out and fix a few areas where elements were misaligned.

Changing the line screen

At all four output resolutions I noticed that wherever thin white lines lay across the gray areas of a TIFF the lines were distorted. This happened because I forgot to specify a line screen for the TIFFs and they printed at a coarse default of 53 lines per inch. I reset the line screen to 120. After adjusting the screens, I had the poster printed again on a Linotronic, at full size and 1270 dpi. ▌ *To apply a screen to a bitmap element, select it, choose Element Info from the Element menu and type into the Image dialog box that appears. You can choose a line or a dot screen and can specify the angle and line ruling desired.*

In retrospect

Looking back on this project, I think being limited to black-and-white made the poster design stronger. It's easy to be seduced by the richness of on-screen color. But without the immediate sensual appeal of a range of hues, I was forced to think more about the structure of the composition and the use of value contrasts.

It was also interesting to think and plan very directly concerning the features that FreeHand provides and to design graphic elements that would use those features well. Though PostScript illustration is very flexible, it does have its own strengths and weaknesses and its own "look." It felt comfortable to let the PostScript medium shape the style and rendering of the poster. The same text and photo material might have given rise to a very different composition if executed by silkscreen or watercolor, for instance.

Another thing I appreciate about the computer in general is that it enables me to work and be creative in a small space. Working with conventional art media is wonderful, provided you have the room to use it, the luxury of spreading out your materials and the time these materials require. But for those who work at home, as I do, and especially when there are children underfoot, paints, inks and scissors are more difficult to manage. The computer almost magically contains the extra space, materials and time I need to execute complex and satisfying work that would not otherwise be possible.

Janet Ashford

"I have done art work all my life — painting, drawing, silkscreening and so forth. These media are wonderful but require a lot of room, equipment and time. And once you've committed many hours or days of effort to a painting or design, it's hard to turn back. The computer makes it possible to create — and then change — without losing any of the work already done. The computer does not afford the beautiful textures and subtleties available with traditional, "wet" media. But it's a very flexible medium nevertheless and comes equipped with dazzling electronic paints as well as very sophisticated drawing tools and functions. I find PostScript programs to be perfect media for illustration and a good place to start when working out compositions that will later be rendered with pencil or brush."

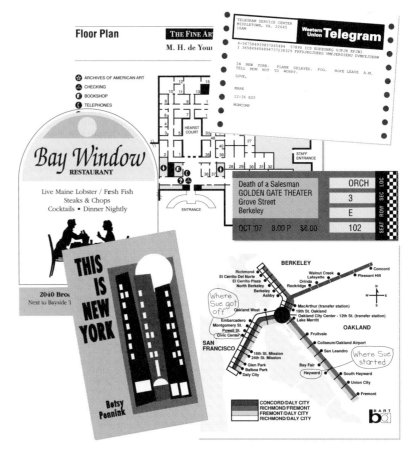

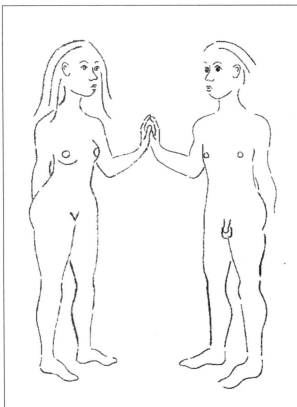

The figure of a woman was drawn with the freehand tool in FreeHand. She was copied and flipped vertically. Strategic lines were altered or moved to create the male figure. The FreeHand drawing was printed, traced over with pencil to roughen the line, and then scanned as line art and saved as a TIFF file.

The illustrations above were made in FreeHand for a book teaching English to foreign students. The museum floor map and BART map were traced from scanned templates. In the book, each illustration includes a drop shadow to make it pop off the page when placed in the book's PageMaker layout.

This portrait of Lincoln was made for a workbook on American history. The portrait was rendered as a high-contrast drawing in FreeHand using a scanned photograph as a template for tracing.

A greeting card illustration made in FreeHand features a simple drawing of a chair, tiled floor and wallpaper made using shapes with a blue outline.

This poster employs a TIFF scan in two ways. The line drawing above was drawn over a TIFF used as a template in FreeHand. The 2-point black line was cloned, styled as a 3-point mauve line and offset 1 point to the right and the bottom. The image below uses the same TIFF, saved as a MacPaint document in ImageStudio and made transparent in FreeHand.

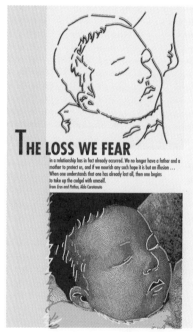

A FreeHand illustration of an African woman giving birth was based on a 19th century drawing by Robert Felkin, a British physician and traveler. The drawing was scanned and used as a template for tracing. The lines of the figures were drawn as shapes and filled with color. The decorative border at the top was drawn with the freehand tool, and then copied, reflected vertically and positioned as the bottom border. Detail was then added to both borders, so that they weren't exact copies of each other.

C H A P T E R   9

Creating an Imaginary Landscape

Artist

Tom Gould went to school at San Diego State College and worked in several studios in the San Diego area before becoming art director of *Psychology Today* magazine from 1968 to 1975. He has worked as a freelance designer since then, concentrating on publication design. His work has included annual reports, textbooks and a two-year stint as art director of *San Diego Home and Garden* magazine.

Project

The project was to create an illustration for the cover of *Verbum* magazine that would showcase the capabilities of PostScript illustration in color. *Verbum* is a magazine devoted to the exploration of microcomputer art, especially graphics. Both the publisher and the art director were eager to use a PostScript application, in this case FreeHand, to create a complete cover, including illustration and type, and to output the final color separations directly from the program.

I used a Mac II with 2 MB of RAM and a 60 MB hard drive, an Apple color monitor and a LaserWriter. Color proofs and final output were made through a service bureau using a QMS ColorScript 100 PostScript printer and a Linotronic L-300 imagesetter, respectively.

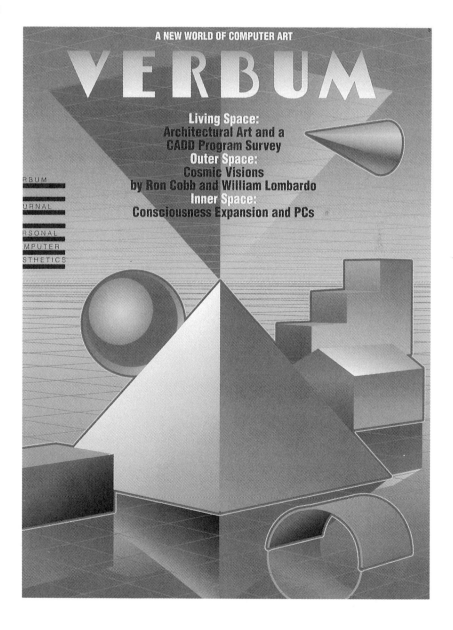

Design process

My cover design was to be used for an issue devoted to exploring "space," inner, outer and architectural. I formulated my first ideas with this theme in mind, beginning with thumbnail sketches. I began working with geometric shapes expressed as architectural forms. I wanted to place the shapes on a grid, real or underlying, both because of its graphic appropriateness to the subject and because I like the space-creating precision that grids make possible. The earliest solution was an evolutionary architectural sequence going from a basic cube to an arched span, defined by an isometric grid. But the geometric alignment of the forms did not settle down enough to allow the exploration of transparencies that I envisioned, so I looked into an alternate visual image. The pyramid has always been a visually and mystically potent form. I liked the symmetry of the single pyramid, and then somewhat arbitrarily added a second one reflected up into the sky in a sort of gravity-defying balancing act. I created a loose computer "sketch,"

showing the basic colors and composition I intended to use. After approval of a color proof by the publisher and art director, I redrew the image more precisely. I created a limited color palette of warm and cool colors and relied on graduated color fills to create the look of three-dimensional objects. This cover was my second attempt to output four-color separations from the Macintosh. I had been working with a Macintosh for three or four months, trying to stay ahead of my clients' requirements while also learning the software. There had been little or no chance to experiment. But I had been using FreeHand and was impressed by its precise line handling and the potential of graduated fills in color.

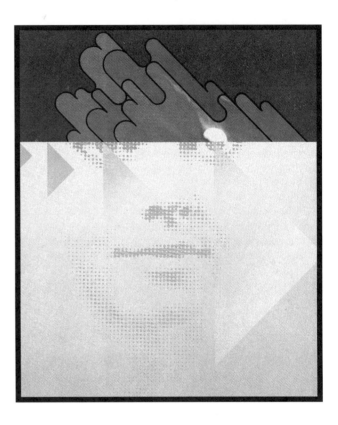

I like to use an isometric perspective because of the possibilities for creating ambiguous space. This is for me a virtue, because reversible figures maintain the integrity of the picture plane while exciting the eye with their simultaneous projection into and out of space. In this sketch, I visualized a sequence of basic architectural forms aligned on a 30 degree axis. I thought that a fine linear structure could support some transparent planes of color, created with graduated fills. Unfortunately, the geometry constrained the overall image into something overly complex and unattractive in shape.

I had been intrigued by the ambiguous nature of a pyramid aligned point-on-the-horizon, as seen in this illustration from a 1970 issue of *Psychology Today*. This image was created well before the advent of the Mac, but it employed many of the techniques now being done with computer graphics, including graduated mechanical screens, inserted images, "bitmaps" (oversize 0 degree halftone screens), and found four-color images.

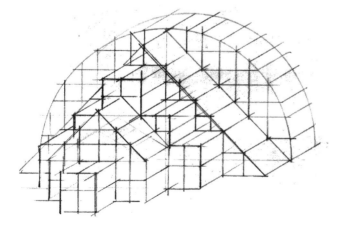

This was another early idea. The grid at the top was drawn first and then cloned and scaled with 100 percent horizontal and reduced vertical values. These two grids were then cloned and reflected across the horizontal axis. The idea of one horizon, as a dimensionless line, was taking form.

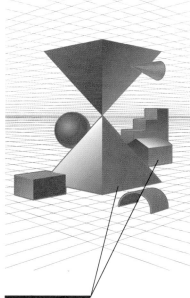

The sequence above shows how the final design evolved. A pyramid is aligned to the horizon and a second one perches on the tip of the first. The grids create ground and sky planes. The grid lines continue through the upper pyramid, creating visual ambiguity by flattening the shape into two dimensions, and at the same time allowing it to be "read" as a spatial solid.

The grid lines served only as an organizing structure, not as a reliable guide for perspective. (For example, the small house is 1 grid segment long and the pyramid side is 3 grid segments wide. But the house length is greater than ⅓ the length of the pyramid base.)

The finished *Verbum* cover includes custom-made type for the title. The black type below the title is the only black used in the illustration. I've found that mixing black in process colors can create moiré patterns when printed.

A NEW WORLD OF COMPUTER ART

$7

VERBUM

Living Space:
Architectural Art and a
CADD Program Survey
Outer Space:
Cosmic Visions
by Ron Cobb and William Lombardo
Inner Space:
Consciousness Expansion and PCs

ERBUM
3
OURNAL
F
ERSONAL
OMPUTER
ESTHETICS

After experimenting with pencil sketches, I fired up the Mac and began the FreeHand imaging. I first zoomed out to Fit In Window to position a good baseline for my two-point grid. This was generated by drawing a horizontal line at midpoint, extending from the left "vanishing point" to beyond the opposite margin. I cloned the line, selected its right end point and pivoted the clone by moving the end point up a few points, using the Move command. I repeated this process, each time increasing the distance in an arithmetic progression to create a diverging sequence of angled lines radiating from a single point (Figure 1). This sequence was then grouped, cloned and reflected to the bottom and to the right to form the grid upon which the remaining design was built (Figure 2). A true perspective grid would be created by using a geometric progression to increase the distance between the lines as they move toward the foreground. My grid is an expedient that serves as an organizing structure for the purposes of my illustration. It allows objects placed on it to appear to be in perspective, but it couldn't be used as a reliable guide for drawing the objects. The grid is distorted, with the squares becoming larger rather than smaller as they recede toward the horizon. So I had to fudge the dimensions of the background shapes relative to the grid to make them look smaller than those in the foreground.

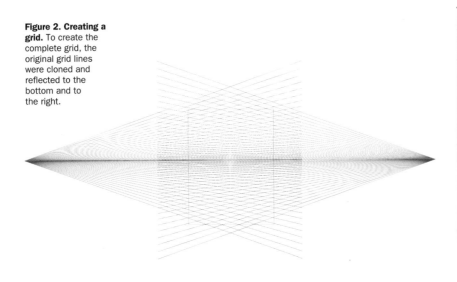

Figure 1. Drawing perspective lines. FreeHand's Clone and Move functions were used to create a sequence of angled lines radiating from one point.

Figure 2. Creating a grid. To create the complete grid, the original grid lines were cloned and reflected to the bottom and to the right.

Figure 3. Preparing a comp. A QMS color proof was made of the FreeHand "rough" to check color values and get approval from the publisher and art director.

Figure 4. Choosing colors. Since most of the objects were colored with graduated fills, I could use strong or complementary colors for the beginning and ending hues, allowing the gradation to mix and diffuse the raw colors. I used a range of blues in all values for structure, with oranges and reds in the high and medium values for warmth. I omitted black entirely, to avoid moiré patterns. I drew squares, filled them with my graduated fills and placed them on the pasteboard to act as color swatches for reference as I worked. To make sure I was not misled by on-screen color, I checked the final color mix percentages against a process color book.

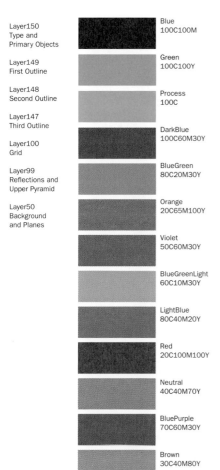

Layer150
Type and
Primary Objects

Layer149
First Outline

Layer148
Second Outline

Layer147
Third Outline

Layer100
Grid

Layer99
Reflections and
Upper Pyramid

Layer50
Background
and Planes

Blue
100C100M

Green
100C100Y

Process
100C

DarkBlue
100C60M30Y

BlueGreen
80C20M30Y

Orange
20C65M100Y

Violet
50C60M30Y

BlueGreenLight
60C10M30Y

LightBlue
80C40M20Y

Red
20C100M100Y

Neutral
40C40M70Y

BluePurple
70C60M30Y

Brown
30C40M80Y

A FreeHand "rough"

At this point I began applying colors and fills to the background to create both atmospheric and geometric space. I decided to superimpose the grid over the "sky" and its miragelike pyramid, but allowed the foreground "real" shapes to lie in front of the grid. The whole piece was composed on the screen, rather loosely and without much attention to color and line style names or to the use of FreeHand's layering capabilities. When the basic design was established, I had a QMS print made to see how my screen colors would translate to four-color print (not very well in FreeHand 1.0) and to show the art director and publisher what I intended to do (Figure 3).

After approval I redrew the entire page, starting with the grid, in order to make adjustments in spacing and to clean up some of the simplistic or overly complicated solutions I had used the first time. I defined colors to create a limited color palette, providing myself with warm and cool tones in dark and light combinations, with a few accents to spark up the limited structural palette. I avoided using black in my colors. Some of my colleagues have made pioneering efforts to push the envelope of Mac color. They've learned that the use of black in process colors can result in unfortunate moiré patterns due to the limitations on PostScript-defined screen angles.

The colors were placed as swatches off the image area for reference, along with notes about what layers were used for various elements (Figure 4). FreeHand allows the use of 201 layers, as if the design were being done on a tracing pad of 201 perfectly transparent pages. In addition, the usual front-to-back interleaving of objects can be done within each single layer, offering infinite levels of control, as well as an infinite number of ways to become confused. I found it useful to assign different planes of the illustration to different layers. This kept things in relative positions. By choosing Layer Control from the View menu, I could isolate individual layers and work on them separately. ■ *Making notes off-image on the pasteboard helps keep track of which elements are assigned to which layers.*

Painterly fills

The color fills were applied to the geometric shapes to create "painterly" accents and emphasis. For example, the floating cone was filled with three shapes, each shape filled with a highlight, a middle tone, a core shadow and reflected light analogues (Figure 5). ■ *Angling the fills slightly creates subtle breaks in the transition between fills to avoid the mechanical airbrushed look that many computer-aided designs have (see "Creating a 'painterly' impression" on page 104).*

I decided to add reflections to the ground plane (further mixing the metaphor of the upside-down pyramid "reflection"). These were plotted and colored with cool variations of their primary color schemes, but still within the limited palette. Elements were butted together in zoom-in mode and colored with fills. Using overlaid radial fills resulted in a somewhat clumsy rendering of

Creating a "painterly" impression

The Impressionist painters, in their attempts to render visual reality and the qualities of light in space and on objects, employed a style of brushwork called "broken," in which the local color of the object is rendered in complementary, vibrating hues that mix in the eye of the viewer. The use of the dragged brush to produce nuances of color and to direct the viewer's attention by the direction of the stroke became an end in itself in the Action Painting of this century, in which a painterly quality was much admired. There are also Gestalt studies of the perception of objects that suggest that emphasis of edge contrasts makes for strong visual spatial cues. By combining these aspects of aesthetic and perceptual theory, I feel that the painterly use of graduated fills, easily and elegantly accomplished in FreeHand, can provide an analogous device for creating spatial shapes, without the rubbery airbrushed look that so often results from the smooth transitions the computer creates.

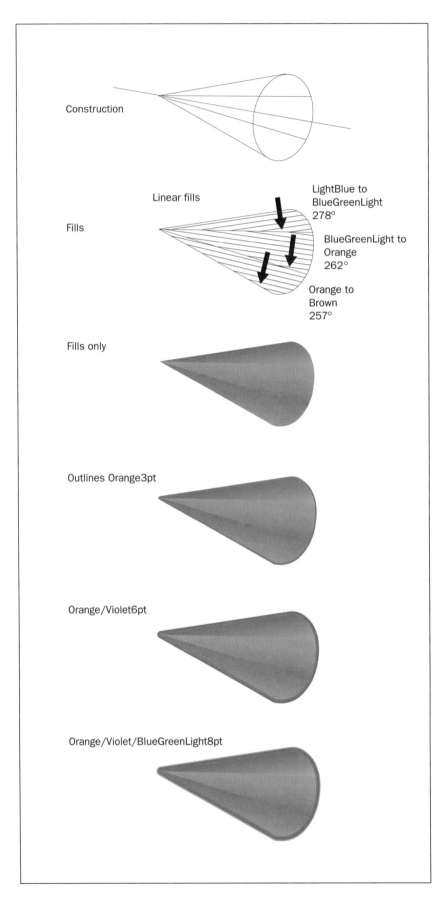

Figure 5. "Painting" the shapes. Each cone shape is filled with three separate filled shapes in order to achieve a more painterly look.

a spherical highlight on the sphere that floats to the left of the pyramids. If I were doing the illustration today, I would use the Paste Inside masking function (it was available in FreeHand 1.0, but I didn't realize it) to offset the radial fills, but I would still employ the subtle intuitive alignment of fills to create a non-mechanical shading.

Experimenting with color contrast

A contour line was drawn around the group of "real" shapes. This was cloned twice, varied in width and color, and layered to create a halo of complementary colors. I feel that the contrast of colors was not successful, possibly due to the limitations of process color printing. The brilliance and vibration that I envisioned and that appeared on the screen were missing. If I were doing it again, I would try to use value rather than color contrasts to get a shimmering effect.

Custom lettering

I tried a number of Adobe typefaces as logo possibilities, but none seemed appropriate (*Verbum* redesigns its logo with each issue to complement the cover design). I also experimented with drop shadows reduced in size to align with the central perspective, but this wasn't satisfactory either. I decided that type with graduated fills would work well. Outline fonts were not available to me at the time, so I decided to "hand letter" the logo. I chose a variation of Broadway, an old favorite for its malleability and ease of construction, and also for its reference to the streamlined 1930s, when airy fantasies of architecture and geometry were in their heyday. The six letters in "VERBUM" were without internal negative shapes except for the B. I drew it as a single closed path, to allow the background to show through the negative space inside the B (Figure 6). A soft blue at the top shaded into white, with no outline. I created a template of lines to maintain consistency in angle and line widths (Figure 7). I later devel-

Figure 6. Making the counters unfilled. The letter B was derived from the R. The line that defined the bowl was curved around to meet the vertical stroke, but not joined, in order to maintain a closed shape with a single outline. If the strokes had been joined, the counters, or spaces inside the letter, would have filled in. The outline was a white line at first, but I couldn't be sure that it would disappear, even in the white of a graduated fill. So I selected None in the line menu. A logarithmic fill, light blue to white, gave the letters a floating feeling.

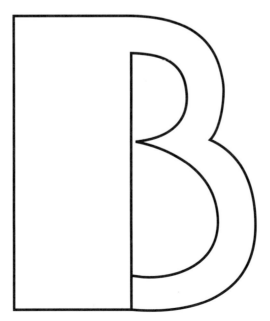

oped the rest of the alphabet in FreeHand (Figure 8). Since most of the design decisions had already been made, this was a task of a few hours.

I now had the design completed on-screen to my satisfaction, and it was time to send it to the Linotronic for color separations. I selected each color in turn, went to Edit Color from the Color menu and revised the percentages according to a color tint guide (printed samples of screens of colors in 10 percent steps, mixed in all combinations of CMY). I attempted to match the colors in the book to the colors I had seen on the screen and also varied percentages to avoid poor value contrasts. This was a somewhat intuitive process, although I knew enough to avoid using black in my colors. I didn't know at the time that I could adjust my monitor to get more faithful color rendition. But I find that even with screen adjustments, cyan is still not very accurate, and I always use color guides to check color before sending for a QMS proof. The QMS proof of my final cover design came out okay, and the art director added display type, after which the cover art was output as four pieces of film and ran without problem on the four-color press.

In retrospect

If I were doing this illustration again, I would probably wish to adjust some colors. The lack of high-resolution color-proofing systems with fidelity to process color mixtures is an on-going problem. Color monitors by their nature can't give an adequate picture of how ink will lie on paper, so until we're working in an all-electronic environment, we'll have to make that final intuitive mental visualization before sending PostScript files for film output. This is no different than what had to be done before the computer, but it's often easy to be seduced by brilliant RGB color and apparent finish on-screen. It's still important to think like a printer in order to get the most out of any graphic design for print. ∎ *Color-picking systems like TekColor (see page 55) are beginning to help with the visualization process.*

We're always being reminded, sometimes cruelly, that the bounty of capabilities we enjoy via the Macintosh is the result of a haphazard growth from much more modest beginnings, when the availability of three or four typefaces was considered a great leap forward. There are aspects of prepress work

Figure 7. Aligning letterforms. After the first simple letters were created by eye, the line weights and angles were duplicated as grouped elements, which could be moved around to align the letterforms for consistency.

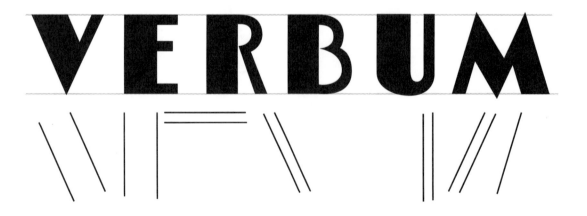

(trapping, for instance) that need much more attention. In its marketing strategy, the computer industry works hard to convince buyers that anyone can do wonderful design on the desktop. This creates problems for the advanced and experienced artist, because the industry would rather not point out problems that the newcomer is unlikely to encounter.

A unique situation exists right now in computer design, profoundly different from anything past or present. A single generation of designers has experienced the use of hot type/letterpress (not all that different from something Gutenberg would recognize), has passed through cold type/photo-offset, and is now grumbling and fumbling its way through the electronic (actually digital) revolution in creating marks on paper. We must guard against solving problems of the new medium in old ways. And the new breed of designers growing up with computers needs to acquire the breadth of hard-won insights into what it means to communicate with design. The curve and swell of a line, produced by the trained twist and drag of a quill or reed pen, still speaks to us in ways we can't ignore.

Figure 8. Developing an alphabet. Shown here are two versions of the Verbum alphabet, one in a default halftone (at top) and one in a line screen (at bottom). The six letters I had created initially served as templates for the rest of the alphabet, with essentially only the O and the S requiring unique new patterns.

PORTFOLIO

Tom Gould

"The computer has transformed my design practice on a day-to-day, nuts-and-bolts level. What I wish for now is an opportunity to explore some of the possibilities of the medium without the constraints of commercial work."

This apple was done in FreeHand in a workshop to explore some of the painterly color treatments described in this chapter. It was done quickly, was composed on the monitor, and would have benefited from some forethought and planning.

A magazine illustration dealing with wine shows an exploitation of FreeHand's Paste Inside function, with up to three graduated fills in some of the checker squares.

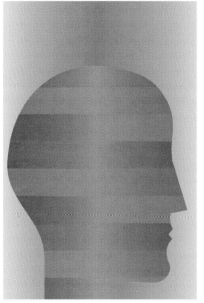

A personal Christmas card shows FreeHand's Blend function in action. By selecting as reference points for the blend the tip of the dove's left wing and the tip of the first star point to the left of the top center point, I created a blend with a spiral effect.

This preliminary illustration for a psychology textbook shows the use of graduated fills butted together along a central vertical line.

This FreeHand adaptation of a Soviet Georgian cloisonné icon was used on a souvenir coffee mug for the San Diego Soviet arts festival. It employs a straight-forward use of objects colored with flat fills and a thick outline in a contrasting color.

C H A P T E R   1 0

A Figure Study in Layers of Color

Artist

David Brickley received a Bachelor's degree in Communication Design in 1987 from the Art Center College of Design in Pasadena, California. He worked as a freelance art director for several major San Francisco advertising agencies and now provides consulting and computer illustration for advertising, editorial and trade show demonstrations.

Project

The project was to create a complex illustration that would demonstrate the capabilities of Corel Draw, a new PostScript illustration program for IBM and compatible systems. I had met the people at Corel Systems in Ottawa, Canada, and when they saw the kind of work I was doing with computer graphics, they encouraged me to use their program to create something special for them. Corel set no limits on subject matter or time. I began in March of 1989 and delivered a finished drawing five months later.

I used a Dell 386/16 computer, equipped with 1 MB of RAM and a 70 MB hard disk, an extended VGA adapter with a 14-inch multifrequency monitor, a math coprocessor and a Microsoft mouse. At one time I was a devoted user of the SummaSketch tablet. But during the development of the illustration for Corel I found the mouse more accurate and less tiring to work with. Final output was to a Hewlett-Packard PaintJet printer, a Linotronic L-300 imagesetter and a Matrix QCRZ film recorder.

Design goals

I wanted to create a piece that would look like it was made by an illustrator, but that could not have been executed without the special capabilities of a computer. I chose a figure study because it's perhaps the most difficult art to execute, with or without a computer. I was excited by Corel Draw's many features, especially the availability of graduated fills. I hoped to create a piece that would fully use these features and still achieve an "artistic" look.

PostScript illustration has a look of its own — crisp edges, clean lines and opaque colors. This look, combined with PostScript's opaque layering of elements, determined that the diver piece be constructed of many overlapping objects that give the visual impression of form and light.

A photo of the screen shows the completed Diver piece. Working at high resolution, I was able to achieve effects that looked great but were difficult to output.

A color proof was printed using a Hewlett-Packard PaintJet printer.

Final PostScript output of three divers, but not the background, was generated using Linotronic color separations. The complete illustration proved too complex to print.

Corel Draw lets you view the drawing in preview mode while you work in keyline mode, as shown in this photo of the screen.

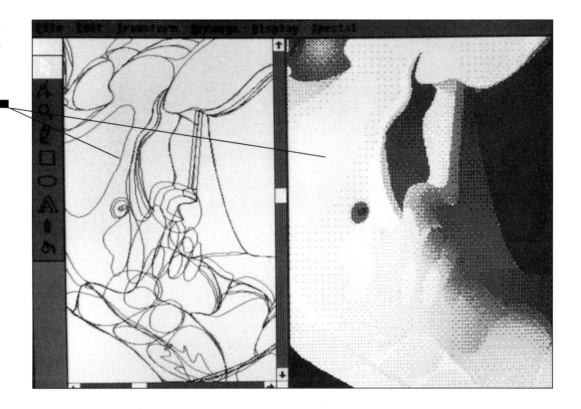

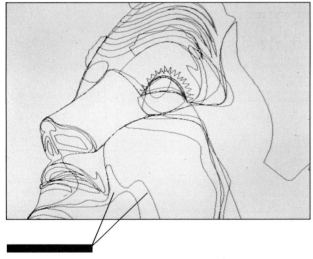

A close-up of the diver's face in keyline shows the many overlapping objects used to create it.

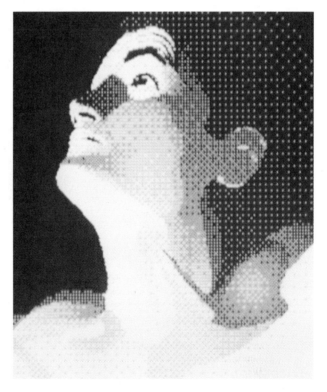

When viewed in color, the layered objects in the diver's face give the impression of contour and shading.

With complete freedom to choose a subject and unlimited time in which to execute it, I decided to challenge the PostScript medium by attempting a complex figure study. The figure was based on a small photograph of an Olympic diver in mid-air. My design plan included a surreal, imaginary landscape of water, mountains and sky, with the diver and a series of receding duplicates positioned against this background.

Creating the background

"Diver" was drawn in two parts: the figure and the background. The background was done first, to help establish the mood and scale of the piece.

The sky is one large rectangle that stretches the width of the horizon. It's colored with a gradient fill that moves diagonally from light blue at the lower left corner to dark blue at the upper right. To create the fill I chose the Paint icon from the toolbox, specified the beginning and ending colors for the fill, and then specified the direction of the ramp by entering an angle number. The colors and angle of the fill suggest a late afternoon sky. The water is also a large rectangle whose width matches that of the sky. To create a sense of perspective, the color is graduated from a deep blue at the bottom to a slightly lighter blue at the top (Figure 1).

The mountains were drawn as one irregular shape and given a flat fill. To give three-dimensional form to the peaks, I added highlight shapes that simulate the way light from a low sun might fall on mountain surfaces. The

Figure 1. Creating the background. The sky and the water are both a rectangle colored with a gradient fill. The mountains are a single irregular shape overlaid with highlight shapes that define shadows.

highlights were all colored with a graduated fill that's dark red at the bottom and light orange at the top. This technique made it look as if all the peaks were lit by the same light source (Figure 2).

Without a picture reference, I had to play with shapes to get the look of a rocky bluff. I used the draw tool and the node-editing tool. The draw tool can be used to place specific points one at a time or it can be used to generate a freehand path with points automatically assigned by the program. A node-editing tool is used to add or delete individual points from a path. ▍ *Paths drawn "freehand" in PostScript often contain many more points than are necessary to define the desired lines, and their complexity can lead to printing problems.*

The clouds were created from about five or six basic shapes that were altered and scaled differently and colored with slightly varying radial fills. I used this theme-and-variations method because I wanted the clouds to look as amorphous and random as possible yet have the same style. Almost all of the "puffs" have a radial fill, from blue-green at the outside to a near-white at the center. The center of the fill is positioned in a different place within each cloud shape. To do this I first created a cloud shape and filled it with a radial fill. Then I drew a tiny line segment some distance from the cloud, depending on how I wanted the center of the fill to be offset. I selected the line, then selected the cloud shape (it has to be done in that order) and chose Combine from the Arrange menu. This caused the center of the radial fill to shift to the center of the new grouped object, even though the fill does not extend beyond the

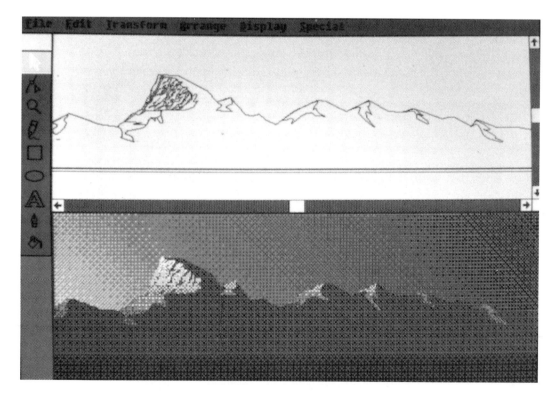

Figure 2. Detailing the peaks. The flat-color mountain shape is given dimension by highlight shapes that define the lighted sides of the peaks.

boundaries of the cloud shape. The clouds were colored according to their orientation to the sunlight. Those in shadow were given darker fills of blue-green. I also paid attention to the altitude; the higher clouds are whiter (Figure 3).

Assigning colors

In Corel Draw colors are created only when an object to be colored is selected. For example, to color the mountain shape I drew it, selected it, and then clicked on the Paint icon in the toolbox to view a fly-out menu of options, including a palette of gray values, a PMS option, options for spot and process color, and options for graduated fills. I chose process color, which led to a dialog box in which I specified the desired percentages of cyan, magenta, yellow and black. Colors are not given names and cannot be chosen again from a menu. In Corel Draw, the color becomes part of the paint attributes for the selected object. ▌ *To use a color or other specified style again, select the object that will incorporate the style , then choose Copy Style From from the Edit menu. Select the attributes you wish to copy (color, fill pattern, line weight and so forth), and then select the object who's style you wish to copy. The chosen attributes will be automatically transferred to the object that was selected first.*

Creating the figure

Although there's an autotrace feature in Corel Draw, I didn't use it to create the diver. The diver's body was drawn freehand, beginning with an outline shape that contains a graduated fill that changes from a dark flesh tone at the toes to a lighter tone at the head. This coloring helped me determine how the figure would fit in with the background (Figure 4). As I worked on the figure, I rotated it into different orientations — upside down, backwards and so forth — to find the one that looked best against the background. The fill

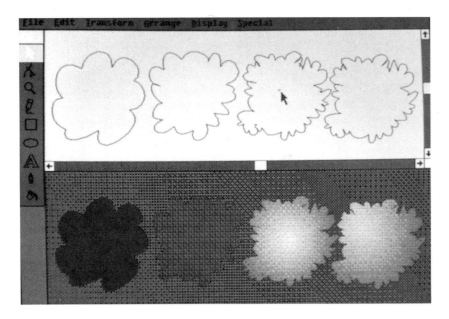

Figure 3. Creating the clouds. Five or six basic cloud shapes were created and then altered slightly, resized and colored differently to create a bank of varied cloud shapes. Most clouds are colored with a radial fill.

within the diver retained its orientation relative to that shape, even when the shape was rotated.

Skin tone

Light and shadow, shape and form, the skin and bone of the diver, are all defined by values of skin tone. Corel Draw does not currently provide logarithmic gradient fills or a blend function that fills in intermediate steps in the transformation from one object to another. So in a number of areas I achieved the effect I wanted by layering many objects, each with a different color and a different role in defining a shape (Figure 5).

The features of the diver's body were created working from the head to the toes. The head was rendered first, because I always feel better about a figure drawing once the face is done. The figure as a whole required over 200 separate objects.

Working in fine detail

Most of the drawing was created with as much magnification as was comfortable to work in. For example, at the setting I used, the eye of the diver would fill the screen. This allowed me to create very fine detail. My intent was to create an illustration for printing as a medium-sized poster. But some printers can output color images that measure 60 inches across. Detail and accuracy may not be apparent at smaller sizes, but the potential for larger output is always there. Printers seem to operate according to the unwritten law that every misaligned shape or mismatched seam will be emblazoned across the

Figure 4. Fitting the figure with the background. To provide a sense of how the figure would fit with the light source in the background, a base contour shape was drawn, colored with a gradient fill, and then rotated until it looked right.

Figure 5. Using opaque layers. Because Corel Draw didn't include a blend function, a "blended" effect was simulated by layering many objects that varied subtly in shape and color.

paper for all the world to see. It seemed much easier to create the shapes accurately as I worked, than to try to "clean up" the drawing later. But my attention to detail, and the screen display that made it possible, created an illustration file that later proved difficult to print.

Printing

My first attempt at color output was via a Hewlett-Packard PaintJet printer. To help speed the printing process I first recorded the image data on a floppy disk. This process took 12½ hours (I let the computer run overnight). The diver piece contains many graduated fills, which require a great deal of processing time.

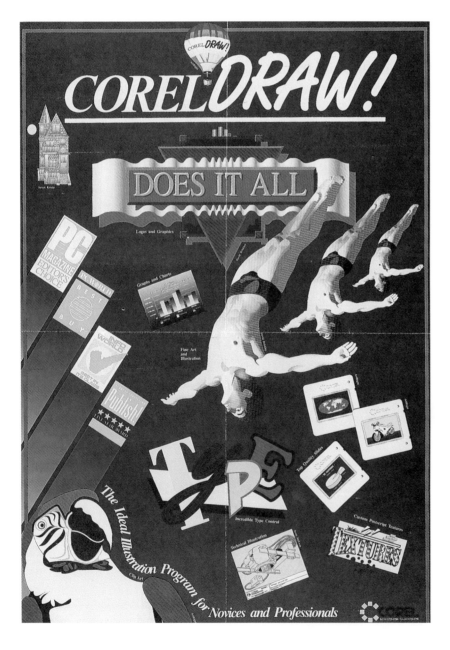

Figure 6. Printing part of the file. A PostScript color separation generated by a Linotronic L-300 was used to produce the image of three divers for a Corel promotional poster.

Printing time depends on the device and the resolution used. In this case the file that took over 12 hours to store on a floppy was printed in about 2 minutes on the Paintjet.

The next step was to print color separations through a Linotronic L-300, so that the image could be printed and used by Corel. But at this point the process stalled. In the end the illustration proved to be too complex to print. We were able to get Lino color separations of the figure of the diver and two of the clones, but could not also get the background to print. The three figures were eventually used on a Corel Draw promotional poster (Figure 6).

It was probably all those freehand curves that caused the problems. My illustration contains more complex paths, with more points, than can be processed. One solution would be to modify the illustration, perhaps redrawing some elements or removing points. But for an illustration with so many components, this task seemed daunting.

I attempted to print a PostScript slide of the complete illustration using a Matrix QCRZ film recorder running Freedom of Press software, which interprets the PostScript code in a way that can be understood by the non-PostScript film recorder. But this device and software combination could not handle the complexity of the image.

In retrospect

Central to the creation of this piece was the very fact that it was "computer art" — that is, art created with electronic technology rather than with brush and paint on canvas. Until recently art created with a computer has looked unmistakably like "computer art." But as the technology has progressed and hardware and software have improved, the technology is getting out of the way.

Ironically, as the software provides more and more features, it's easy to be misled by the facile screen display into creating illustrations that are too complex to print at higher resolutions. At this point the diver piece exists as a data file, as a 72 dpi screen display and as a low-resolution Paintjet image. None of these is of sufficient quality for use as an end product. My experience with the diver has taught me not to be quite so ambitious until the output capabilities catch up with the screen interface.

David Brickley

"When I was 11 years old someone gave me a "Visible V-8" model. The idea was to learn the inner workings of a V-8 engine by putting the model's hundreds of small parts together. Through working on this model, I learned not to be intimidated by a big, long-term project. The persistence, patience and attention to detail I learned then have served me well in the creation of computer art."

This Cobra sports car was drawn with GEM Artline. The contour of the car was traced from a scanned image.

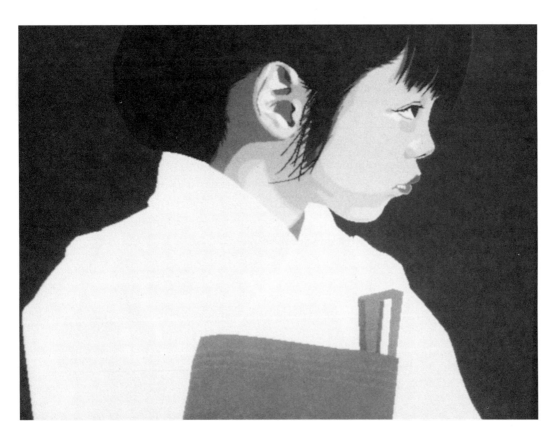

The Geisha girl was made with Lotus Freelance as an illustration for *PC World.* Freelance allows use of only 12 colors at a time. To edit colors you must exit the program and use a separate utility.

This drawing of a balloon was created using Corel Draw. It contains over 100 objects, all colored with gradient fills. The effect of direct sunlight on a round surface was achieved by pushing the range of colors; for example, by going from almost white to almost orange within the yellow band.

CHAPTER 11

Invitation to a Dance

Artist

Geoff Schwartz grew up in Southern California and received a B.A. in art with an emphasis in graphic design from San Diego State University. After graduation he worked as an intern and then as a designer with Calvin Woo Associates (CWA, Inc.), a marketing communications and design firm in San Diego. He began using a Macintosh in 1988 and was instrumental in CWA's transition from traditional to electronic media.

Project

The project was to design and illustrate an invitation, reply card, and envelopes for an annual dinner sponsored by the San Diego Trial Lawyers Association to benefit the St. Vincent de Paul/Joan Kroc Center for the Homeless. The dinner featured a performance by a group of Samba dancers, so the client wanted illustrations keyed to a theme of festive, South American music. The Association had received donated design work in the past, but this year had a small budget to hire a designer. Because the printing budget was also small, the design was created to fit the limitations of working with only two colors, paper plates and inexpensive paper.

Preliminary drawings were made with pencil and marker pens. Thunderscan was used to scan drawings for use as templates. The final illustrations and some type elements were created in Illustrator 88 on a Macintosh Plus and the final layout was done in PageMaker 3.0. A LaserWriter Plus was used for proofs and final output was high-resolution paper through a Linotronic L-300. The lino output was altered by hand with white and black ink and was mounted and marked for spot color with a tissue overlay.

Design process

The Trial Lawyers Association representative, Sharon Blanchet, was an interesting, dynamic person with a wonderful sense of color and design. She wanted the invitation for their annual benefit dinner to include lively images of South American dance. She specifically wanted to incorporate stars and moons to convey a sense of festive, nighttime entertainment. But beyond that, she left the design up to me, saying "Go have fun." I spent some time at the library researching images of Rio and of Brazilian Samba dancing. I then made a series of pencil sketches to work out the image of a dancer, stars and moons, and other decorative elements. My final drawings were scanned and used as templates for tracing in Illustrator. I made several preliminary drawings on the computer and tried a few different page layouts. These were presented to Sharon and finally we settled on a design. The final Linotronic output looked somewhat stiff, so I painted on it by hand to produce the look of a woodcut.

To begin the design process, many pencil sketches were made of dancers, revelers, stars and other decorative elements.

The outside of the invitation features a drum image and a border placed over a sky shape filled with a 256-step blend. The sky wraps around to the back of the invitation when the card is folded.

Design:

Geoff Schwartz

CWA Inc., / HumanGraphic

The San Diego

Trial Lawyers Association

Presents

The Fifth Annual

Red Boudreau

Memorial Dinner,

"Cinco de Boudreau"

An outer envelope and smaller reply envelope incorporated the stars and moon motif and staggered type that was developed for the invitation. The reply card also featured the stars and moon. These pieces were assembled in PageMaker, using the graphic elements created in Illustrator.

Non Profit Organization
U.S. Postage
PAID
Permit No. 1563
San Diego, California

Red Boudreau Memorial Dinner

San Diego Trial Lawyers Association

2247 San Diego Avenue, Suite 136

San Diego, California 92110

"Cinco de Boudreau"

Red Boudreau Memorial Dinner

Please reserve

_____ seats at $125.00 $ _____

_____ tables at $1,250.00 (table of 10) $ _____

I cannot attend but enclosed

is a donation of $ _____ for the homeless.

Name _____

Phone _____

Address _____

City _____ Zip _____

Firm _____

Make checks payable and return to: Please seat me with:

"Red Boudreau Memorial Dinner"   _____

2247 San Diego Avenue, Suite 136   _____

San Diego, California 92110   _____

(619) 299-7757   _____

RSVP by August 28, 1989

The final Linotronic paper output of the invitation's inside spread was hand-painted with ink and correction fluid, to produce the flecked and chipped look of a woodcut print.

B enefitting
St. Vincent de Paul / Joan Kroc
Center for the Homeless

September 9, 1989
U.S. Grant Hotel

6:00 p.m.   *Cocktails*
7:30 p.m.   *Dinner*
7:30 p.m.   *Memorial Tribute in honor of*
             Reeves Jacques (1941-1987)
8:30 p.m.   *Comedy of the Three Amigos*
             L.A. Samba Floor Show
9:00 p.m.   *Mar Dels*

Fabulous raffle prizes including a
glass sculpture by Christopher Lee.

Black tie optional or
South of the border attire.

Tickets: $125.00 per person,
$1,250 per table, (table of ten).

Chairmen: Sharon Blanchet, Steven Boudreau,
Thomas Sharkey, Honorable Robert C. Coates

I try not to jump on the computer immediately when working out a design. For this job I wanted to first develop a feeling of the atmosphere and wild dancing in Rio at Carnival time. My colleagues at Calvin Woo Associates emphasize the importance of research. Working with them has taught me to explore as many ideas as possible before settling on one that feels worthwhile. So I made many preliminary sketches in pencil to work out images for a dancing figure and other decorative elements (Figure 1).

Creating the drum element

A drum image was chosen for the cover of the card, to convey a sense of excitement and invitation to the dance. The drum image was drawn with white lines and shapes on a black rectangle. Because I was working with a black-and-white monitor, I didn't attempt to differentiate between colors at first. Decisions about color were made later as all the design elements were assembled in PageMaker. The design appeared on screen as areas of solid white and black. I purposely kept the solid color areas separated from each other with white lines and borders, knowing that the registration tolerance of a quick printer using paper plates would be low (Figure 2).

The vertical triangle borders around the drum were created by drawing one triangle with the pen tool, duplicating it, and positioning the copies in a vertical row. This was done by eye at high magnification, using a non-printing vertical line as a guide (Figure 3). ▌ *Illustrator does not include guidelines for the alignment of elements. However, a line can be drawn and specified with a stroke of None to serve as a guide. It will be visible in keyline mode and elements can be positioned against it. But the line will not appear in preview mode or when the illustration is printed.*

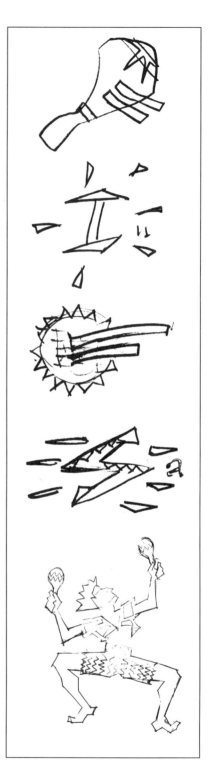

Figure 2. Anticipating registration problems. Different color areas in the drum image were not butted together, but were separated by white lines and shapes to reduce the likelihood of misregistration problems.

Figure 1. Making preliminary drawings. After research into images of Rio and Samba dancing at the library, several pencil sketches were made of figures and decorative elements. One sketch of a dancing figure was scanned and used as a template in Illustrator.

Figure 3. Stacking a row of triangles. To create the first side of a border for the drum image, a single triangle was drawn with the pen tool, filled with black, and then copied eight times. The copies were stacked on top of one another, with a non-printing line as a guide.

Figure 4. Copying and reflecting. The first row of triangles was copied and the copy was reflected across the vertical axis with the reflect tool.

Figure 5. Finishing the border. The top and bottom sides of the border were created in the same way as the left and right sides, with a triangle from the vertical sides that was copied and rotated 90 degrees. A slightly larger triangle was drawn, copied and rotated three times. The four triangles were positioned as caps at the four corners of the border.

Figure 6. Creating a preliminary figure. The first dancing figure created in Illustrator featured shapes filled with both black and white and many decorative elements. The figure was positioned over a graduated background.

The vertical stack of triangles was copied and flipped across the vertical axis to create the opposite side (Figure 4). To make the top and bottom sides, a triangle copy was rotated 90 degrees using the rotate tool, then copied and positioned horizontally in the same way as for the vertical sides. I let the length of the triangles determine the dimensions of the design, adjusting the image in the center to fit. A larger triangle was drawn to serve as a cap for the four corners of the border. It was copied and rotated three times to align with the orientation of each corner (Figure 5).

Drawing a dancing figure

Sharon and I decided to use the image of a Samba dancer for the inside of the card. I made several pencil drawings of dancers before settling on a design I liked. I created a marker pen sketch and then a final pencil sketch, which was scanned with ThunderScan and used as a template in Illustrator. Because I was trained in traditional art methods, my tendency is to be very representational and to create modeling in my figure drawings. But once my drawing template was in the computer, I found I could not easily render the modeling using solid color shapes and lines. The computer forced me to make the drawing more abstract and this was an advantage for this project, as I wanted the design to be simple and gutsy.

My first figure drawing in Illustrator featured a fairly realistic rendering of the arms and legs and many decorative elements on the clothing (Figure 6). After conferring with the client, we decided to try an even more abstract rendering. I broke the figure up into segments and drew them using only straight lines. Other ornamentation was eliminated. This produced a stronger, less cluttered design with a lively, dancing feeling (Figure 7).

Figure 7. Drawing the final figure. The final dancing figure was composed entirely of black-filled angular shapes. The finished design is stronger, less cluttered and more abstract than the preliminary figure.

Making a type design

The benefit dinner was titled a "Cinco de Boudreau" celebration so these words were to be set as a title beneath the dancer. I decided to create each letter as a reversed character within a black rectangle. I used Futura Book to set the first letter, a C, and used the scale tool to make it taller and narrower (Figure 8). ▌ *To scale a text or graphic element, select the object, click on the scale tool, and position its dotted cross icon at a point from which the object should be scaled. The dotted cross will change to an arrowhead icon. As you hold down the mouse and drag the arrowhead away from or toward the origin point, the object is scaled accordingly. Objects can be scaled nonuniformly (with the horizontal and vertical dimensions varying independently) or proportionately. Holding down the Shift key while dragging the arrowhead constrains the changes to a proportional scale. Objects can also be scaled by typing numbers into the Scale dialog box that appears when you hold down the Option key and click with the scale tool icon.*

The C was specified as a 20-point character with a white stroke. It was aligned to the center, which helped with positioning it within a black rectangle. I selected the C and the rectangle and duplicated them to produce the other 15 type elements. I then edited the type by selecting the C within each box and typing the appropriate new letter in the Type dialog box that appeared when I chose Type from the Style menu (Figure 9). Each new letter retained the distortion that had been originally applied to the C. Each letter was then individually positioned within its black rectangle.

I positioned the type elements in two staggered lines to fit below the figure of the dancer (Figure 10). But Sharon felt this design was hard to read, so I repositioned the letters on a simpler curve (Figure 11). To make reading easier, the top and bottom lines were specified to be printed in different colors.

Figure 8. Distorting the type. A C set in Futura Book was made taller and thinner by dragging it with the scale tool.

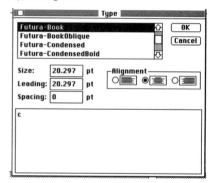

Figure 9. Editing the type elements. The C within each type element duplicate was selected and edited through the Type dialog box.

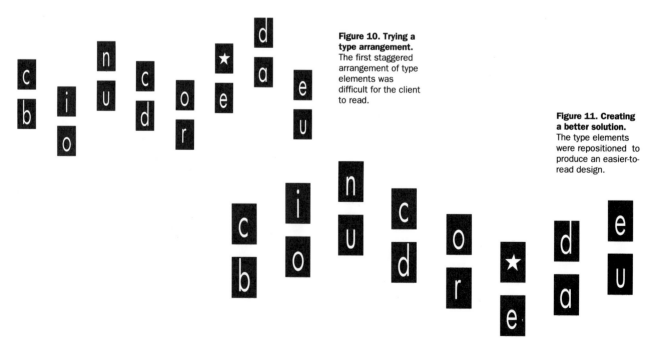

Figure 10. Trying a type arrangement. The first staggered arrangement of type elements was difficult for the client to read.

Figure 11. Creating a better solution. The type elements were repositioned to produce an easier-to-read design.

Creating a background

To provide a background for the drum image and the dancing figure, I created a "sky" made of a colored shape with a horizontal top and a jagged bottom, suggesting a mountain horizon. White stars and a white quarter moon were placed in front of the sky. On the inside of the card the sky is filled with a solid color. On the front cover it's filled with a blend that graduates from black to white. The gradation was created in Illustrator by drawing a 5-point black line and blending it to a 5-point white line in 256 steps (Figure 12) (see "Producing smooth gradations" on page 67). However, the final Linotronic output showed a slight amount of visible banding, which was compounded when the piece was printed with a too watery ink, resulting in some streaks (see page 124).

Masking the sky shape

The rectangle containing the blend was masked by drawing a negative shape to fit the positive sky shape I wanted to leave visible. The masking shape was filled with white and placed on top of the blend (Figure 13).

Figure 12. Creating a blend. To produce the effect of a very smoothly graduated fill, a 5-point black line was blended to a 5-point white line in 256 steps.

Figure 13. Masking the blend. A "negative" shape was drawn (left), given a white fill and no stroke, and positioned over the blend element. This created a sky-over-mountains shape (right).

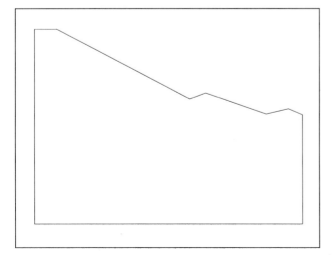

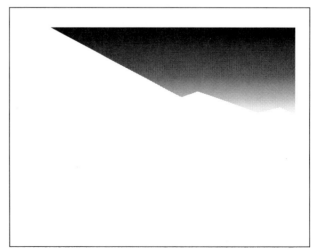

Drawing stars and moon

The stars were drawn roughly, to give them an irregular look. I drew the stars in the same way I used to as a child, making straight lines from point to point (Figure 14). When the final point was placed on top of the first one, a closed path was created and Illustrator filled the entire shape with the white fill I specified, ignoring the overlapping of the lines (Figure 15). I could have drawn the stars from angle to angle but the child's way was easier and more fun.

I drew the quarter moon with angular curve segments, to fit with the woodcut look that was beginning to evolve for the whole piece. The sky shapes and the positioning of the stars and moon are slightly different for the front and inside of the card (Figure 16). These elements were used again, along with the Cinco de Boudreau type on the return envelope, the outer envelope and the reply card (see page 125).

Page layout

The final card layout was done in PageMaker by importing the graphic elements from Illustrator and positioning them with type created in Page-Maker. My original design called for a gatefold on the card because I really like the idea of unwrapping something to see the inside (Figure 17). But the client and I decided to use a single fold instead, to save money on the folding costs.

The type for the cover was created in Illustrator using Garamond bold italic, in 9 points on 18-point leading. A 16-point reversed initial cap was placed in a black rectangle (Figure 18). PageMaker was used to create the type for the inside of the card, which includes a solid initial cap set in a white rectangle. I was not happy with the short, squat Garamond capital B and at the last moment, while waiting for the printer to pick up the boards, I went

Figure 14. Drawing the stars. To achieve an irregular look, the stars were drawn quickly and roughly from point to point with the pen tool.

Figure 15. Filling the stars. Because the star shapes were drawn with a line having a stroke of None, the lines that crisscrossed the interior of the star don't print. The stars were filled with white and placed over a dark background.

Figure 16. Creating two sky shapes. Two slightly different sky shapes were created for the invitation. The shape for the outside (above) features a blended background. The one for the inside (below) is filled with solid color. The same moon and star elements were used on both, but were scaled and positioned differently.

back to Illustrator and used the scale tool to stretch a B. There wasn't time to incorporate this into the PageMaker layout, so I printed the letter on the LaserWriter at 200 percent, then ran downstairs to our stat camera, shot it down to size, and pasted this small element on the final layout. In general I felt limited by the small number of fonts. Though we had 50 fonts in our system, I would have liked more choice.

Planning for the printer's limitations

When I first positioned the drum element over the bottom of the sky shape in PageMaker, I realized I might be creating a difficult registration problem for the printer. I had intended to print the triangle border in a different color than the sky and butting these two colors next to each other might exceed the registration tolerance of paper plates and a quick printing environment (Figure 19). So I went back to my Illustrator file of the drum element and drew a zigzag shape along the edges of the upper half of the triangle border and filled it with white. This created a white line border to separate the solid color triangles from the gradation in the sky (Figure 20). As it turned out, both border and sky were ultimately printed in the same color, but I retained the white border as it gave a crisp look to the graphic.

Figure 17. Trying a gatefold. The first invitation layout featured a gatefold opening. But the client's limited budget ruled out using more than one fold. This LaserWriter proof was one of several trial layouts created in PageMaker.

Figure 18. Setting type in Illustrator. Type for the invitation cover was created in Illustrator, using Adobe's Garamond bold italic. A large initial cap was reversed and placed in a black box. Other type for the invitation was set in PageMaker, where the final layout was created.

Hand work on the computer output

Sharon and I agreed that the final proof of the card's inside spread looked too stiff and static. To enliven it I decided to create the look of a woodcut by painting on the final Linotronic output with white correction fluid and black ink. I was a bit intimidated by the thought of fiddling with that perfect-looking lino output, but I think my hand work gave the illustration the spark it needed (Figure 21). I could have tried to add these details in Illustrator, but I thought it would have been too tedious. I would have liked to make a real woodcut of the design, but the client's limited budget didn't allow me the time to do this. As it was, I spent 35 hours on the design, far exceeding the budgeted time. The extra work was done after hours, because I was committed to seeing my design through to the best possible final execution.

Preparing art boards and spot color instructions

The final layouts for the folded card, reply card and envelopes were printed as composites through a Linotronic L-300. The paper output, altered with my hand work, was pasted up on traditional art boards and a tissue overlay was made to indicate colors. Pantone color swatches were affixed to show which colors were to be used. I could have created a spot color separation through PageMaker, but I was accustomed to preparing boards and tissue overlays and it seemed easier to do it this way. I had presented Sharon with some color

Figure 19. Butting colors together. Placing the drum element over the sky shape could have created registration problems if the two elements were printed in different colors.

Figure 20. Separating color areas. To reduce the likelihood of misregistration, the drum element was altered to include a zigzag white border around the upper half. This separated the color areas of the border and the sky.

possibilities, and together we chose a purple for the sky areas and a deep red for accents and some type elements. The colors were a bit brighter than I would typically choose, but the final printed piece looked very festive and attractive. I was glad to be working with a client who had a good color sense and strong ideas about what she wanted.

In retrospect

If I can swing from the ceiling, or close my eyes, or do anything else to jolt myself out of my design norms, I'll try it. We're very chained to our habits, and my habit from art school is to use modeling and try to make things look real. So when I'm called upon to make a drawing that's more abstract than my usual style, I use the peculiarities of PostScript illustration to force myself into a different way of drawing. This approach worked well to create a strong graphic style for the Samba dancer.

But it's important to realize that the computer can't do everything. Sometimes it can be a very powerful tool, but for some types of illustration the computer is limiting. It's good to break away from electronic media sometimes. If a certain style can't be done well in Illustrator or FreeHand, then I don't try to do it that way. Sometimes it's appropriate to take the computer output and play with it, even alter it by hand if necessary.

Figure 21. Altering the computer output. The final output of the invitation's inside spread was altered by using black ink and white correction fluid to paint in the small flecks and chips characteristic of a woodcut print.

Geoff Schwartz

"The Macintosh is a very exciting and powerful tool, yet it has a limited place in the creative process. Sometimes I'm so entranced by the machine that I glue my face to its screen for hours and days at a time. To refresh the creative spark that makes me want to draw and paint in the first place, I'm going to take my surfboard to Indonesia for a while and watch the locals make art with nothing but their hands. I hope I won't spend too much time wondering what the coming upgrades of PageMaker and Illustrator will be able to do. Selamat Tinggal!"

"Leaping Leroy" is a character created for a fantasy book as a self-promotion. I used Thunderscan to scan a 19th-century etching of a male figure. The scan was used as a template in Illustrator 88 and the elephant's head and tail were added. It took quite a long time to create this illustration with the Macintosh, but once I had it on disk the applications were endless.

Illustrator 88 was used to create the graphic elements for this display panel for a health food wafer. Calvin Woo was art director for the project. PageMaker 3.02 was used to lay out the complete panel with text. The biggest challenge of the illustration was to show only the torso of a human body without having it look as if the limbs had been cut off. I used curving shapes to define the lines of the body and tapered these to points at the ends.

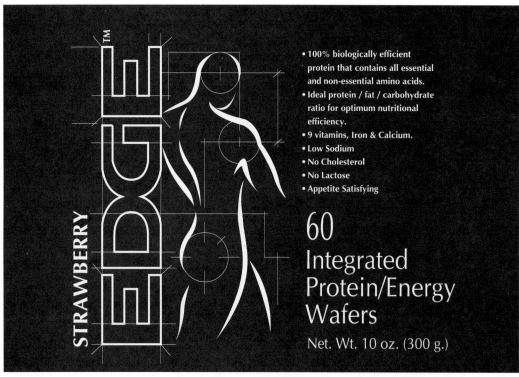

STRAWBERRY EDGE™

• 100% biologically efficient protein that contains all essential and non-essential amino acids.
• Ideal protein / fat / carbohydrate ratio for optimum nutritional efficiency.
• 9 vitamins, Iron & Calcium.
• Low Sodium
• No Cholesterol
• No Lactose
• Appetite Satisfying

60 Integrated Protein/Energy Wafers

Net. Wt. 10 oz. (300 g.)

A business card for
John Bradshaw
incorporates 5 of the
28 symbols designed
for use in his
business. The
graphic elements
created in Illustrator
88 were composed
in PageMaker.

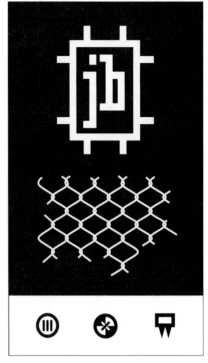

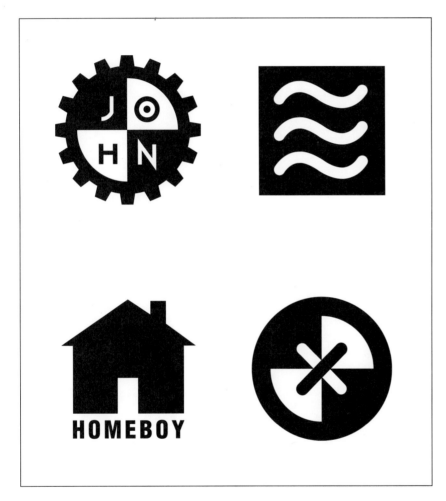

For some people one
logo isn't enough!
These are 4 of 28
symbols created in
Illustrator 88 for
artist John Bradshaw.
The symbols will be
used to make metal
stamps, stickers and
custom-color
rubdowns for a variety
of projects.

This logo for the
Graphic Design
Group at San Diego
State University was
originally designed
and inked by hand. I
used Thunderscan to
scan the original
logo, and then
rendered it in
Illustrator 88, using
the blend tool to add
graduated grays to
the ends of the
letters.

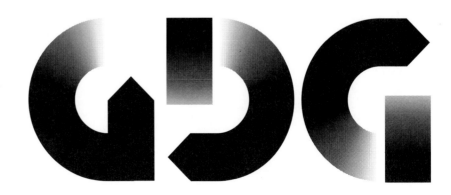

CHAPTER 12

Clean and Simple Spot Illustrations

Artist

Don Baker grew up in rural Idaho. He decided to become an illustrator during the second grade. After he created a dazzling bunch of orange carrots with a bold black outline, Don's mother told him he could become a *commercial artist*. Those were the biggest words Don had heard and he accepted them as his destiny. Don completed a three-year course in advertising art in 1978 and has freelanced as an illustrator in Seattle for the past six years. He shares studio space on the waterfront with his wife, Kolea, an artists' representative. The Bakers bought their first Macintosh computer on October 19, 1987, the day the stock market crashed. Today Don spends roughly half his time illustrating with the computer. He also enjoys making experimental music, and he produces a limited-edition computer art/art/literary art rag called *Eulipian*. It was recently accepted into the periodicals collection of the Museum of Modern Art in New York.

Project

The assignment was to create a series of small, black-and-white illustrations for a travel magazine. The art director suggested topics to depict — an airplane in the clouds, an African scene, the coastline and so forth.

The illustrations were made using FreeHand 2.0 with a Macintosh II. Proofs were made on a LaserWriter II and final output was generated on a Linotronic L-300 imagesetter. The illustrations range in size from 7K to 16K.

PROJECT OVERVIEW

Design process

I always begin an illustration assignment by developing the idea and doing a tight pencil sketch of my proposed solution. Regardless of how I plan to finish the piece, I work out the details at my drawing table until I'm pleased with it. Then it's sent to the client for approval.

For this assignment, I was hired by John Askwith, art director for *Outside* magazine, to create a series of travel images to be used in the "Active Traveler" section of their magazine, as a part of the magazine's redesign. Because the illustrations would be reproduced at a very small size (½ X 1-inch) it was critical to describe the subjects with a single, dominant element and a minimum of detail. I chose to design them with askew, random borders to enhance the feeling of movement and adventure.

The opening page of *Outside's* "Active Traveler" section shows one of the spot illustrations in place.

Highlights on the engines are shapes filled with a graduated fill that radiates along a line exactly perpendicular to the straight edge of the shape.

The cloud shapes are divided into two parts so that one half can be filled with a flat fill and the other half with a graduated fill.

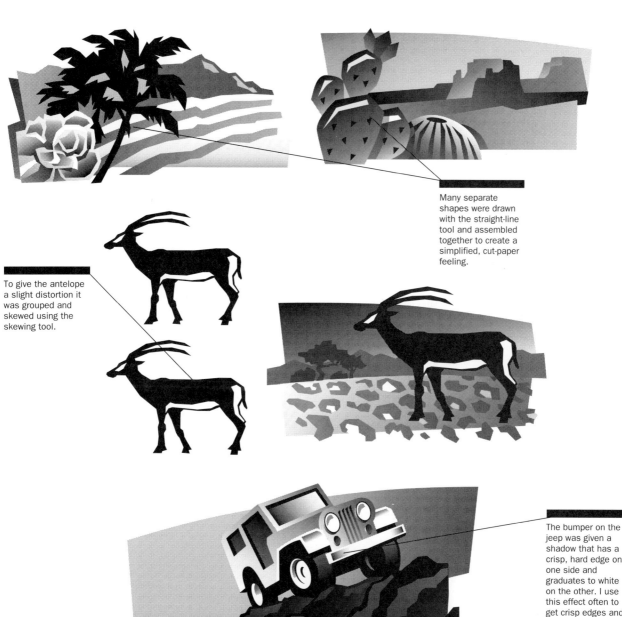

Many separate shapes were drawn with the straight-line tool and assembled together to create a simplified, cut-paper feeling.

To give the antelope a slight distortion it was grouped and skewed using the skewing tool.

The bumper on the jeep was given a shadow that has a crisp, hard edge on one side and graduates to white on the other. I use this effect often to get crisp edges and soft shadows.

The wavy line was first drawn using the Snap To Grid option for perfect placement of points. I used the rulers to measure the width and depth of the curve I wanted. I then duplicated the line, positioned it below the first line and drew end lines to connect them. I joined the end lines and curves to form a closed path using the Join Elements feature. I checked the finished shape by selecting it and calling up the Element Info dialog box to make sure the Closed box was checked. Then I duplicated the shape once, positioned the new wavy shape under the first, and then repeated the duplicate function two more times. I selected all four shapes and rotated them to the preferred angle using the rotation tool and then dragged them into position in the picture.

After the client gave me the green light on my pencil sketches, I sent them to a service bureau to be scanned. For use in FreeHand I have my sketches scanned as line art and saved in a TIFF format; then I place each scan in a new document, assign it to layer 0 and make it inactive. This grays the scanned image back and allows me to use it as a template to draw over (Figure 1). Eventually, when the drawing is completed, I delete the scan.

Working in layers

I began my work by drawing shapes and lines over the template and assigning each group of similar elements to a different layer. I generally allow extra layers between elements so I can add highlights or shadows in between later. I find that the layering approach helps to keep the image organized in my mind (see "Layering" on page 141).

After I've finished drawing all the parts of an illustration, I create the colors or gray values to use as fills (see "Working in color" on page 142). I find the most efficient way to do this is to assign a fill or line to every piece in the artwork, even if I'm not sure what I want at first. I do this preliminary work in FreeHand's keyline mode, and then switch to Preview mode and correct gray values to get what I want. In FreeHand, if you don't assign a fill or line to a shape, you can't see it or select it in Preview mode. So, to avoid bouncing back and forth in and out of Preview mode, I find it easier to give everything a fill at the outset.

Figure 1. Making a template. The original sketch was scanned as a TIFF and placed in FreeHand's background layer to serve as a template. PICT and TIFF formats work equally well as templates, but sometimes the PICT files take up more memory.

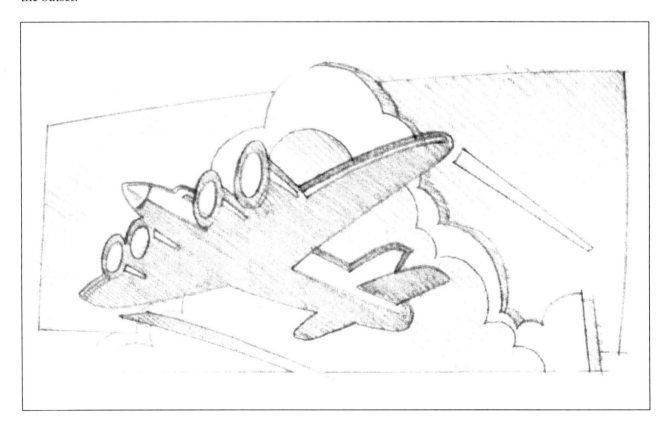

■ Layering

FreeHand provides 200 printing layers and one nonprinting layer to aid in organizing an illustration. Elements drawn or placed in layer 0 do not print. Templates and guides can be stored here. Layers 1 through 200 are stacked on top of layer 0, with the elements in the higher-numbered layers obscuring elements on the layers below. Elements can be drawn in any layer and sent to any layer, using the Send to Layer command. Within a single layer elements can be stacked using the commands Send To Front, Send To Back and Bring Forward and Send Backward. The Layer Control dialog box can be used to make different layers visible or invisible, active or inactive. Inactive layers can be seen but not selected or edited. It's handy to render lower, background layers inactive while drawing foreground elements. This prevents accidentally selecting previously drawn elements while drawing new ones.

Creating the airplane

I began the airplane illustration by drawing the oval for the largest engine prop, using the oval tool. I rotated it into place using the rotation tool, cloned it and used the scale tool to make the clone smaller. I gave the outside oval a fill of black and no line weight and the inside oval a white fill and no line weight. I assigned the white oval to a higher layer, so it would always appear in front of the black oval. I selected both ovals, grouped them and then duplicated and sized them down to create the next prop. I repeated this process until all four props were done (Figure 2).

Next I drew the wings and body of the plane, going back to carefully edit the curves. I drew the highlights on the wings and the white areas of the body and nose. Last, I added the window and the highlights on the engines (Figure 3).

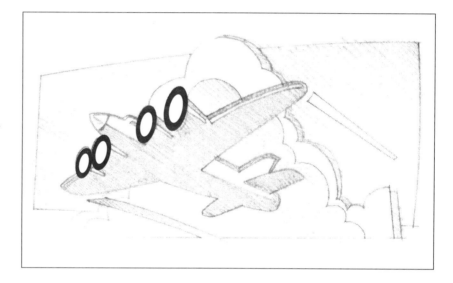

Figure 2. Drawing propellers. One propeller was drawn and filled. Then it was copied and resized to create the others.

Figure 3. Outlining the plane. Once the propellors were drawn and in place over the template, the outlines and highlight shapes that define the rest of the airplane were carefully drawn.

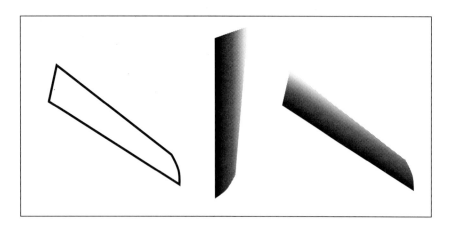

Figure 4. Aligning fills. Highlights were drawn in place, rotated to a vertical axis, filled with a horizontal radial fill and then rotated back to position. The orientation of the fill remains fixed within the shape and rotates with it.

Fitting fills to shapes

To create the graduated fills in the highlights on the engines, I first drew each highlight in place, and then rotated it so that the line that began the fill from black to white was perfectly vertical. I then gave each shape a logarithmic fill from 100 percent black to white at 0 degrees (exactly horizontal), and finally rotated the shape back into position. This ensured that my fill met the background color (in this case black) exactly along the straight edge of the shape (Figure 4). I could have applied a fill to each highlight shape while it was in place, but this would have required specifying a unique fill angle for each highlight.

Working in color

For color illustrations I draw the basic image first and then create a color palette and assign fills to my shapes. I send out for a QMS color test, edit where necessary and get a second color proof if the changes are very substantial. Whenever possible I like to meet with the client in my studio to preview the color art on-screen before I send out for final film. I always recommend that a high-quality color proof like a Cromalin or Matchprint be made from the process negatives before the piece goes to press.

For four-color pieces I generally create the colors using a Pantone Process Color Guide. I find it helpful because I can always go back and check the printed color I've created by looking it up in in the PMS book. My color monitor doesn't create every color well. Some very dark colors, for example, show much lighter than their printed versions and so are misleading. I can always quickly edit a color by looking it up to make sure I'll get the color I want, even if it isn't accurate on the screen.

Pantone uses a four-digit number to describe its colors. The first digit represents yellow, and 1 equals 10 percent, 2 equals 20 percent, and so on all the way up to X, which equals 100 percent. The second digit represents magenta, the third cyan and the fourth black. When I create a color in FreeHand, I name it with the color name, for instance orange, and also give it the formula for how it was created. Therefore, an orange X300 would have 100 percent yellow and 30 percent magenta. A turquoise 3061 would have 30 percent yellow, no magenta, 60 percent cyan and 10 percent black.

For complex color pieces, I include location information in the color names. For instance, if I have a background with a pattern in it, I create and name the color something like BK (for background) blue 0280, to show at a glance that it's a background color. That way, I don't use it anywhere else by accident.

If I need to edit a color, I simply select it, go to Edit Color under the Color menu, and change it to whatever I choose. All areas that have that color immediately show the new edited color. Otherwise, I would have to select each and every shape filled with that color and give them new fills. That can be *very* tedious when you have lots and lots of tiny pattern shapes to edit.

After drawing the streaks coming from the wings, I drew the clouds, using the corner tool for all end points and straight lines, and the curve tool for curves. I've found it very convenient and fast to use the two keyboard shortcuts — keys 8 and 9 — to switch between curve and corner tools. This allows me to quickly place all the right points in the right places. Then I can go back and make any edits I feel necessary. I drew the two main clouds, and then duplicated the largest one and offset it to create the shadow, which was assigned to a lower layer and given a separate fill. With the knife tool I cut away the part of the shadow that was hidden behind the main clouds, and redrew it to follow the contours of the edge of the foreground cloud (Figure 5). ▮ *Trimming shadows and other "underneath" elements is a good habit to develop. It can cut printing time dramatically if the trimmed object includes a graduated fill or a PostScript pattern.*

The smaller cloud in the foreground was cut with the knife tool into two shapes, so that I could give the right half a flat fill and give the left half a graduated fill (Figure 6). The white cloud in the background was treated in a similar way. It was cut near the right side to allow the very far right to graduate to a light gray.

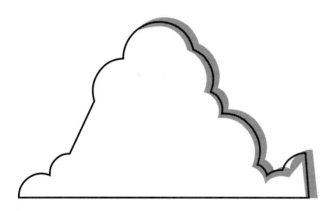

Figure 5. Creating shadows. The shadow behind the white cloud was created by copying the cloud, filling it with gray, and then cutting away the portion that falls beneath the cloud. Trimming the shadow close to the edge eliminated a large portion of gray fill that would not be seen. Because a monotone gray screen was used in this case, trimming did not reduce printing time. But it's a technique that's become a habit.

Figure 6. Using two fills for one object. The gray cloud was cloned from the white cloud, and then divided into two pieces. A straight line was added to each piece, in order to create two separate closed paths that could be filled.

To create the background I drew a rectangular shape, assigned it to a lower layer, cut it and redrew it in two pieces behind the clouds. I did this in order to control the visual blend of the graduated fill. The left shape contains a fill that graduates from 20 to 60 percent, and the right shape graduates from 60 to 100 percent (Figure 7). If I had retained the background as a single shape containing a fill that graduated from 20 to 100 percent, the gray values would have changed too rapidly in the area behind the cloud.

Careful proofing

When my drawing on-screen was complete, I proofed it on the LaserWriter II, checking the gray values and looking for anything that was missing or didn't line up exactly. Finally, I sent the illustration document to a service bureau for a black-and-white paper test at the resolution and dpi specified for the final output. Everything looked fine, so this was my final test. I then ordered final film, according to the client's specifications. ▮ *For black-and-white illustrations, I order a repro positive along with the film, so that the client will have a high-quality proof for reference and to show to the printer.*

In retrospect

Looking back, these travel illustrations seem very simple and straightforward. Yet I learned many new techniques that I've employed in projects since then:

• Reducing unnecessary fill area for complex fills such as gradations, speeds up the screen redraw and printing processes.

• Drawing with fewer points (see "Reducing the number of points" on page 145) cuts down on imaging time.

Figure 7. Interrupting a graduated fill. The background shape was also cut in two and redrawn into two separate shapes so that each could contain its own fill. Applying a fill to a single background shape would have resulted in too rapid a change in gray values in the area that's obscured by the cloud.

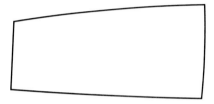

▮ **The limits of computer output**

I do print tests often in order to learn the limitations of the imagesetter. How is printing affected by the size of the output paper or film? How complex can my illustration be? When will visible banding occur? I find that PostScript illustration software allows you to create images that are difficult, sometimes impossible, for an imagesetter to output. And considering that the level of expertise varies from service bureau to service bureau, it's important to test new procedures before implementing them in work for clients.

Providing trap is an ongoing concern. I've had very good results from four-color process printing so far, without providing trap. I think that sending film without providing for trapping is asking a lot of a printer, however, and does not allow for paper stretch or other things that might affect registration. FreeHand doesn't automatically provide trapping for objects that are butted against each other. I can create a trap myself in certain areas of an illustration, but not in others. For instance, it's not possible to provide a trap for a graduated fill. The amount of trap required varies too, depending on the specific piece of art, the colors involved and so forth. I feel that providing trap is a technical manipulation that is best done by the printer and not left to the artist. Trapping is the printer's responsibility when the artist provides camera-ready art. But when the artist provides the printer with color-separated negatives generated by a PostScript illustration program, technical responsibilities are shifted. At this point, I work without trap and leave it to the printer to let me know if there's a problem and how much trap I should add to solve it.

Reducing the number of points

The *Outside* magazine spots were small and simple, but for more complicated pieces I try to draw shapes using fewer points to achieve the same effect. Instead of using curve points, I draw all the corner points of an image first, and then pull out the handles while holding the Option key down. That allows me to create many of the curves I need without adding curve points. I can save sometimes close to half the total number of points by doing this, thus conserving memory and minimizing outputting time.

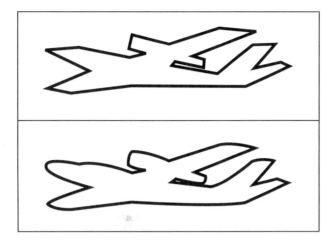

• While "layering" is useful for constructing drawings, it also has disadvantages. Using many layers can increase imaging time. The use of layers also requires careful checking of illustrations in Preview mode when making last-minute corrections, because when elements from different layers are joined to each other or grouped together, the new composite element is automatically assigned to layer 100. This can cause some elements to be unintentionally obscured. It's a good idea to combine more elements on a single layer before making final corrections and printing, and to use fewer layers in general.

• Like graduated fills and PostScript patterns, blends are complex elements that can slow the screen redraw process. For quicker redraw, create blends, adjust the colors and shapes, and then delete the blend and retain only the starting and ending objects. When the illustration is finished, go back and recreate the blends.

• Laser proofs can often be deceptive in black-and-white contrast. Illustrations that had plenty of punch in a laser proof often looked washed out at the finer resolution of a Linotronic print. It's possible to compensate for this in FreeHand by changing the setting of the Transfer Function in the Print Options dialog box that appears when you click Change in the Print dialog box. The default setting assumes that proofs and final output will be sent to the same printer. Choosing Normalize causes the program to compensate for the value density differences between the laser printer and the imagesetter.

It's often time-consuming to make illustrations fit the limitations of the software and output devices. But once I learn a new technique, I simply bite the bullet and incorporate it into my working style until it becomes routine. I insist that my computer-generated work look as good as work I could generate by hand, so I try hard to make sure my PostScript illustrations make the best use of the technology.

Don Baker

*"I feel confident that I can produce good
art on the computer because I've spent
years developing the fundamental skills of
design and production through doing mechanically separated art, silhouette images
and flat graphics in general. I think it's
important to employ the software in a way
that best uses its strongest features. I
consider it a compliment when someone
mistakes one of my computer-generated
pieces for airbrush, mechanical art or
something else.*

*I think microcomputer artwork will truly
become a part of mainstream graphic art
when it can match the current industry
standards of high-end prepress color
systems like Scitex. This is beginning to
happen with Visionary, Handshake and
other "linking" software. With a Scitex, a
piece of PostScript art can be choked and
spread and color-corrected, and it can be
output to a printer's specifications
concerning emulsion, line screen or the requirements of a specific press. I'm very
eager to see this interface develop further.*

*I find it exciting that artwork, typesetting,
graphics and page layout can all be
created in a common language, so that the
barriers and mysteries held by each
disappear."*

This color illustration
was used with an
article in *Personal
Computing* magazine.
To create the pattern
to the left of the
computer I used
FreeHand's autotrace
tool to trace a
scanned sketch.

This art for the A-P
Business Service
Printers calendar for
1990 illustrates a
belief by the Mayan
Indians of Mexico
that the world rests
on the backs of two
giant alligators
floating in a great
pond. Four PMS
colors were used in
the image.

The legs of the table above symbolize the four areas served by Aldus products: publishing, digital photography, presentations and illustration. The piece uses primarily flat fills, except for some graduated fills on the table top. The background elements were drawn with the straight line tool. This color illustration was used as a cover for *Aldus* magazine.

These color spot illustrations are similar in style and technique to the *Outside* magazine spots featured in this chapter. The agency especially liked the askew borders and playfulness of the images. The illustrations were used in a vacation planner brochure for Doug Fox Travel.

I wanted a woodcut look, so I used flat fills and hard, straight edges for most elements. This color illustration was used with an article in *Personal Computing* magazine.

CHAPTER 13

Exotic and Mountainous Maps

Artist

Jill Malena received a B.A. in Graphic Design from California State University, Chico in 1987. During her last year of school she began using a Macintosh computer for page design and illustration. After graduation she worked for a year doing typesetting and design on a Macintosh Plus for a small print shop in Sacramento. She now works as a freelance designer and production assistant for John Odam Design Associates in Del Mar, California.

Project

The project was to create a series of color tour maps for the Journeys travel company catalog. I was hired by John Odam to design and produce the maps under his art direction. They were to be created in FreeHand for placement in a PageMaker layout. I used a Macintosh IIcx with 4 MB of RAM and an 80 MB internal hard drive. Scans were made with an AppleScanner and proofs were printed on a LaserWriter II NTX. Color proofs were run on a QMS ColorScript 100 printer, and final film output was to a Linotronic L-300 at high resolution.

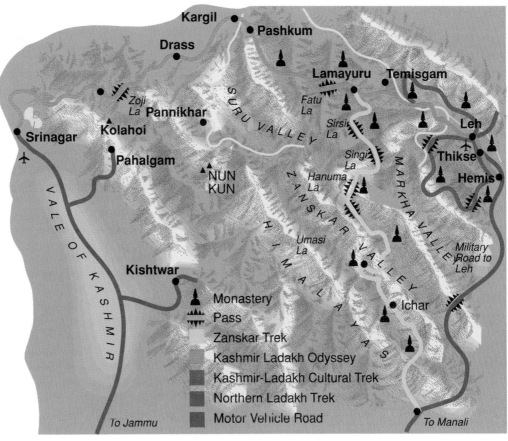

**PROJECT
OVERVIEW**

Design process

The Journeys travel company provides trekking trips in exotic and mountainous areas in Asia, Africa and Central and South America. They wanted a new, consistent look for their tour maps and requested that the mountain ranges be shown in a textured and topographic relief. The maps needed to convey a sense of adventure and excitement to prospective tourists.

John Odam and I examined the eleven tour regions and made pencil sketches to determine how we would treat various elements, such as countries bounded by water, borders between countries and so forth. We decided to do each map as a country silhouette, rather than place the country within a rectangular border, because the irregular shapes of the countries gave a more dynamic look to the page layout. We chose a palette of "safari" colors — khakis, deep greens, muted browns — to fit with the style of the trips. I created a preliminary map of Ladakh and then viewed it with John on his 19-inch color monitor. He made suggestions about images to add or change. After these revisions, we had a QMS color proof made and then negatives for a color key to check our color scheme and style. After further suggestions and approval from John and the client, I completed the remaining 10 maps.

Costa Rica Tropical Odyssey
Tortuguero Jungle Odyssey
Wildlands Camping Safari
Mountain Bike Odyssey

To indicate ocean water along the coast, a line copied and cut from the country outline was cloned and colored in two shades of blue, in two thicknesses. The darker line sits on top of the lighter one, and they both are placed behind the country.

To indicate mountain elevation, as in this map of Japan, a texture drawing was made by hand on tracing paper, scanned as a bitmap, and placed in the FreeHand map document.

To create the effect of a two-color line for the air route on this map of Tanzania, the original line was cloned and changed to a dashed line in another color.

FreeHand's Join function was used to join the text for the two oceans to diagonal, slightly curving paths.

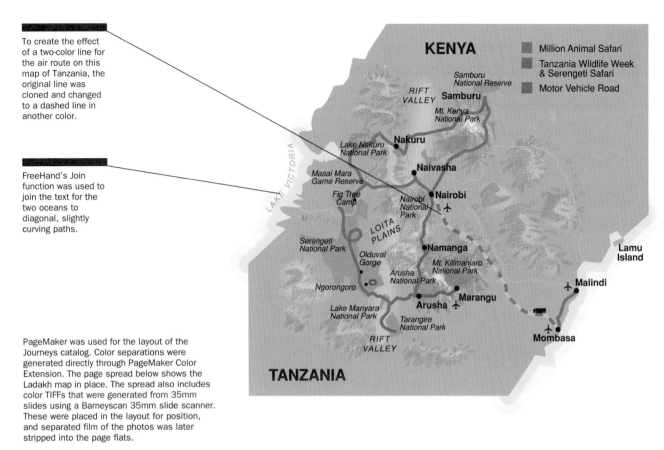

PageMaker was used for the layout of the Journeys catalog. Color separations were generated directly through PageMaker Color Extension. The page spread below shows the Ladakh map in place. The spread also includes color TIFFs that were generated from 35mm slides using a Barneyscan 35mm slide scanner. These were placed in the layout for position, and separated film of the photos was later stripped into the page flats.

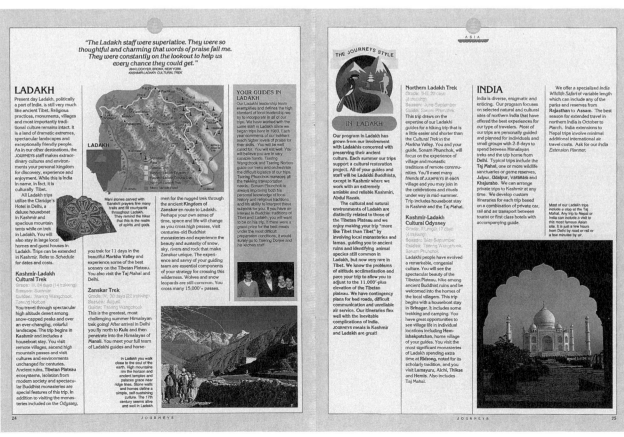

The map resource material was supplied to us by the client in two forms: as Illustrator 88 documents (Figure 1) and as hard copy from other sources (Figure 2). There were a total of six maps already created in Illustrator 88, which had been used in the company's newsletter and for route planning. I opened each Illustrator map, removed extraneous information, saved it as a 1.1-compatible document, and then reopened each as a FreeHand document. ▌ *To convert an Illustrator 88 file for use in FreeHand, open it, choose Save As from the File menu, and check the Illustrator 1.1 box in the Save dialog box. Then open FreeHand, choose Open from the File menu, and select the Illustrator 1.1 document you've created. The illustration will be automatically converted by FreeHand and will open with all its anchor points, ready for further editing.*

I scanned the hard-copy maps and used them as templates for tracing in FreeHand. I referred to an atlas for details that weren't clear. Much of the geographical rendering was left to my discretion. After working with all the resource material, I completed a series of 11 base maps in FreeHand, each one consisting of a country outline filled with a background color, lines indicating rivers and some travel routes, and type elements indicating city names, points of interest and so forth (Figure 3).

Specifying colors

Once we decided on a basic color scheme, I created a palette of four-color process colors and gave most of them names corresponding to their use; such as Base, Ridge, Mountains, Rivers and so forth. ▌ *Only cyan, yellow and magenta were used in the color mixes, as experience has taught us that the use of black in four-color process colors can cause moiré patterns when printed.*

Figure 1. Working with reference material. Some of the maps— Madagascar, for example— had already been created for the client in Illustrator 88. These were converted for use in FreeHand.

Figure 3. Producing the base map. After all the map reference material had been provided, a base country outline for each map was produced in FreeHand. The one shown here is for Ladakh.

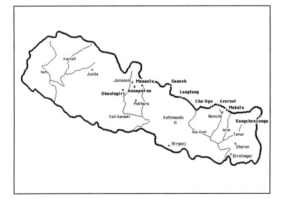

Figure 2. Scanning. About half of the map reference material was supplied in the form of photocopies. These were scanned and used as templates. Shown here is the scan of Nepal.

Giving each color a name made it easier to find the color needed in the color menu, and also simplified color changes. ▍ *To change the specifications or name of a color, select or create an element that contains that color and choose Edit Color from the Color menu. Enter the changes into the dialog box that appears.*

I also created palettes of lines to be used for trails and rivers. These color and line palettes were created in the first map document I worked on. To provide each of the other 10 map documents with the same color and line palettes, without having to type the color specs into each one in turn, I used a tip from John. I kept my small color samples on the pasteboard of each map document, so that as I went on, I could easily select and copy the "palette" and paste it into the next map, without having to go back to the original map in which the palette had been created (Figure 4). ▍ *To transfer a palette from one document to another, draw a square or line in each color or style and place these elements in the pasteboard area of the document. Select and copy all of these to the clipboard, open a new document and hit Command-V (or choose Paste from the Edit menu) to paste in the shapes. Once these elements are part of the new document, their color and style specifications automatically appear in the appropriate menus.*

Making the type size consistent

In order to keep the type size consistent on each map, I decided to work on each at "actual size" in FreeHand. To determine the size I placed each map outline in the rough catalog layout, reduced it to fit, and then measured it and adjusted the FreeHand file accordingly. Some maps were created before the final page layout was determined, so I had to adjust the type size later, when I knew what the final illustration size would be. We used 5- and 6-point Helvetica type on all the maps — we wanted the type to be readable but small enough so that the map wouldn't look cluttered. About half of the Illustrator 88 maps contained the necessary type; the rest I keyed in myself.

Figure 4. Transferring color and line palettes. To transfer the color and line palettes from one document to another, swatches were drawn in each style, copied and pasted into the next document. The color and line styles appeared automatically in the appropriate menus.

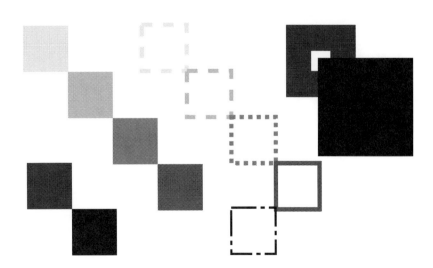

Coloring the coastlines

To create a two-tone blue outline to indicate ocean water against a coastline, I selected the country outline, cloned it and then gave the clone a fill of None and a line of Basic (it was a default 1-point black line) so that I could more easily see and select it (Figure 5). I used the knife tool to cut the outline at the beginning and end of the coastline, and then deleted the unwanted segment (Figure 6). I selected the remaining line and specified a new line style called Ocean Front (a 12-point line in light blue). I sent it to layer 70, to sit behind the country outline (Figure 7). I cloned this line and created another new line style called Ocean Depth (24-points in a darker blue). I then sent it to layer 60 to move it behind the Ocean Front line (Figure 8).

Figure 5

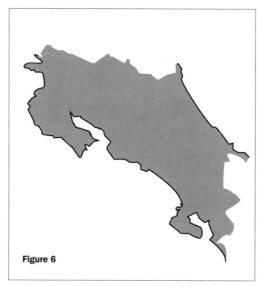

Figure 6

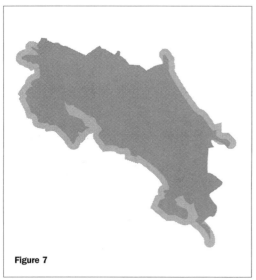

Figure 7

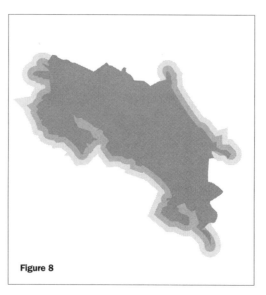

Figure 8

Figure 5. Defining the coastline. The country outline was cloned and changed to a 1-point black line with no fill.

Figure 6. Cutting the line. The knife tool was used to cut the black line clone in four places. The line was then de-selected, and the unwanted "non-coast" portion was selected and deleted.

Figure 7. Placing the line behind the country. The coast-line segment was styled as a 12-point blue line and sent to a layer behind the country outline.

Figure 8. Creating a second line. The 12-point blue line was cloned, changed to a 24-point line in a lighter blue, and this new clone was sent to a layer behind the first blue line.

Figure 9. Creating a relief texture. Pencil and tracing paper were used to draw a cross-hatched texture to delineate the mountain slopes and shadows. The pencil drawing was scanned on the Apple Scanner.

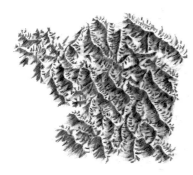

Creating the effect of a relief

The client wanted the mountain ranges to look three-dimensional, with some indication of the topography. To create this effect, I placed a piece of tracing paper on a laser print of the map outline and used a pencil to sketch in the mountain ridges and a cross-hatched texture of shading along the western sides of the mountains (Figure 9). The newspaper weather map served as the model. Using an Apple Scanner and the AppleScan software, I scanned my texture drawing as a 75 dpi grayscale bitmap and then selected Adaptive from the Filters menu. This "dithered" the scan, giving it a stippled effect (Figure 10). (We tried applying some of the dithers available in ImageStudio, but finally decided the AppleScan dither looked best.) I saved the dithered mountain scan as a MacPaint file, placed it in the FreeHand map document, and made it transparent. (The ability to make bitmaps transparent is a new feature of FreeHand 2.02.) ∎ *To make a bitmap element transparent, select it, choose Element Info from the Element menu and check the Transparent box.*

I placed the mountain texture in layer 90, above the base layer of the map outline. I gave it a blue color to differentiate it from the green of the background (Figure 11).

After seeing a proof of this mountain treatment, the client asked for more detail on the eastern sides of the slopes and suggested using a second color. This would have been cumbersome to execute because we would have had to create two separate texture drawings, one for each half of the slope, then import both into FreeHand and give each a different color. We were trying to keep the maps simple, both in style and technique. We were especially concerned about creating an illustration file that might be too complex to print. So John and I worked together to adapt our original relief treatment. John made some pencil sketches to indicate the mountains' eastern slopes. I saw what he had in mind and altered the existing relief drawing, implementing more angular and coarse pencil strokes on the eastern side slopes (Figure 12). I rescanned, dithered and then placed the amended relief in FreeHand. After approval by Journeys, I drew and scanned 10 more texture sheets, one for each map.

Figure 10. Dithering the texture. The Apple Scanner's Adaptive Filter option was used to apply a dither to the mountain texture drawing.

Figure 11. Placing the texture in the map. The dithered texture bitmap was placed in the FreeHand map, specified as transparent and colored blue.

Figure 12. Defining the eastern slopes. A close-up of the final texture drawing shows the treatment of the eastern slopes, the effect of coarse, angular pencil strokes.

Styling the route lines

Each map includes 2-point lines that indicate the different tour routes offered by Journeys. These were rendered in bright, hot colors (reds, oranges, yellows) to make them easily visible against the muted backgrounds. In all, we specified seven different trail colors. Each map incorporates all or some of these colors, depending upon how many different tours are given in that country. The trail routes were identified by color on a map legend.

We also created special line styles to indicate ancillary air, water and train routes, to clearly show that these were part of a particular tour. I was able to create the effect of a two-color line for the air route by drawing the route first in the appropriate color, and then cloning that line and specifying it as a dashed line in a blue color. The dashed blue line sat directly on top of the route line below, allowing the route color to show through between the dashes (Figure 13). I drew in most of the trails by hand with the freehand tool, using my eye to follow rough maps supplied by Journeys. In this case my contour drawing experience combined well with my hand skill with the mouse.

Along with the dashed lines, we used small dingbat symbols (typographic ornaments) of a plane and a boat to indicate the air and water routes. Because the Carta font does not include a symbol for a train, I drew a stylized train myself and reduced it for use on the train route line (Figure 14).

In some cases more than one tour followed the same route in sections. In order to lay down the trail lines so they were precisely butted alongside each other, I cloned the first trail, specified its new color, and then used the Move function to move the new line exactly 2 points up or down from the first line. I then used the knife tool to cut away all but the section that the two trails had in common.

Figure 13. Creating a two-color line. To create the effect of a two-color line, the original solid line was cloned and then changed to a dashed style in a different color.

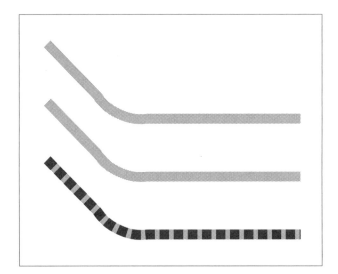

Figure 14. Defining line styles. Line styles and colors were developed to indicate the trails and the air, water and rail routes that connect to them. Airplane and boat symbols were created as type elements using the font Carta and placed on the appropriate route lines. A special train symbol was drawn in FreeHand and reduced to fit the route size.

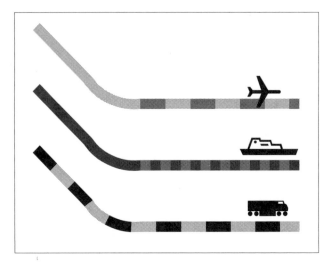

Organizing with layers

My work on the preliminary map helped me organize how best to manage my execution of the rest of the maps. For example, the first map was created with front-to-back interleaving in one layer, but I quickly learned that this was too difficult to manage. FreeHand's layering capability was a big help in organizing map elements. I placed the country outline and base fill on layer 80, the mountain scans on 90, the trails and routes on 100, and the type and any other symbols on layer 110.

Creating additional topographical relief

The client was happy with our final treatment of the mountain range textures, but wanted more color and drama to suggest the different elevations of the mountains. John and I discussed how to achieve this effect and decided to blend a base "valley" element (in a darker color) with a "peak" element in a lighter color. This blended element sat beneath the mountain texture to suggest increasing height. I created these elements using the bitmap relief as a guide. I drew a shape around the outside edges of each mountain section and colored it Base, then a drew a smaller shape along the ridge of that section and colored it Ridge. These two shapes were selected and blended in three steps to create an element with a subtle gradation of color. I selected all the parts of this new element — the outside outline, the ridge outline and the blend element — grouped them, and sent them to layer 80, where they sit just in front of the country base outline (Figure 15).

For low mountain ranges, like those in Africa, I created a softly curving, foothill effect by drawing the outline shapes with the FreeHand tool. For the higher mountain ranges I created a more jagged, deeply etched outline by using the corner point tool. For the higher elevations, for instance the Himalayas, the client wanted to use lighter, cooler colors. For the lower mountain ranges in Africa we used warmer reds and browns. For the medium-range elevations in Japan, for instance, we used greens.

Figure 15. Suggesting mountain elevation. To give an additional feeling of height to the mountain ranges, a blended element that changes from a darker color at the base to a lighter one at the ridge, was created to sit behind the texture bitmap.

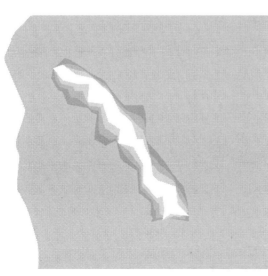
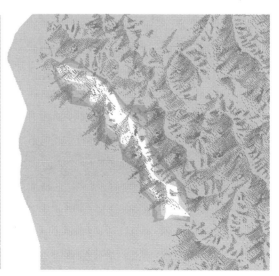

Using the Move function

The client later wanted to change the ridge colors of some of the blended elements, so I had to ungroup them, change the color of the ridge outline, and redo the blend. It was confusing visually to do this now that the blends were sitting behind the texture bitmap. So I moved the bitmap temporarily out of the way by selecting it and choosing Move from the Edit menu. I moved it by a large, easily remembered distance, for instance 300 points to the right, and then edited the blend and regrouped the blend elements, without the bitmap in the way. When I was finished I brought the bitmap element back into position by moving it 300 points to the left.

Text along a path

The type for the names of rivers and mountain ranges was joined to paths drawn along the contours of those geographical features. For the curving or sideways type elements we decided to use all caps with space between the letters (Figure 16). ▌ *To create spaces between letters, enter the text without spaces in the Text dialog box, close the box and then drag the middle handle at the right or left of the element box. This results in spreading out the letters, without increasing the type size or distorting the letters (see "Working with text" on page 91).*

I spread out the type until it looked like it was the same length as the path I planned to join it to. Then I joined the two elements by selecting them and choosing Join Elements from the Special submenu under the Element menu (Figure 17).

It was often necessary to go back and edit these type elements for typos or text changes. The Type dialog box does not open when you double click on a joined text-path element. So at first I had to unjoin the elements, and then double click on the text element to edit it. This was a cumbersome process. Eventually, we discovered that it's possible to edit text that's joined to a path by opening the Text Along A Path dialog box. ▌ *To edit text after it's been joined to a path, select the joined text-path element and choose Element Info from the Element menu. Then click Edit Text in the Text Along A Path dialog box that appears. This will open the Type dialog box containing the original text, which can then be edited.*

The Text Along A Path box also provides options for aligning the text to the path along its baseline, ascenders, or descenders. You can also choose whether the text characters are rotated around the path (the vertical orientation of each character is perpendicular to the path at every point), or vertical (all the characters remain vertical even when aligned to a curving path), or are skewed horizontally or vertically.

Ganging color proofs

To save on the cost of QMS color proofs, we ganged two maps in each 8½ x 11-inch document. Before ganging two different maps, I had to be sure to

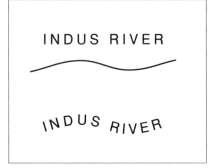

Figure 16. Spreading type. To add space between the letters of river and mountain names, the Type Element box was stretched by dragging the middle handle on the right or left side.

Figure 17. Joining text to a path. A line was drawn following the curve of the river. Then the rivers's name was entered in the Type dialog box. After the text was spread to an appropriate length (see Figure 16), the line and the text were selected and joined, creating one curved text element.

rename certain elements in the color palette so they would retain the correct values. ▌ *FreeHand gives priority to the color spec in the newly opened document and alters any colors with the same names in the illustrations that have been pasted into it.*

In some cases the client had asked for color changes in the blended topo elements that sit behind the bitmap mountain relief texture. So in some documents the color spec for Ridge was different than in the original map. I renamed the Ridge colors — calling them Rwanda, Ladakh and so on — to differentiate them. This way each color printed with its own process color specs intact.

In retrospect

This map project was complex and highly customized for the client, but because of FreeHand's extraordinary capabilities I was able to complete the project in only about 80 hours. It would have taken much longer to produce these maps by conventional means.

In thinking back over the process, I discovered that I'd learned a few techniques I could have used to make the map production a little easier. For instance, rather than move the bitmap texture layer out of the way when doing the color changes on the blend elements, I could have used Layer control to render the layers above 80 inactive and invisible. A wonderful characteristic of FreeHand is that it's often possible to execute the same thing in several different ways, even if some methods are less elegant than others.

For an illustration with so many elements, FreeHand was the perfect tool. The layering capability made it possible to organize all the elements, without having to shuffle through a big pile of papers, as with conventional media. It was relatively easy to go back in and make changes and corrections as the client requested them. On the down side, I had to worry about the possibility of corrupted files, or the peculiarities of the software.

The computer also helped me to communicate effectively with the art director. I designed the preliminary map following the sketches and styles we worked out together, and then showed John a full-color comp on-screen. John could quickly see the solutions I had come up with and could critique and edit my design on-screen, in color, to clearly show me what revisions he wanted.

PORTFOLIO

Jill Malena

"While I was attending Chico State, a friend in a design class created a comp for an assignment using the school paper's Macintosh and laser printer. The instructor tore her apart because she hadn't inked everything by hand! Once I began using a Mac, I knew there was no turning back to conventional media. Learning the fundamentals of graphic design in a traditional setting was an invaluable experience, and I'll never throw away my X-acto knife. But I'm amazed that so many designers are still using conventional layout and paste-up.

Electronic design is the best thing that's happened to my career. I'm able to try graphic solutions that I would never try otherwise and get an immediate result. The computer lets me shine as a designer much more than if I were using conventional means. I'm confident that I can use the computer to execute any design a client might want. Even if I'm not sure at first how to achieve a particular effect, I'm certain that somehow, some way, I can do it using the current graphic software.

Working in San Diego I feel that I'm on the cutting edge of this technology. It's also very exciting to be a woman in this field that has been primarily dominated by men. Computer graphics has created a powerful network in the design community. Before the computer, designers rarely consulted each other about how to do their work or use their tools. But now it's commonplace to get phone calls from other designers with questions about how the computer software and hardware work. We're all learning together."

This logo for a wedding invitation and sweatshirts was done in FreeHand 2.02. The camelia was traced from an encyclopedia, scanned, autotraced in FreeHand and edited.

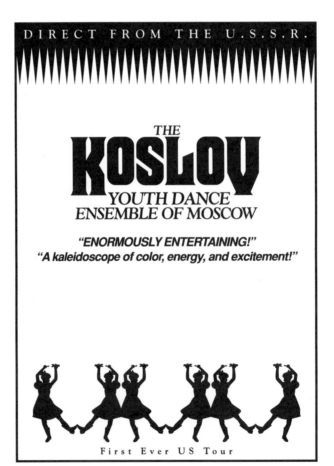

This advertising slick for an international dance company was done in FreeHand 2.02. The Koslov mark was recreated by scanning a printed version and using it as a template for tracing. The dancing figure was based on a color photograph supplied by the client. One figure was drawn and copies were reflected to create the paper doll effect. The teeth at the top were created by drawing a rectangle filled with a graduated fill from black at the top to white at the bottom. I then chose Halftone Screen from the Special submenu under Element and specified a screen at 5 lines per inch and 0 degrees.

This logo for an open house was created in FreeHand 2.02. The building shape was drawn using the corner point tool and the confetti and lettering were drawn using the freehand tool.

This page folio was created in FreeHand for *Step-by-Step Electronic Design* newsletter. The design needed to look "pixelly" so I set the Snap To Grid option to a comfortable size (a 6-point grid) and drew the squares with the rectangle tool while holding down the Shift key to constrain them to squares. The grid made the squares snap to a uniform size and made it easy to align them.

A logo for Spencer Nilsen, a composer and producer, was based on an autotrace of his scanned signature, touched up in FreeHand.

These two-color book covers were developed in FreeHand as part of a series of 12 theosophical manuals. Designs were derived from Adobe patterns (below middle) and borders (below left) as well as printed reference materials, which were scanned and used as templates (below right).

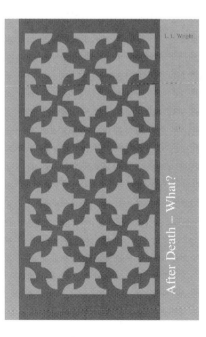

CHAPTER 14

Detail and Depth in a Crystal Ball

Artist

Michael Scaramozzino created his first computer graphics in 1981 with "ArtSketch," a program he wrote while studying computer science at the University of California, San Diego. He earned a Bachelor of Fine Arts in illustration from Rhode Island School of Design and became director of their newly founded Academic Computer Center. He served as vice president of software development for a computer consulting company before founding DreamLight Incorporated three years ago in Providence, Rhode Island. DreamLight is a design studio focusing on corporate ID/logo design and illustration ranging from simple black-and-white line drawing to full-color photorealistic rendering. All work at DreamLight, from concept to completion, is done digitally.

Project

"Lucid Beginnings" was designed as a promotional piece for my design studio, DreamLight. The piece contains elements created in a bitmap paint program, in a grayscale paint program, and in a PostScript illustration program. We wanted to push the limits of black-and-white illustration before moving on to the new color technology.

I worked on this project over a full year (actually about 200 hours done after work and on weekends), so the equipment evolved as the image did. It was started on a Macintosh Plus and finished on a Macintosh II with 5 MB of RAM. We used a Nutmeg full-page display, a Nova 20 MB hard disk, and a 12" SummaSketch tablet (hijacked from our PC-based paint system). It was proofed on an Apple Laser-Writer and a service bureau's Linotronic L-300. The final image was output on a Varityper 4300 at another service bureau. A Practical Peripherals 2400 baud modem and Red Ryder were used to communicate with the service bureaus. The image was created with FreeHand (version 1.1, then version 2.0), ComicWorks (now called GraphicWorks), ImageStudio and PageMaker 3.0. The file is over 1 MB and took about 45 minutes to output as an 11 X 17-inch 2400 dpi image on the Varityper imagesetter.

Design goals

As the Macintosh community began to
work with color, I decided to see how far I
could push the black-and-white technology
before moving on to color myself. My
focus was an illustration for a promotional
piece that would look back at our studio's
beginnings and also convey a sense of our
forward thinking. I admire Escher's work
and thought an Escher-like crystal ball
done in this new medium would reinforce
the past/future theme. Through the
illustration we gaze into a crystal ball,
back to the time when DreamLight
consisted solely of myself, a PC-based
paint system, and a single black and white
Macintosh Plus. Thus the name "Lucid
Beginnings."

"Lucid Beginnings"
includes a crystal
ball created in
PostScript illustra-
tion, that rests on
a base created in a
bitmapped paint
program. Grayscale
painting was used
to create the
shadowed area
beneath the base.
The images were
combined in a
page layout
program.

The crystal ball,
created in
FreeHand, is an
ambitious, black-
and-white rendering
of images of the
artist's studio,
including a self-
portrait.

The self-portrait head was sketched first in a paint program, imported into, and then drawn over as a template in Free-Hand. The body was drawn directly in FreeHand and the two elements were combined.

Blends and masking were used to create the effect of spot-lights illuminating the walls.

L ucid Beginnings" is the third and final image in a series of black-and-white explorations of PostScript illustration. In "Scroll" I explored the possibilities of realistic shading. It was done in Illustrator 1.1, which could not create blends or graduated fills, so all the shading was done "by hand" (see the "Portfolio" on page 174). I stacked gray shapes on top of one another like a contour map and by varying the value of each successive shape, created the appeance of a shaded area.

The next image, "High Performance," was a Lamborghini Countach, also done in Illustrator 1.1 using the same shading techniques (see "Portfolio"). It was received with mixed reviews. Some people felt the piece was well-executed technically but not very "artistic." For my third effort I wanted to create an image that continued to push the level of realism and detail but would also be a little more varied in style and more spontaneous. I created different parts of the image in different styles, using a bitmapped component, a grayscale area, and a high resolution PostScript illustration. Both of the previous images were also included in "Lucid Beginnings" as prints hanging on the walls of the studio.

Resource material

The first step was to find a real crystal ball. After some searching I was able to borrow one from an associate. Since I knew the project would stretch over some time, I worked from a photograph of the ball as well as from life. When

Figure 1. Sketching.
Initial sketches were made in ComicWorks, a bitmapped paint program that provides "easels" for the separate control of different parts of the image.

I placed the ball on the table near my desk, I was amazed to find that the half of the studio behind me was reflected by the top of the crystal and the other half was refracted and inverted through the bottom. There was an additional ghost image that was a combined reflection and refraction. By putting black mat board under the ball and carefully arranging the studio lights I was able to get everything that I wanted to show in the ball. I set up a camera on a tripod to shoot over my shoulder and snapped a picture with a self-timer. I worked from the real ball as long as I could, and then switched to the photograph when I returned the crystal a few weeks later.

Initial sketches

Some designers like to sketch on paper and then scan their drawings into the computer. But I find sketching directly with the computer gives me more flexibility. My favorite program for sketching is ComicWorks (now called GraphicWorks). Its biggest strength is its use of easels that allow you to isolate overlapping objects and play with the composition much as you would with tracing paper. The initial conceptual sketches were drawn freehand in ComicWorks using a stylus and drawing tablet (Figure 1). Originally I had included several more objects in the painting, but at this point I really liked what was happening in the base area and decided to focus in on the ball and base alone. I felt this would provide a good visual contrast between the high-contrast bitmapped base and the high-resolution, fully rendered crystal ball that was to come.

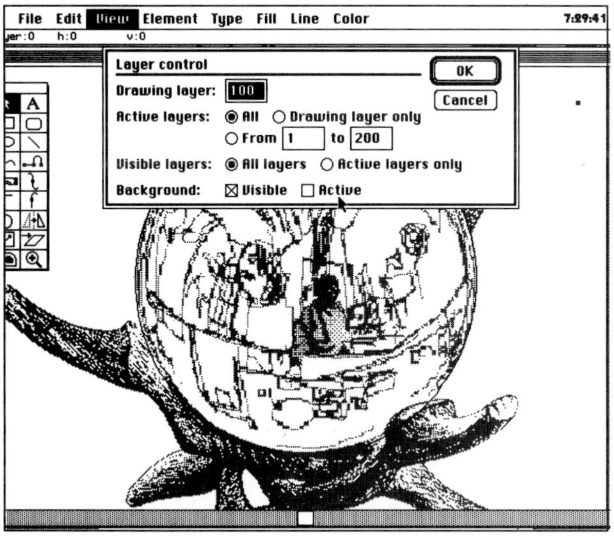

Figure 2. Importing a template. Placing the sketch in the background in FreeHand and making it visible but inactive made it possible to draw on top of it.

Beginning the crystal ball

I saved my sketch as a MacPaint document and placed it into FreeHand as a template (Figure 2). The sketch was used primarily for rough proportions. Most of the details were worked out in FreeHand using the photograph as visual reference. No part of the image was scanned.

I began by defining some of the major areas of the image. FreeHand's layering system made it manageable to work with this extremely complex illustration. Related areas were organized on specific layers according to the natural order of overlapping. For instance, since the figure was to overlap the door behind it, the figure was placed on layer 175 while the door was placed on 150 (Figure 3). By assigning elements to their own layers I could isolate a single element and work on its details without disturbing any other parts of the image. ∎ *By leaving some room between layers at this stage, you'll have empty layers to use later for adding highlights or shadows that fall between images.*

To bring the earlier illustrations, "Scroll" and "High Performance" into the crystal ball, I opened the original files and removed some of the small details that wouldn't be visible in the finished piece. The gray shades of the remaining shapes were adjusted to fit in. For instance, since "High Performance" was placed in a relatively dark area of the crystal ball, each of its gray shades was made about 5 percent darker than in the original image.

The next step was to distort "High Performance" to match the curve of the ball. This was accomplished by skewing the image, ungrouping all of its elements, selecting all the points in the left 95 percent of the image and rotating them about 2 degrees around a pivot point slightly above and to the right of the image. This procedure was repeated using 90 percent of the points, then 85 percent, and so on, all the way down to about 10 percent of the points in 5 percent increments. The final effect simulates how the image would look through the ball (Figure 4). Even though most of these items would actually be reversed in a crystal ball reflection, I took the liberty of making them right-reading. I was more interested in the final visual image than in rendering true reflections and refractions.

Richness of detail

The computer allowed me to bring a degree of detail to the piece that I couldn't have matched using traditional media. Much of the detail I added was not even visible in the resource photo. Though a lot of the fine work is not clearly seen in the finished piece, I think the eye notices the visual variety, which heightens the sense of depth and realism in the image. To achieve this level of detail I worked on individual sections at a very large scale.

Figure 3. Layering the images. Major areas of the crystal ball were defined and the organization of layering was determined. The figure was placed on layer 175, and the door behind it is on 150.

Figure 4. Distorting an image. The image of "High Perform-ance" was skewed, and smaller and smaller groups of points were progressively rotated farther and farther to give it a smoothly curving distorted effect. The type was bound to a curved line, grouped and then skewed to match the distortion.

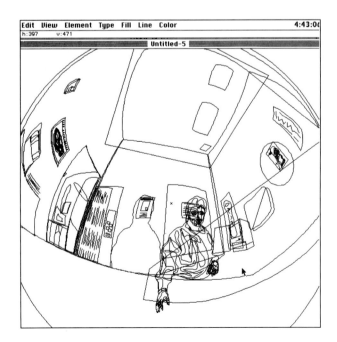

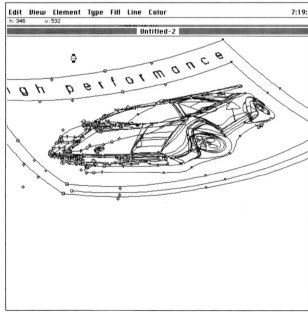

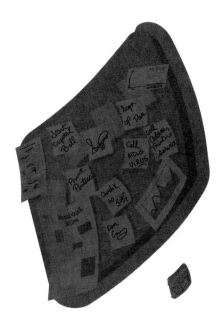

Figure 5. Paying attention to detail. A great deal of detail was brought to the piece. For example, the notes posted on the bulletin board are actually readable when enlarged. The freehand tool was used with the stylus to put handwriting on each note.

Combining separate files

Since FreeHand is limited to an 800 percent zoom, some sections were done individually in separate files. The bulletin board is a good example. I copied the simple outline done initially (see Figure 3) and pasted it into a new blank document (Figure 5). After enlarging it as much as possible, I worked on the details, grouped the elements, reduced the image back to its original size, copied it and pasted it back into the original file. This method also allowed me to print detailed items by themselves, which saved quite a bit of time. "Lucid Beginnings" was so complex that I printed literally hundreds of laser proofs.

▍*Though you can assign elements to different layers in FreeHand, you can't currently print the contents of only one layer.*

I had some difficulty with the self-portrait because working directly in FreeHand isn't spontaneous enough. To loosen up, I did some face studies in ComicWorks, using a mirror for reference (Figure 6). When I felt comfortable with one portrait, I pasted the bitmap into a new FreeHand drawing and used it as a template for the high-resolution version, which was then reduced and placed into the crystal ball (Figure 7).

Using blends and fills

To create the effect of soft lighting, I made extensive use of blends, graduated and radial fills, and clipping paths. For instance, to light the walls I made a large circle that's offset, with its center falling over what I thought should be the lightest area of the image. I filled the circle with a radial fill and pasted this inside the wall outline, which clipped the radial fill to fit.

The bright spotlights were created with blends. The largest area of light dispersal was drawn in a dim shade of gray, the hotspot was drawn on top of

Figure 6. Drawing the face. To render the self-portrait more accurately, a face study was first painted in ComicWorks and then placed into FreeHand and used as a template.

Figure 7. Assembling the figure. The finished head was placed on the finished body (originated in FreeHand) and the entire figure was pasted back into the crystal ball.

that with a very light gray, and the two were blended together with 50 to 100 steps intervening, depending on the distance covered (Figure 8). Sometimes, if there was a radial fill on the wall behind it, a blended spotlight appeared to have a dark edge around part of it where fills intersected. In this case I pasted the blended spotlight inside the largest of the spotlight's shapes and adjusted the edges of that shape to clip out the dark edge and let it match the background shade (see "Editing a clipping path" on page 171). The many complex blends and gradations give the ball most of its depth and richness.

Shadows or transparencies can be simulated even though PostScript works in opaque layers. For example, I used clipping paths to create the cast shadow that falls across the DreamLight logo.

The finishing touches on the crystal ball were the addition of the inverted ghost image of the figure and the highlights around the edge of the ball. To create the ghost image I cloned the figure, inverted it and enlarged it. After moving it into position I traced the highlights that lie on top of the figure and blended each one to the background shade. Once they were blended, I removed the cloned figure from beneath, creating the effect of highlight reflections fading into the background (Figure 9). The highlights at the edge of the ball are simply thin abstract shapes of light gray that help give the feeling of smooth glass.

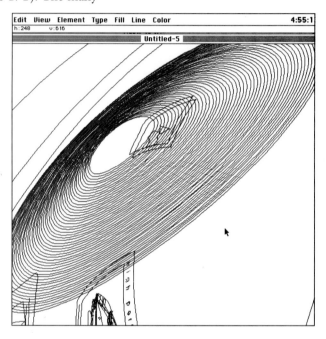

Figure 8. Lighting the room. Blends, radial and graduated fills, and clipping paths were used to create a feeling of soft spotlighting. A spotlight like the one shown here is a blend with over 40 steps.

Combining elements from different programs

The completed ball was saved as an encapsulated PostScript (EPSF) file. The bitmapped base was opened in ImageStudio, where a gray background screen and shadows under the ball were painted around it. This combined image was saved as a TIFF file with a 60-line screen at 45 degrees. We wanted to clearly show the difference in resolution possible between bitmapped and PostScript images. Using PageMaker 3.0, I combined the background and the EPSF ball. At this point I hit an annoying snag: one part of the base is meant to be in front of the ball, but none of the programs I used could create a bitmap that was opaque inside but transparent outside the image area. The ImageStudio TIFF placed in PageMaker as an opaque object within an opaque white box around it. Even though I hadn't drawn in the parts of the base that would be obscured by the ball, I needed to place the EPS file of the ball on top of the TIFF in order to get a clean edge on the globe. To reclaim the small obscured sliver of the base, I opened FreeHand, set the grid to 1 point and traced the small part of the base that was to overlap the ball, constructing it of small squares to simulate the "bits" in the original. I exported this as an EPS file, which was opaque but not surrounded by an opaque white square (Figure

When an object is masked with a clipping path, the resulting object can be edited by changing the outline shape of the clipping path. For example, if a TIFF image is pasted inside a rectangle, the amount of the image that shows through the mask can be increased or decreased by dragging a corner point of the rectangle. But if the masked element is grouped, dragging a corner handle will resize the image but not change how much of the image shows.

10). This technique was not one I would enjoy using over a large area but it was quite handy for this little piece. █ *A paint document will place in FreeHand surrounded by an opaque white bounding box. With the item selected, choose Element Info from the Element menu and check the Transparent box to eliminate the box and make the element transparent.*

The ability to combine pieces from various programs is one of the Macintosh's most powerful features. We also have a high-end dedicated turnkey paint system in our studio. It's capable of producing beautiful paintings but, unlike the Mac, it's incompatible with any other program and thus very limited.

Problems with the RIP

While I was creating this piece, I ran high-resolution proofs at various stages. It's the only way to see exactly how the shading will look. I learned quite a bit in the process. Early in the project I noticed that I needed to specify the Linotronic L-300's highest (2540 dpi) resolution to avoid contour banding on graduated fills and blends. But at 2540 dpi I got unsightly vertical bands across the entire page because the raster image processor (RIP) could not build a raster image for the full page and so it output to the imagesetter piece by piece, about an inch at a

Figure 9. Adding finishing touches. To create the effect of an inverted reflection, the figure was first cloned, inverted, and enlarged. Then the highlight areas were traced and each was blended to the background shade.

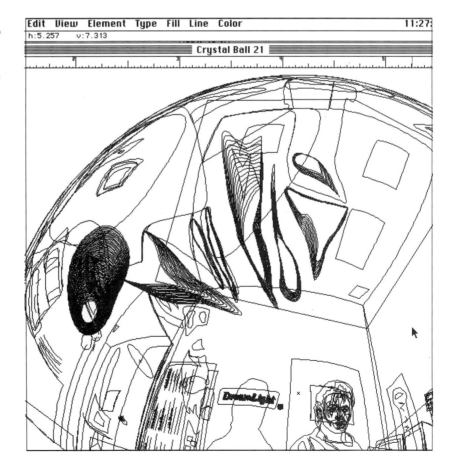

time. This starting and stopping of the imaging mechanism was visible as the banding on the final output, due to a very small change in the laser's intensity between starts and stops. Discussion with the people at Linotype determined there was no way to avoid this. When the new RIP came out, I tried again. The banding wasn't as apparent, but it still existed. I tried using the Varityper 4300, which has an image buffer on a dedicated hard disk. The Varityper did the trick. This imagesetter builds the raster image for the entire page, stores it on a dedicated image disk, and then sends the entire bitmap to the imagesetter. It's imaged in one pass, thus avoiding any banding problems. Linotype has subsequently licensed "Lucid Beginnings" to use in testing their future high-end RIP.

Figure 10. Duplicating pieces for layering. When the base and ball elements were combined in PageMaker, the ball obscured a small sliver of the base. FreeHand was used to draw a small shape duplicating the missing sliver.

Flatness and limitcheck errors

As I neared completion of the image, I hit another problem in printing. I got a "limitcheck" error message, indicating a PostScript error due to the complexity of a path or outline. This can be remedied by increasing the flatness of the troublesome path. But by now there were well over 1000 different paths in the image and I didn't know which one to flatten. The image took about 40 minutes to output before it would crash. Tracking down the offending path (or paths) would cost a fortune in processor time at the service bureau. I needed to reset the flatness of the entire ball globally, a function that's not possible through a FreeHand command. Instead I exported my illustration document as a text file and studied the PostScript code in a word processor.

■ *To export and open a FreeHand illustration as a text file, choose Print from the File menu, click OK and immediately press the F key. This will print the illustration to disk as a text-only document. It can be opened and edited in a word processing program.*

Accessing the PostScript code

The solution was actually rather simple. I created a new PostScript text file in a word processor and named the file UserPrep. I put it into my System folder and removed the UserPrep file that comes with FreeHand and usually resides in my FreeHand folder. In the new UserPrep file I typed the single PostScript command: */df 6 def.* This defines a default flatness of 6 for all paths. I found the effect of using the value 6 to be unnoticeable at resolutions above 1200 dpi. ■ *If necessary, you could go a bit higher. But if you go too high, your curves will print with flat facets (see "What is flatness?" on the next page).*

Next I defined a PostScript fill in my illustration document to act as a signal to FreeHand to load UserPrep. ■ *When FreeHand finds a custom PostScript definition in a document, it will load the UserPrep file; otherwise it won't.*

After exporting the ball with my new UserPrep and reassembling the image in PageMaker everything was fine. ▌ *When using a new UserPrep file, be sure to send a copy of it to your service bureau, along with the application file of the illustration. If your illustration is saved as an EPS file, however, the new UserPrep command(s) will be bound with it and need not be sent separately to the service bureau*

In retrospect

It's not necessary to have a background in computer science to use the computer for design or illustration, but I've found that my technical understanding helps me to use it more efficiently. I can track down and correct problems such as the limitcheck error that would otherwise have crippled the project before completion.

I devoted a lot of time and energy to producing "Lucid Beginnings," in order to show the complexity of which the computer medium was capable. When our studio first began, desktop publishing was in its infancy. As a "computer" service we found we were attracting clients who expected our work to be cheaper and better than (but otherwise much the same as) traditional design. To reposition ourselves as a producer of higher-end illustration, we wanted to create complex and sophisticated illustrations like "Lucid Beginnings." Though it took many hours, we had fun and learned a great deal along the way. The techniques I learned and my mastery of the program have been used many times since then on jobs for clients.

▌ **What is flatness?**

Flatness is a PostScript parameter that determines the smoothness with which curves are rendered when printed. Curved paths are actually approximated with a series of small, straight line segments. The shorter these segments, the smoother the curve will appear when printed. The flatness value determines how long each line segment will be by specifying the distance from each point on the approximated curve to the corresponding point on the true curve. This distance is measured in output device pixels or "dots."

Both FreeHand and Illustrator preset the flatness value at 0. This allows each output device to set its own best value. The screen preview uses a flatness value of 1, and printers use their own preset values keyed to their resolution. A high-resolution printer like a Linotronic L-300 presets a higher flatness value than a laser printer, for instance.

When curved paths in a PostScript illustration are very complex a "limitcheck" error may occur and the illustration will stop printing. One way to overcome this is to cut the path into smaller pieces. Another way is to increase the flatness value of the path, which reduces the number of line segments the printer has to produce. Both FreeHand and Illustrator allow the user to select an object and change its flatness value. However, if an illustration contains many complex paths, this path-by-path editing of flatness can be tedious. In Illustrator it's possible to globally increase the flatness of all paths by choosing Select All from the Edit menu, choosing Paint from the Style menu, and typing a new flatness value in the Paint dialog box. In FreeHand flatness can't be changed globally through the interface but only by changing the PostScript code that describes the illustration. This requires a knowledge of PostScript programming (see "Flatness and limitcheck errors" in this chapter).

Changing the flatness value means balancing computational efficiency against the accuracy of the image. Very low flatness values produce curves that are very accurate and smooth. But accuracy requires the generation of thousands of tiny line segments, which can increase processing time or produce a limitcheck error. For complex images, some trial and error may be required to determine a flatness value that allows the illustration to print, but without noticeable coarsening of the curves.

PORTFOLIO

"Scroll" was done in Illustrator 1.1 for Sprintout, an imagesetting service bureau. The assignment was to come up with an example that would show off the power of the Linotronic L-300 to produce composite images and type.

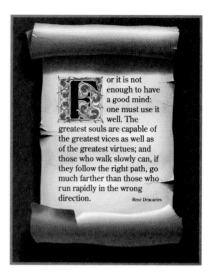

For it is not enough to have a good mind: one must use it well. The greatest souls are capable of the greatest vices as well as of the greatest virtues; and those who walk slowly can, if they follow the right path, go much farther than those who run rapidly in the wrong direction.
—René Descartes

Michael Scaramozzino

"When we provide technical consulting for other studios, I often find that their problems are not actually technical but instead involve their approach to the computer as a design tool. There are two common mistakes in thinking about the computer's use in design. One is "technophobia." A creative staff is often unsure, afraid or resentful of the technology. They see the computer as a machine that saps creativity and removes freedom, or that mechanizes their "art." The computer seems like something out of a science fiction novel, bent on replacing human beings. The other mistake is made by people who think of computers as too restrictive for design, but 'computerize' anyway, not wanting to be left behind. They view the computer as a machine like a Xerox copier or a stat camera and feel that it's useful only for production.

Computer graphics is still in an early stage of acceptance, as the "new" medium of photography once was. At first, chemists were the only people who could do photography, just as programmers were the first to do computer graphics. Early examples of photography were rejected as real art. "Technicians are not artists," people said. But a new breed of artists got their hands on cameras — people who understood aesthetics and enough of the technical aspects to master the new medium. Eventually their works were accepted as art. As artists take computer graphics to new limits, it too will be accepted as a medium.

Some artists excel in oil painting but not in sculpture. Some will take to the new computer medium and others will not. But it's not a case of converting or being left behind. The computer doesn't put a leash on creativity; on the contrary, it unleashes it."

"High Performance" was done in Illustrator 1.1. The shading is built up by drawing overlapping shapes from dark to light, similar to a contour map.

These simple orthographic drawings were done in Illustrator 88 using its ability to constrain lines to specific angles.

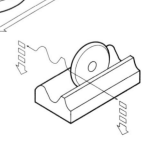

This four-color product illustration was done in FreeHand for the Gtech corporation. The challenge was to bring excitement and life to a static machine. Many of the lighting and shading techniques explored in "Lucid Beginnings" were used.

A four-color promotional illustration for Sprintout was designed to announce the client's new color capabilities while emphasizing their imagesetting expertise. I thought a jungle theme would allow us to make both points in an exciting way. The piece was done in FreeHand 2.02.

A simple black-and-white logo for a small glass and design studio was designed in Illustrator 1.1. This piece was to be elegant yet economical for reproduction.

This logo for a company that imports and exports health, housing and recreation products between the United States and Nigeria was designed in color in FreeHand.

Gallery

On the following pages is a selection of work done in PostScript illustration programs by various artists from around the world.

Deborah Ivanoff
Modern Graphics
Common
Cardiff, California.

Cover Art for a science textbook was rendered using the blend function in Aldus FreeHand 2.02 on a Macintoch IIci.

Louis Fishauf
is creative director of Reactor Art & Design
Ltd., a graphic design and illustration firm
in Toronto, Canada.

Cubist Head was composed on-screen in Adobe Illustrator 88. The shapes that define the features along the front of the face were created by drawing an open, zigzagging path that was colored with a black fill and no stroke. Specifying a black fill caused the program to automatically connect the end points of the path creating a series of solid, black-filled shapes. The curved shapes at the left of the face are single paths stroked with heavy line weights.

Huntress was created as a personal piece in Illustrator 88 and later used in an ad for Adobe Systems. The dog image was taken from a collection of images built up by the artist, that are recycled through various illustrations. Three overlapping, colored blends make up the background elements of sky, trees and wavy ground.

Terry Brown

works as an interface designer for Apple Computer.

Botany Ball was begun in Adobe Illustrator on a Macintosh SE and continued in Illustrator 88 on a Mac II. The blend tool was used to create the soft edges of the background and the shadow beneath the ball. The hundreds of small leaf shapes are clones that have been rotated into many different orientations. "The idea of using a compressed ball of plants instead of a row of potted plants is just to be different," notes Terry Brown.

Laslo Vespremi

Laslo Vespremi has been art director of the Cincinnati Enquirer, the Chicago Sun Times, and the San Francisco Examiner. He was the founding art director of MacWeek magazine and is a regular columnist for MacWeek GA. Vespremi works as a software specialist for EFI (Electronics for Imaging).

MacOffice was created in Adobe Illustrator. It features an intricate interleaving of elements within Illustrator's single drawing layer, with objects in the foreground placed in front of and partially obscuring objects behind them. For example, the Macintosh Plus in the lower right was drawn as a complete object, but is partially covered by the opaque, gray-filled head of its operator.

Bob Lee
*is a freelance illustrator and concrete poet
who works in San Diego, California.*

Tech Seed was
created in FreeHand.
It is built up of many
objects colored with
graduated fills. The
left-hand side of the
cube base contains a
linear fill while the
right-hand side
contains a radial fill.
Each globe at the top
was constructed by
making an arrange-
ment of overlapping,
irregular curved
shapes and pasting
these elements
inside a circle used
as a clipping path.
Some highlights
were added on top of
each globe.

Berlin Series incorporates a TIFF image of Karl
Marx within a series of FreeHand illustrations
depicting the eventual re-unification of East and
West Germany. The first and last images are
shown here. The TIFF, along with two graduated
fills, are pasted inside the triangular shapes
that lie on the clock faces. The stacked black
letters spelling BERLIN were cloned, colored
gray and skewed to create the look of a hinged
shadow. The clone was skewed again in each
successive design, so that the angle between
the two stacks of type appears to decrease.

Dorothy Remington
is a principal in Remington Design, a San Francisco design firm that produces editorial and publication design, annual reports, corporate identity and package design. Remington has taught computer illustration at the College of Arts and Crafts in San Francisco.

Fruit was created in Illustrator 88 as a label for fruit jars. The base of each piece of fruit was constructed of a multistepped blend from the outside outline to a smaller interior shape in a lighter color. The cleft in the apricot was created by positioning two such blend elements on top of each other, with the topmost one set slightly to the right. Each small highlight on the raspberries, strawberries and cucumber is also a subtly blended element.

Checkers was created as a test illustration for the Scitex system of producing color separations and proofs directly from an Adobe Illustrator 88 file on disk. The illustration features checkerboard squares contructed of blends, upon which are placed a variety of abstract shapes and letterforms. The shadows behind the objects were created by copying each one, coloring the copy gray, and then skewing and scaling the copy.

Max Seabaugh
uses a full range of media from traditional to electronic to produce illustrations and graphic design. His company, MAX, provides work for Apple Computer, Letraset, and many small design firms in the San Francisco Bay area.

Graphics, Science
and **Music** are three of 31 generic icons created in Illustrator 88 to accompany software articles in *MacWorld* magazine. Some shapes, like the guitar, for example, were created postively by placing black shapes over colored background shapes. Other shapes, like the inside of the tuba's horn, were created negatively by placing a color-filled shape over a solid black shape.

BAAAAAD CAT

Baaaad Dog (left) and Baaaaad Cat (right) were created in Illustrator 88 as Christmas gifts for the artist's brothers, who own a dog and a cat, respectively. The checkerboard pattern in the background of Baaaad Dog is a single zigzagging path filled with 100 percent cyan and no stroke. When an open path is "filled" in Illustrator, the program automatically connects the two end points to create filled shapes.

Baaaaad Cat's mouth was created by drawing the outside crescent shape and giving it a stroke of 20-point orange and a fill of white. The teeth were created by drawing a negative shape filled with black and placing it over the white-filled mouth shape.

Creative was made in Illustrator 88 to illustrate an article on creativity with computers for a national business news weekly. The design is composed of five black-filled shapes, two of which also define the edges of the woman's hair. Details were drawn as black stroked lines on the white background and as white stroked lines on the black shapes.

Mike Gilmor
received a B.A. in animation from the University of Washington and worked as art director of the AppleCoop/Tech Alliance in Seattle before becoming a computer illustrator and art director for Silicon Beach Software in San Diego.

Interfacing with Midi was created in FreeHand to illustration an article in *Call Apple* magazine. The design was constructed almost entirely of simple geometric shapes. For example, the flute player's right hand is made of circles, ellipses and rectangles filled with white and with a thin black outline. The shapes are interleaved and masked over with other white shapes with no outline to eliminate unwanted black outlines.

Course Builder was created in FreeHand to illustrate an article on education software. The large figure was cloned, reduced and rotated slightly to create the small drawing in the book at lower right. The clouds were created by assembling a group of differently sized white-filled ellipses with black outines. Then a white-filled shape with no outline was drawn to obscure some of the overlap of black outlines at the center of each cloud.

Artificial Intelligence, done in FreeHand, combines a portrait of Albert Einstein with a grid suggesting electronic circuitry. The face is constructed of many irregular shapes, each of which has a portion of the circuit grid pasted inside it. The tonal value of the grid varies slightly in each facial piece.

Hardware Future features three-dimensional type created by stacking three identical type elements, slightly offset from each other. The elements are white at the bottom, black in between, and 60 percent gray on top. The soft edges of the facial features were created by executing a blend between the inner and outer shapes of each feature. The piece was done in FreeHand.

GALLERY

David Doty

is a freelance graphic designer, principally working for publishers in the Chicago area. He specializies in electronic design and implementation of multiple-page documents such as books, workbooks, and training manuals. Doty is also the editor and pblisher of ThePage, a journal for users of the Macintosh computer and page layout software. Doty is a past-president and founding member of A.D.E.P.T. (Association for the Development of Electronic Publishing Technique), a Chicago area group of electronic and desktop publishers.

The illustrations shown on these two pages were created to demonstrate various FreeHand techniques for issue 35 of ThePage. The complete set of illustrations is available for purchase on disk from PageWorks, (see the "Appendix").

The latitude lines on this globe were created by using FreeHand's ellipse tool to draw white ellipses, which were positioned on top of the globe. Once in place, some of the ellipses were cut and the top halves were deleted.

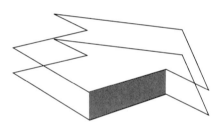

To create the effect of a three-dimensional object, Doty created a skewed outline of the United States, cloned it and positioned the clone slightly below the original. These two outlines were then used as guides for drawing a series of rectangles in varying shades of gray, to give the appearance of thick edges on the shapes. The technique is shown in the figure of an arrow shape above.

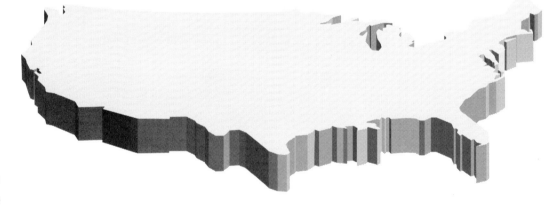

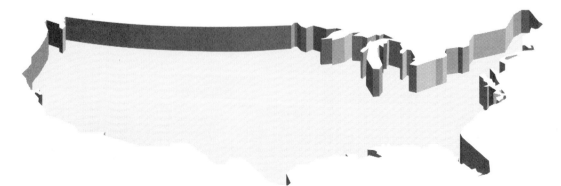

To enclose a sphere within an open-sided cube, the front sides of the cube were drawn as a closed path with overlapping edges, so that the edges could be filled with color and the center remain unfilled and open.

To create the effect of a spiraling star, a large outer star was blended to a smaller inner star shape, with the upper left point of the outer stars and the top point of the inner star selected as reference points. The two star were colored with a black fill and white line. After the blend was executed, the inner star was filled with solid white.

A graduated fill can be turned into a pattern of lines in FreeHand by specifying a coarse line screen in the Halftone Screen dialog box available from Special under the Element menu. Note that the screen rulings remain the same, regardless of the size at which the graphic is used, so plan ahead to make sure the line screen fits with the desired finish size.

Suze Woolf
is a principle in Visible Images, a
computer-based design firm in Seattle.

Blue Line Badge was created in FreeHand to advertise the Base Line company's line of pre-ruled masking sheets, clean-up sheets, and pre-ruled paste-up sheets. The badge features Captain Base Line, a creation of Fran Olson of Visible Images. The motto "Dare to be square" was set in Stencil along an oval path. The black line grid in the background was created by drawing a larger grid of intersecting diagonal lines and pasting it inside an oval with a heavy black outline. The white line grid in the sunglasses was created in a similar way by pasting a grid of white lines inside a black-filled eyeglass shape. The white lightening shapes were placed on top of the finished masked eye pieces.

Olympic Range was created in FreeHand to illustrate a holiday card sent to clients by the Newman-Burrows printing company. The illustration features an outline of the Olympic mountain range below a sky colored with a three graduated fills. The three suns and coronas, also made of graduated fills, show the position of the sun at sunset on the Winter Solstice (left), the Vernal and Autumanal Equinoxes (center) and the Summer Solstice.

Icicle Software logo was created in FreeHand. The zigzagging edge around the logo was created by using the square corner tool to draw an outward pointing angle. The angle was copied and the copies were rotated by the appropriate number of degrees to follow the shape of a circle. The angles were positioned along one quarter of a circle with their end points overlapping, then joined into a single path. This path was cloned and reflected to create the other three quarters, and then all four sections were joined into a closed shape and filled with black. The zigzags on the first circle made in this way were too coarse, so the circle was cloned and rotated so that the points are evenly interspaced.

March 21: Vernal Equinox
September 21: Autumnal Equinox

Sunset on December 21: Winter Solstice

June 21: Summer Solstice

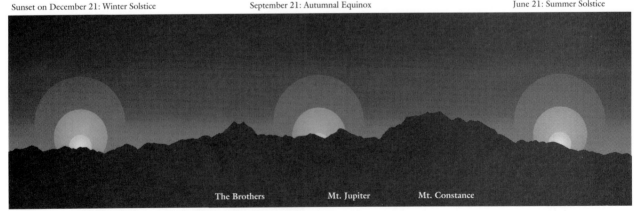

The Brothers   Mt. Jupiter   Mt. Constance

WISHING YOU COLOR ALL YEAR

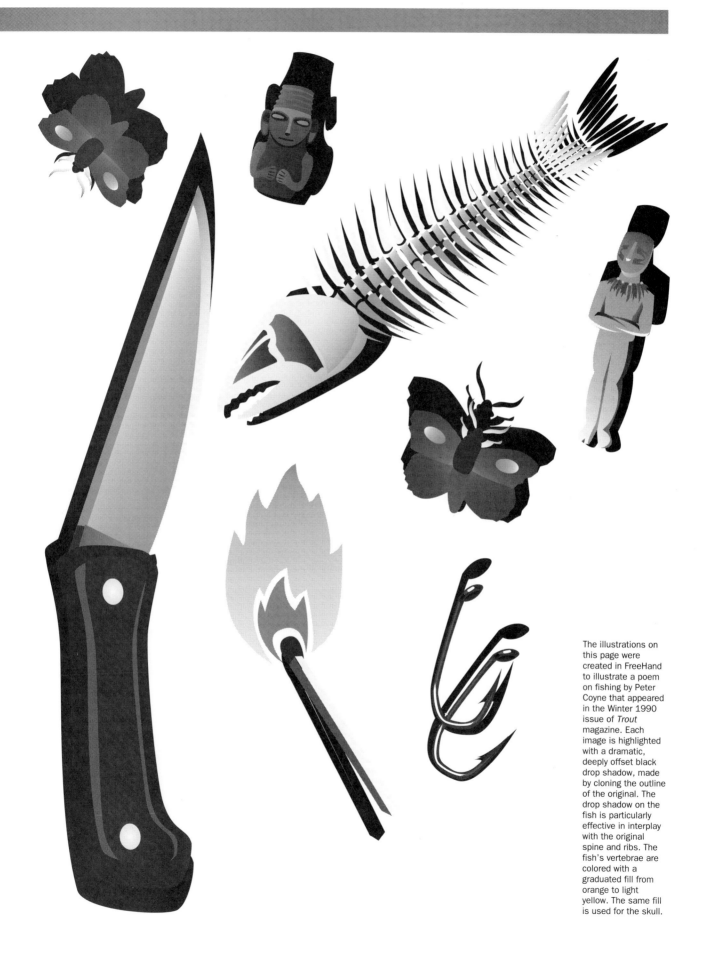

The illustrations on this page were created in FreeHand to illustrate a poem on fishing by Peter Coyne that appeared in the Winter 1990 issue of *Trout* magazine. Each image is highlighted with a dramatic, deeply offset black drop shadow, made by cloning the outline of the original. The drop shadow on the fish is particularly effective in interplay with the original spine and ribs. The fish's vertebrae are colored with a graduated fill from orange to light yellow. The same fill is used for the skull.

Glenn Mitsui and Jesse Doquilo
are principles in M Design of Seattle, a
graphic design firm specializing in
Computer illustration and design. Clients
include Apple Computer, Aldus, Letraset,
Crosfield, Microsoft and Raleigh Bicycles.

Solutions was
created in FreeHand
for an Aldus
conference. To fill
the sphere with a
radial fill that has a
slightly offset center,
a circle containing a
radial fill was pasted
inside another circle
placed over it slightly
off center. The
second circle serves
as a clipping path for
the fill.

M Vision was
created in FreeHand
as a self-promotion
to convey a sense of
design vision in only
black-and-white. The
background is a
PostScript fill,
created by entering
the code (sand) 0
texture in the
PostScript Fill dialog
box. The iris of the
eye is composed of
a series of
overlapped circles
containing graduated
fills from black to
white. Highlights are
created with black
triangles arranged on
nonprinting circles.

HOMING
FOR HAIR

The Homing logo is
contructed of a solid
black vertical
rectangle overlaid
with two groups of
eight thin white
triangles. The
triangles are butted
together like the
teeth of a comb, and
the two white
elements create the
impression of a
letter H.

Z-Space consists of
an arrangement of
simple black-filled
shapes that refer to
architecture (a
triangle template),
housing (roof stair-
step, and window
shape) and also
create the negative
white shape of a
letter Z. The logo
was created in
FreeHand.

The designs on this page are part of a series created for a line of T-shirts and jewelry pins geared to graphic designers. The designs depict the mythical country of Republica of Design, a place in which designers are constantly at war with engineers and accountants and would rather die than submit to practicality. The shirts and pins are sold by a design store in Seattle. The two images below are composed of black-filled shapes, combined with type in the Emigré font, Modula. The flag image at right includes a PostScript Fill background created by typing the code *(heavy-mezzo) 0 texture* in the PostScript Fill dialog box.

Jack Davis

worked in advertising art direction and graphic design using traditional media prior to coming to the Mac in 1984. After completing an MFA in Computer Imagery and Design, he originated the Computer Graphics Department at Platt College in San Diego and became its first director. He is currently graphics editor of Verbum magazine and an international speaker.

The Boy, drawn in Illustrator 88, was traced from a scanned 1950's trademark. Highlights in the hair are white-filled shapes placed over the black. The shear and scale tools were used to give the piece an apparent perspective. The graduated drop shadow was created with the blend tool.

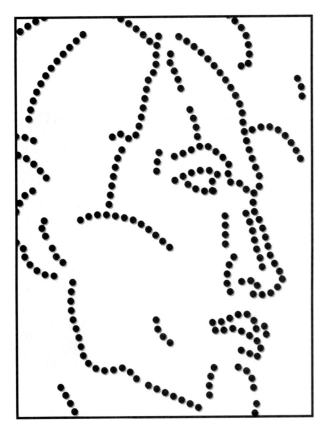

Dot Profile was drawn in Adobe Illustrator, using the dashed line pattern from the Lines menu, with the dash length set at 0 points and with round end caps specified. The profile is actually two copies of the same drawing, a black one offset slightly from the gray one underneath.

The mountains, water and sailboat in this **Logo Design** are formed from sets of repeated shapes. For the sail, for instance, a single black triangle was drawn and repeated. The stacked triangles were then individually modified to form the larger black-and-white shape.

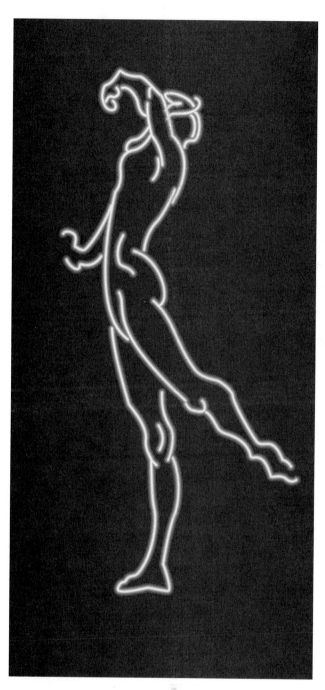

This **Verbum Logo**
was assembled in
Illustrator 88 from
parts drawn in other
programs. The three-
dimensional V was
created in Swivel 3D
and opened in
Illustrator. The type
was set on a circle
with the TypeAlign
desk accessory and
brought into
Illustrator, where it
was skewed with the
shear tool. Each of
the three spheres
was created by
blending from a small
circle to a larger one
in Illustrator.

Neon Dancer was
drawn in Illustrator. A
thick line was
duplicated and the
copy, directly on top
of the original, was
assigned a narrower
stroke and a lighter
color; then the two
lines were blended
to create the neon
tube effect.

GALLERY

David Smith

of Sausalito California is a fine artist and illustrator in traditional as well as electronic media. He is the designer of Adobe Illustrator's tool palette and of training materials for Apple Computer. He also teaches computer illustration workshops for Apple, Stanford University and others.

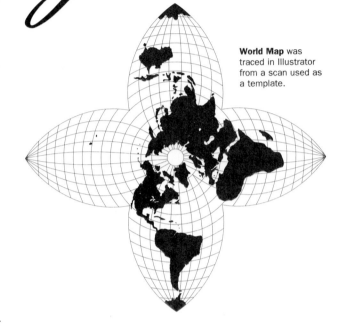

Up & Running was drawn in Illustrator at 400 percent from a scan used as a template. The original art was created from typeset letters and a hand-inked brush script.

World Map was traced in Illustrator from a scan used as a template.

The Flag was produced easily in Illustrator using the Command-D function for duplicating images. The camera-ready image took four minutes to produce.

Lifestyle was drawn in Illustrator 88. Letterforms were traced and then sized, positioned and modified as graphic elements. Standard cover elements for *Verbum* magazine were later added to the original file.

The Rose Café, created in Illustrator, is an example of the inline technique. Each of the shapes that make up the rose consists of three layers. The top white layer sits on an exact duplicate stroked with a thick black line, which in turn sits on another exact duplicate stroked with a thicker white line.

Ku chiu Ping
is owner and creative director of Arrow Productions Ltd. in Hong Kong and is the primary designer for Micron, a company specializing in high-tech business proorducts.

These images were created in Illustrator 88 and used instead of photographs in advertisements for the Micron line.

Pattie Belle Hastings
is a principal of Graphice, a design firm based in Atlanta, Georgia.

Oblique was created in Illustrator 88. The buildings were drawn in vertical and horizontal alignment and then "italicized" using the shear tool. The shadows were created by copying the outline of each building's facade, filling it with gray, skewing it and sending it behind the building. The white-line buildings in the black triangle are rotated copies of the original, unskewed buildings.

The large three-dimensional letters in **Question Marks** were made by tracing a scanned template in Illustrator 88. Each letter was copied and the copy was offset and used as a guide for drawing the shapes that indicate the sides of the letter. These shapes were filled with a darker shade of gray than the letter face.

In the **Training Solutions** logo, the sculpted appearance was achieved by "stacking" two circles with graduated fills in opposite directions.

Mike Uriss

is a San Diego–based freelance illustrator. He has worked extensively with FreeHand, Illustrator and ImageStudio on the Macintosh and Corel Draw on the IBM PC.

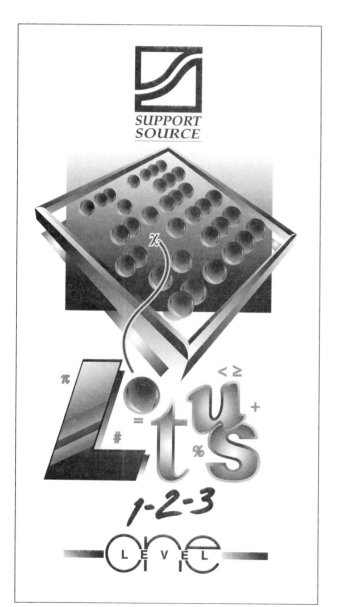

Shark Art was drawn in Corel Draw as part of a series of logos for beachware. It received second place for Commercial Illustration in Corel Draw's 1990 Design Contest.

Lotus 1-2-3 was drawn in Corel Draw as a cover illustration for one of a series of training manuals. The "L" and "o" were created with the drawing tools. Other letterforms were created by modifying characters from the program's resident fonts.

Resources

This appendix lists hardware, software and other resources of use to artists using PostScript illustration programs. The resources are grouped in categories in the following order:

PostScript Illustration Software

PostScript Clip Art

Paint Programs

Draw Programs

Image-Processing Software

Fonts

Font Design and Font Manipulation Software

Page Layout Programs

Prepress Systems

Utilities

Scanners and Digitizers

Monitors

Color Calibration

Storage Systems

Printers and Imagesetters

Film Recorders

Periodicals

Books

Bulletin Board Services

Communication Software

PostScript Illustration Software

Adobe Illustrator
Adobe Systems, Inc.
PO Box 7900
Mountain View, CA 94039-7900
800-344-8335

Aldus FreeHand
Aldus Corporation
411 First Avenue South
Seattle, WA 98104
206-622-5500

Arts & Letters
Computer Support Corporation
15926 Midway Road
Dallas, TX 75244
214-661-8960

Corel Draw
Corel Systems Corporation
1600 Carling Avenue
Ottawa, Ontario, K1Z 8R7, Canada
613-728-8200

Cricket Draw
Cricket Software
40 Valley Stream Parkway
Mallvern, PA 19355
215-251-9890

Cricket Stylist
Computer Associates
10505 Sorrento Valley Road
San Diego, CA 92121-1698
619-452-0170

GEM Artline
Digital Research, Inc.
70 Garden Court
Monterey, CA 93940
408-649-3896

Micrografx Designer
Micrografx, Inc.
1303 Arapaho Road
Richardson, TX 75081-1769
800-272-3729

Smart Art, Volumes I, II, III
Emerald City Software
1040 Marsh Road, Suite 110
Menlo Park, CA 94025
415-324-8080

Streamline
Adobe Systems, Inc.
PO Box 7900
Mountain View, CA 94039-7900
800-344-8335

PostScript Clip Art

Adobe Illustrator Collector's Edition
Adobe Systems, Inc.
PO Box 7900
Mountain View, CA 94039-7900
800-344-8335

Art Nouveau Images
Silicon Designs
PO Box 2234
Orinda, CA 94563-6634
415-254-1460

Artagenix
Devonian International Software Company
PO Box 2351
Montclair, CA 91763
714-621-0973

ArtClips
Tactic Software
13615 South Dixie Highway, Suite 118
Miami, FL 33176
305-378-4110

ArtRoom
Image Club Graphics, Inc.
1902 11th Street, S.E.
Calgary, Alberta, Canada T2G 3G2
403-262-8008

Arts & Letters
Computer Support Corporation
15926 Midway Road
Dallas, TX 75244
214-661-8960

ClickArt EPS Illustrations
T/Maker Co.
1390 Villa Street
Mountain View, CA 94041
415-962-0195

Clip Art for Ministry
The Church Art Works
875 High Street, N.E.
Salem, OR 97301
503-370-9377

Clip Art Libraries
Stephen & Associates
5205 Kearny Villa Way, Suite 104
San Diego, CA 92123
619-591-5624

Clip Charts
MacroMind, Inc.
410 Townsend Avenue, Suite 408
San Francisco, CA 94107
415-442-0200

APPENDIX

Cliptures
Dream Maker Software
4020 Paige Street
Los Angeles, CA 90031
213-221-6436

Designer ClipArt
Micrografx, Inc.
1303 Arapaho Road
Richardson, TX 75081
800-272-3729

DeskTop Art
Dynamic Graphics
6000 N. Forest Park Drive
Peoria, IL 61614
800-255-8800

Digiclips
U-Design, Inc.
201 Ann Street
Hartford, CT 06102
203-278-3648

Digit-Art
Image Club Graphics, Inc.
1902 11th Street, S.E.
Calgary, Alberta T2G 3G2, Canada
403-262-8008

Flash Graphics
Flash Graphics
PO Box 1950
Sausalito, CA 94965
415-331-7700

Illustrated Art Backgrounds
ARTfactory
414 Tennessee Plaza, Suite A
Redlands, CA 92373
714-793-7346

Images with Impact
3G Graphics
11410 NE 124th Street, Suite 6155
Kirkland, WA 98034
206-823-8198

Metro ImageBase Electronic Art
Metro ImageBase, Inc.
18623 Ventura Blvd., Suite 210
Tarzana, CA 91356
800-525-1552

Moonlight Art Works
Clip Art Collections
Hired Hand Design
3608 Faust Avenue
Long Beach, CA 90808
213-429-2936

Pro-Art Professional
Art Library Trilogy 1
Multi-Ad Services, Inc.
1720 West Detweiller Drive
Peoria, Il 61615
309-692-11530

PS Portfolio, Spellbinder Art Library
Lexisoft, Inc.
PO Box 5000
Davis, CA 95617-5000
916-758-3630

TextArt
Stone Design Corporation
2425 Teodoro N.W.
Albuquerque, NM 87107
505-345-4800

Totem Graphics
Totem Graphics
5109-A Capitol Blvd.
Tumwater, WA 98501
206-352-1851

Type Foundry
U-Design, Inc.
201 Ann Street
Hartford, CT 06102
203-278-3648

Vivid Impressions
Casady & Greene, Inc.
26080 Carmel Rancho Blvd., Suite 202
Carmel, CA 93923
800-359-4920

Works of Art
Springboard Software
7808 Creekridge Circle
Minneapolis, MN 55435
612-944-3915

Paint Programs

LaserPaint
LaserWare, Inc.
PO Box 668
San Rafael , CA 94915
800-367-6898

MacPaint
Claris Corp.
440 Clyde Avenue
Mountain View, CA 94043
415-962-8946

SuperPaint 2.0
Silicon Beach Software
9770 Carroll Center Road, Suite J
San Diego, CA 92126
619-695-6956

Draw Programs

Canvas 2.0
Deneba Software
7855 N.W. 12th Street
Miami, FL 33126
800-622-6827

MacDraw
Claris Corp.
440 Clyde Avenue
Mountain View, CA 94043
415-962-8946

Swivel 3D
Paracomp, Inc.
123 Townsend Street, Suite 310
San Francisco, CA 94107
415-543-3848

Image-Processing Software

Digital Darkroon
Silicon Beach Software
9770 Carroll Center Road, Suite J
San Diego, CA 92126
619-695-6956

ImageStudio
Letraset USA
40 Eisehower Drive
Paramus, NJ 07653
201-845-6100

Picture Publisher
Astral Development Corp.
Londonderry Square, Suite 112
Londonderry, NH 03053
603-432-6800

Fonts

18+ Fonts
18+ Fonts
337 White Hall Terrace
Bloomingdale, IL 60108

Adobe Type Library
Adobe Systems, Inc.
PO Box 7900
Mountain View, CA 94039-7900
800-344-8335

Bitstream fonts and
Fontware Installation Kit
Bitstream, Inc.
215 First Street
Cambridge, MA 02142
800-522-3668

CG Type
Agfa Compugraphic Division
90 Industrial Way
Wilmington, MA 01887
800-622-8973

**Corel Headline, Corel Loader,
Corel Newfont**
Corel Systems Corporation
1600 Carling Avenue, Suite 190
Ottawa, Ontario, Canada K1Z 8R7
613-728-8200

Em Dash fonts
Em Dash
PO Box 8256
Northfield, IL 60093
312-441-6699

Fluent Laser Fonts
Casady & Greene, Inc.
26080 Carmel Rancho Blvd., Suite 202
Carmel, CA 93923
800-359-4920

Font Factory Fonts (for LaserJet)
The Font Factory
13601 Preston Road, Suite 500 W
Dallas, TX 75240
214-239-6085

Font Solution Pack
SoftCraft, Inc.
16 N. Carroll Street, Suite 500
Madison, WI 53073
608-257-3300

FontGen IV Plus
VS Software
PO Box 165920
Little Rock, AR 72216
501-376-2083

**Hewlett-Packard Soft Fonts
(for LaserJet)**
Hewlett-Packard Co.
PO Box 60008
Sunnyvale, CA 94088-60008
800-538-8787

Hot Type
Image Club Graphics Inc.
1902 11th Street S.E.
Calgary, Alberta, Canada T2G3G2
800-661-9410

**Kingsley/ATF typefaces
(ATF Classic type)**
Type Corporation
2559-2 E. Broadway
Tucson, AZ 85716
800-289-8973

Laser fonts and font utilities
SoftCraft, Inc.
16 N. Carroll Street, Suite 500
Madison, WI 53703
800-351-0500

Laserfonts
Century Software/MacTography
326-D North Stonestreet Avenue
Rockville , MD 20850
301-424-1357

Monotype fonts
Monotype Typography
53 W. Jackson Boulevard, Suite 504
Chicago, IL 60604
800-666-6897

Ornate Typefaces
Ingrimayne Software
PO Box 404
Rensselaer, IN 47978
219-866-6241

Typographic Ornaments
The Underground Grammarian
PO Box 203
Glassboro, NJ 08028
609-589-6477

URW fonts
The Font Company
12629 N. Tatum Boulevard, Suite 210
Phoenix, AZ 85032
800-442-3668

Varityper fonts
Tegra/Varityper
11 Mt. Pleasant Avenue
East Hanover, NJ 07936
201-884-6277

VS Library of Fonts
VS Software
PO Box 165920
Little Rock, AR 72216
501-376-2083

**Font-Design and
Font-Manipulation Software**

Art Importer
Altsys Corporation
720 Avenue F, Suite 109
Plano, TX 75074
214-424-4888

Family Builder
Altsys Corporation
720 Avenue F, Suite 109
Plano, TX 75074
214-424-4888

FontLiner
Taylored Graphics
PO Box 1900
Freedom, CA 95019
408-761-2481

FontMaker
The Font Factory
13601 Preston Road, Suite 500 W
Dallas, TX 75240
214-239-6085

Fontographer
Altsys Corporation
720 Avenue F, Suite 109
Plano, TX 75074
214-424-4888

FontSizer
U.S. Microlabs, Inc.
1611 Headway Circle, Bldg. 3
Austin, TX 78754
512-339-0001

FontStudio
Letraset USA
40 Eisenhower Drive
Paramus, NJ 07653
201-845-6100

LetraStudio and LetraFont Library
Letraset USA
40 Eisenhower Drive
Paramus, NJ 07653
201-845-6100

LetrTuck
EDCO Services, Inc.
12410 N. Dale Mabry Hwy.
Tampa, FL 33618
813-962-7800

**Pairs Professional Kerning Editor
and Kerning Tables**
Pairs Software, Inc.
160 Vaderhoff Avenue, Suite 201
Toronto, Ontario, Canada, M4G 4B8
416-467-81978

Publisher's Type Foundry
ZSoft Corporation
450 Franklin Road, #100
Marietta, GA 30067
404-428-0008

Type Align
Emeral City Software
PO Box 2103
Menlo Park, CA 94026
415-324-8080

APPENDIX

Type Director
Hewlett-Packard Co.
3000 Hanover Street
Palo Alto, CA 94303-0890
415-857-1501

TypeStyler
Brøderbund Software
17 Paul Drive
San Rafael, CA 94903-2101
415-492-3200

Page Layout Programs

DesignStudio
Letraset USA
40 Eisenhower Drive
Paramus, NJ 07653
201-845-6100

PageMaker
Aldus Corp.
411 First Avenue South
Seattle, WA 98104
206-622-5500

Personal Press
Silicon Beach Software
9770 Carroll Center Drive
San Diego, CA 92126
619-695-6956

QuarkXPress
Quark, Inc.
300 S. Jackson Street, Suite 100
Denver, CO 80209
800-543-7711

Ready,Set,Go!
Letraset USA
40 Eisenhower Drive
Paramus, NJ 07653
201-845-6100

Ventura Publisher
Xerox Product Support
1301 Ridgeview Drive
Lewisville, TX 75067
800-822-8221

Prepress Systems

Crosfield
Crosfield Systems, Marketing Division
65 Harristown Road
Glen Rock, NJ 07452
201-447-5800, ext. 5310

Freedom of Press
Custom Applications, Inc.
900 Technology Park Drive, Bldg 8
Billerica, MA 01821
508-667-8585

Lightspeed Color Layout System
Lightspeed
47 Farnsworth Street
Boston, MA 02210
617-338-2173

Printware 720 IQ Laser Imager
Printware, Inc.
1385 Mendota Heights Road
Saint Paul, MN 55120
612-456-1400

SpectreSeps PM
Pre-Press Technologies, Inc.
2441 Impala Drive
Carlsbad, CA 92008
619-931-2695

Visionary
Scitex America Corp.
8 Oak Park Dr.
Bedford, MA 01730
617-275-5150

Utilities

Adobe Type Manager
Adobe Systems, Inc.
PO Box 7900
Mountain View, CA 94039-7900
800-344-8335

DiskTools Plus
Electronic Arts
1820 Gateway Drive
San Mateo, CA 94404
800-245-4525

Exposure
Perferred Publishers, Inc.
5100 Poplar Avenue, Suite 706
Memphis, TN 38137
901-683-3383

Font/DA Juggler Plus
Alsoft, Inc.
PO Box 927
Spring, TX 77383-0929
713-353-4090

QuicKeys
CE Software
PO Box 65580
W. Des Moines, IA 50265
515-224-1995

Screen-to-Pict, public domain
Educorp
531 Stevens Avenue, Suite B
Solana Beach, CA 92075
800-843-9497

SmartScrap
Solutions International
30 Commerce Street
Williston, VT 05495
802-658-5506

Suitcase II
Fifth Generation Systems
10049 N. Reiger Rd.
Baton Rouge, LA 70809
800-873-4384

Scanners and Digitizers

Abaton Scan 300/FB and 300/S
Abaton Technology Corp.
48431 Milmont Drive
Fremont, CA 94538
415-683-2226

Apple Scanner
Apple Computer, Inc.
20525 Mariani Avenue
Cupertino, CA 95014
408-996-1010

Dest PC Scan 1000 and 2000 series
Dest Corporation
1201 Cadillac Court
Milpitas, CA 95035
408-946-7100

Howtek ScanMaster II
Howtek
21 Park Avenue
Hudson, NH 03051
603-882-5200

HP ScanJet Plus
Hewlett-Packard Co.
700 71st Avenue
Greeley, CO 80634
303-845-4045

JX-300 and JX-450 Color Scanners
Sharp Electronics
Sharp Plaza, Box C Systems
Mahwah, NJ 07430
201-529-8200

MacVision 2.0
Koala Technologies
70 N. 2nd Street
San Jose, CA 95113
408-438-0946

Microtek Scanners
Microtek Lab, Inc.
16901 S. Western Avenue
Gardena, CA 90247
213-321-2121

ProViz Digitizers
Pixelogic, Inc.
800 W. Cummings Park, Suite 2900
Woburn, MA 01801
617-938-7711

ThunderScan
Thunderware, Inc.
21 Orinda Way
Orinda, CA 94563
415-254-6581

Monitors

Amdek Corp.
3471 N. First Street
San Jose, CA 95134
800-722-6335

Apple Computer, Inc.
20525 Mariani Avenue
Cupertino, CA 95014
408-996-1010

E-Machines, Inc.
9305 S.W. Gemini Drive
Beaverton,OR 97005
503-646-6699

MegaGraphics, Inc.
439 Calle San Pablo
Camarillo, CA 93010
805-484-3799

Mitsubishi Electronics
991 Knox Street
Torrance, CA 90502
213-217-5732

Moniterm Corp.
5740 Green Circle Drive
Minnetonka, MN 55343
612-935-4151

Nutmeg Systems, Inc.
25 South Avenue
New Canaan, CT 06840
800-777-8439

Radius, Inc.
1710 Fortune Drive
San Jose, CA 95131
408-434-1010

RasterOps Corp.
2500 Walsh Avenue
Santa Clara, CA 95051
408-562-4200

SuperMac Technology
485 Portrero Avenue
Sunnyvale, CA 94086
408-245-2202

Color Calibration

The Calibrator
Barco, Inc.
1500 Wilson Way, Suite 250
Smyrna, GA 30082
404-432-2346

PrecisionColor Calibrator
Radius, Inc.
1710 Fortune Dr.
San Jose, CA 95131
408-434-1010

TekColor
Visual Systems Group
5770 Ruffin Road
San Diego, CA 92123
619-292-7330

Storage Systems

Jasmine Technology, Inc.
1740 Army Street
San Francisco, CA 94124
415-282-1111

Mass Micro Systems
550 Del Ray Avenue
Sunnyvale, CA 94086
800-522-7979

SuperMac Technology
485 Portrero Avenue
Sunnyvale, CA 94086
408-245-2202

Printers and Imagesetters

4693D Color Image Printer
Tektronix, Inc., Graphics Printing &
Imaging Division
PO Box 500, M/S 50-662
Beaverton, OR 97077
503-627-1497

BirmySetter 300 & 400 Imagesetters
Birmy Graphics Corp.
PO Box 42-0591
Miami, FL 33142
305-633-3321

CG 9600/9700-PS Imagesetters
AGFA Compugraphic Corp.
90 Industrial Way
Wilmington, MA 01887
800-622-8973

Chelgraph A3 Imageprinter
Electra Products, Inc.
One Survey Circle
N. Billerica, MA 01862
508-663-4366

Chelgraph IBX Imagesetter
Electra Products, Inc.
One Survey Circle
N. Billerica, MA 01862
508-663-4366

ColorQuick
Tektronix, Inc.
Graphics Printing & Imaging Division
PO Box 500, M/S 50-662
Beaverton, , OR 97077
503-627-1497

Compugraphic Imagesetters
AGFA Compugraphic Corp.
200 Ballardvale Street
Wilmington, MA 01887
508-658-5600

CrystalPrint Publisher laser printer
Qume Corp.
500 Yosemite Drive
Milpitas, CA 95035
800-223-2479

DeskWriter
Hewlett-Packard Co.
PO Box 60008
Sunnyvale, CA 94088-60008
800-538-8787

Fujitsu RX7100PS laser printer
Fujitsu America, Inc.
3055 Orchard Drive
San Jose, CA 95134
408-432-1300

APPENDIX

GoScript
LaserGo
9235 Trade Place, Suite A
San Diego, CA 92121
619-530-2400

HP LaserJet Series II
Hewlett-Packard Co.
PO Box 60008
Sunnyvale, CA 94088-60008
800-538-8787

HP PaintJet
Hewlett-Packard Co.
PO Box 60008
Sunnyvale, CA 94088-60008
800-538-8787

ImageWriter II
Apple Computer, Inc.
20525 Mariani Avenue
Cupertino, CA 95014
408-996-1010

JLaser CR1
Tall Tree Systems
2585 Bayshore Road
Palo Alto, CA 94303
415-493-1980

LaserColor
LaserColor
3875 Nautical Drive
Carlsbad, CA 92008
619-434-7718

Lasersmith PS-415 Laser Printers
Lasersmith, Inc.
430 Martin Avenue
Santa Clara, CA 95050
408-727-7700

LaserWriter II family of printers
Apple Computer, Inc.
20525 Mariani Avenue
Cupertino, CA 95014
408-996-1010

Linotronic imagesetters
Linotype Company
425 Oser Avenue
Hauppage, NY 11788
516-434-2000

LZR Series Laser Printers
Dataproducts
6200 Canoga Avenue
Woodland Hills, CA 91365

Mitsubishi G330-70
color thermal printer
Mitsubishi Electronics America Computer
Peripherals Products
991 Knox Street
Torrance, CA 90502
213-515-3993

Omnilaser Series 2000
Texas Instruments Inc.
12501 Research
Austin, TX 78769
512-250-7111

Pacific Page
(PostScript emulation cartridge)
Golden Eagle Micro, Inc.
8515 Zionsville Road
Indianapolis, IN 46268

QMS ColorScript printers
QMS, Inc.
1 Magnum Pass
Mobile, AL 36618
800-631-2693

QMS-PS Series Laser Printers
QMS, Inc.
1 Magnum Pass
Mobile, AL 36618
800-631-2693

Series 1000 Imagesetters
Linotype Company
4215 Oser Avenue
Hauppauge, NY 11788
516-434-2014

Tektronix printers
Tektronix, Inc.
PO Box 1000 M/S 63583
Wilsonville, OR 97070-1000
800-835-6100

Turbo PS Series Laser Printer
NewGen Systems Corporation
17580 Newhope Street
Fountain Valley, CA 92708
714-641-2800

UltreSetter
Ultre Corporation
145 Pinelawn Rd.
Melville, NY 11747
516-753-4800

Varityper printers
Varityper, A Tegra Co.
11 Mt. Pleasant Avenue
East Hanover, NJ 07936
201-884-6277

Film Recorders

Agfa-Matrix Film Recorder
Agfa
1 Ramland Road
Orangeburg, NY 10962
914-365-0190

Periodicals

Aldus Magazine
Aldus Corp.
411 First Avenue South
Seattle, WA 98104
206-622-5500

Colophon
Adobe Systems, Inc.
PO Box 7900
Mountain View, CA 94039-7900
800-344-8335

Font & Function
Font & Function
1584 Charleston Road
Mountain View, CA 94039-7900
800-833-6687

MacUser
Ziff-Davis Publishing Co.
One Park Avenue
New York, NY 10016
800-627-2247

Macworld
IDG Communications, Inc.
501 Second Street
San Francisco, CA 94107
800-234-1038

PC Magazine
Ziff-Davis Publishing
One Park Avenue
New York, NY 10016
800-289-0429

Personal Publishing
Hitchcock Publishing Company
191 S. Gary Avenue
Carol Stream, IL 60188
800-727-6937

Publish!
PCW Communications, Inc.
501 Second Street
San Francisco, CA 94107
800-222-2990

Step-by-Step Electronic Design
Dynamic Graphics, Inc.
6000 N. Forest Park Drive
Peoria, IL 61614-3592
800-255-8800

U&lc
International Typeface Corporation
2 Hammarskjold Place
New York, NY 10017
212-371-0699

Verbum Magazine
Verbum, Inc.
PO Box 15439
San Diego, CA 92115
619-233-9977

Books

Expert Advisor: Adobe Illustrator
Addison-Wesley Publishing
Jacob Way
Reading, MA 01867

Making Art on the Macintosh II
Scott, Foresman and Company
1900 East Lake Avenue
Glenview, IL 60025

PostScript Language Reference Manual
Addison-Wesley Publishing
Jacob Way
Reading, MA 01867

PostScript Type Sampler
MacTography
326D N. Stonestreet Avenue
Rockville, MD 20850
301-424-1357

Ventura Tips and Tricks, 2nd Edition
Peachpit Press
1085 Keith Avenue
Berkeley, CA 94708
415-527-8555

Bulletin Board Services

Compuserve Information Services, Inc.
5000 Arlington Center Blvd.
Columbus, OH 43260
800-848-8199

**Connect Professional
Information Network**
Connect, Inc.
10161 Bubb Road
Cupertino, CA 95014
408-973-0110

Desktop Express
Dow Jones & Company
Princeton, NJ 08543
609-520-4000

Genie
GE Information Services
401 N. Washington Street
Rockville, MD 20850
800-638-9636

MCI Mail
MCI Mail
1150 17th Street N.W., Suite 800
Washington, D.C. 20036
800-444-6245

Communication Software

Microphone II
Software Ventures
2907 Claremont Avenue, Suite 220
Berkeley, CA 94705
800-336-6477

Red Ryder
Free Soft
150 Hickory Drive
Beaver Falls, PA 15010
412-846-2700

This book was designed and produced primarily on Macintoshes, although several other kinds of computer systems were used. Text was input primarily in Microsoft Word on a Macintosh IIci and a Mac Plus. Other computers used in design and production of the book included two Mac IIs, a second Macintosh IIci, a IIcx, an SE and a Plus.

Text files supplied by artists were converted, if necessary, to Microsoft Word format on the Mac. Files were checked with Word's Spelling function; the Change (search-and-replace) function was used to find and eliminate extra spaces and to insert *fi* and *fl* ligatures.

Pages were laid out and styled using PageMaker 3.02 Color Extension. Body text was set in Adobe's Galliard (10/14½), and captions in Franklin Gothic (8/11). Zapf Dingbats were used for the "hint" symbol.

Illustrations for the project chapters and gallery were created as described in the text and in most cases were supplied by the artist as application files. Most artwork was saved in TIFF, EPS, or PICT format and placed in the PageMaker files. Screen shots to show software interfaces were made using the Command-Shift-3 screen snapshot function or the Camera desk accesory on a Mac Plus.

An Apple Scanner and a Microtek grayscale scanner were used to scan nonelectronic artwork, such as original pencil sketches, as low-resolution TIFFs to indicate position for artwork to be stripped in. Some nonelectronic line art was scanned and saved as high-resolution TIFFs to provide final art that could be permanently placed in the electronic pages.

During final layout and production, files were stored on 45 MB removable hard disk drives. A LaserWriter Plus, a IINT, and two IINTXs were used for proofing pages. Files for final pages were stuffed and segmented (using StuffIt) and stored on floppy disks for delivery to the output bureau. Pages were output on a Linotronic 300 imagesetter. Pages with type and line art only were output at 1270 dpi on resin-coated paper; pages with screen tints or grayscale images were output at 2540 dpi as negatives. Color pages were separated using Adobe Separator and output as negatives at 2540 dpi.

In some cases artwork was provided to the printer as Linotronic negatives or as original laser, inkjet or imagesetter prints, or as final printed pieces (such as magazine pages, stationery items and brochures), which were reproduced by conventional means and stripped into the page negatives. For example, because their custom patterns would have required very long imagesetter output times, several of the shoe patterns in Chapter 5 were laser printed (which was the mode of output originally used by the artist), and the prints were reproduced conventionally. Most of the illustrations in Chapter 10 were supplied as 35mm color photos of screen displays. These and other color photos used elsewhere in the book were separated conventionally from the 35mm transparencies.

The cover (including the spine and back cover) was developed in FreeHand 2.02 on a Macintosh IIcx. Color separations, generated by the program, were output on a Linotronic 300 imagesetter as 2540 dpi negatives.

SUBSCRIBE!

KEEP YOUR EDGE!

CHANGE THE WORLD!

"The emergence of good taste... these guys are very serious about doing things right." – John Dvorak, PC Industry Analyst

"If I were stranded on a desert island, this is the magazine I'd want with me" – Bob Roberts, *MIPS Journal*

"Artists are grabbing the cursor and spawning a distinct design sense, which this classy journal explores." – *Whole Earth Review*

PUSH THE ENVELOPE!

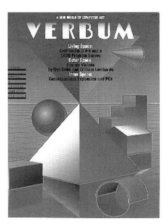

GET RICH!

"I love your inspiring use of media...what should we call this? 'Magazine' hardly seems appropriate." – Chuck Pratt, subscriber, University of Texas

MULTI YOUR MEDIA!

THE JOURNAL OF PERSONAL COMPUTER AESTHETICS

Join the inner circle of electronic art, design and multimedia professionals who've counted on *Verbum* since 1986 to deliver the cutting edge: the Verbum Gallery, regular columns, feature stories, new products, ideas, insights — *synergy*. *Verbum* is both substance *and* style — each issue uses the latest tools and programs to push the limits of desktop publishing.

Verbum Stack 2.0 1990 version of the famous Verbum Stack with usable start-up screens and icons, as well as tons of great bitmap art, sounds, animations and surprises. Shipped on two 800k floppies.

Verbum Digital Type Poster Designed by Jack Davis and Susan Merritt, this deluxe 5-color, 17 x 22-inch poster showcases the variety of digital type effects possible on the Macintosh. Produced on a Mac II with Page-Maker 3.0, output on a Linotronic L-300 and printed on a 100 lb. coated sheet. Text explains the history of initial caps in publishing, and how each sample letter was created. A framable "illuminated manuscript" for every electronic design studio! Limited edition of 2000. Shipped in capped tube.

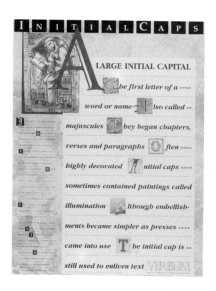

Keep abreast of technology and creativity...

Subscribe to VERBUM, order back issues and products by filling in this user-friendly form and we'll keep you up-to-date on the latest in pc art and news!

Name _____   Organization _____

Address _____   Phone _____

City _____   State _____   ZIP _____   Country _____

☐ **ONE YEAR/4-ISSUE SUBSCRIPTION** – $24; Canada & Mexico – $36 US funds; all other countries – $45 US funds

☐ **TWO YEAR/8-ISSUE SUBSCRIPTION** – $46; Canada & Mexico – $72 US funds; all other countries – $90 US funds

☐ **BACK ISSUES** – $7 each: (circle issue/s)   1.1   1.2   1.3   2.1   2.3   3.1   3.2   3.3   3.4   4.1   4.2

☐ **VERBUM STACK 2.0** – $12 (includes lifetime registration for add-on releases)

☐ **VERBUM DIGITAL TYPE POSTER** – $10 (including tube and shipping)

TOTAL AMOUNT (plus $2.50 shipping for products and back issues)   **$** _____
California residents please add 7¼% sales tax for products and back issues.

☐ **Check enclosed**

☐ **VISA/MC #** _____   exp _____

Send to: VERBUM, PO Box 15439, San Diego, CA 92115 or call 619/463-9977 with credit card number. Allow six weeks for delivery.

PS Book